Poe's Pervasive Influence

Perspectives on Edgar Allan Poe

Series Editor: Barbara Cantalupo
Pennsylvania State University, Lehigh Valley

The Perspectives on Poe series includes books on new approaches to Edgar A. Poe, his work and influence; all perspectives—theoretical, historical, biographical, gender studies, source studies, cultural studies, global studies, etc.—are invited.

Titles in the Series

Poe's Pervasive Influence, edited by Barbara Cantalupo

http://inpress.sites.lehigh.edu/

Poe's Pervasive Influence

Edited by Barbara Cantalupo

LEHIGH UNIVERSITY PRESS
Bethlehem

Published by Lehigh University Press
Co-published with The Rowman & Littlefield Publishing Group, Inc.
4501 Forbes Boulevard, Suite 200, Lanham, Maryland 20706
www.rowman.com

10 Thornbury Road, Plymouth PL6 7PP, United Kingdom

Figures 1 and 2 from Fernando Pessoa's archive reprinted by permission of The National Library of Portugal.

British Library Cataloguing in Publication Information Available

Library of Congress Cataloging-in-Publication Data
Poe's pervasive influence / edited by Barbara Cantalupo.
p. cm.—(Perspectives on Poe ; 1).
Includes bibliographical references and index.
ISBN 978-1-61146-126-8 (cloth : alk. paper)—ISBN 978-1-61146-127-5 (electronic)
1. Poe, Edgar Allan, 1809-1849—Influence. 2. Poe, Edgar Allan, 1809-1849—Criticism and interpretation. I. Cantalupo, Barbara.
PS2638.P73 2012
818'.309—dc23
2012028390

♾️™ The paper used in this publication meets the minimum requirements of American National Standard for Information Sciences Permanence of Paper for Printed Library Materials, ANSI/NISO Z39.48-1992.

Printed in the United States of America

Contents

Introduction

Barbara Cantalupo

The essays, interview, and set of poems in this collection all emerged from the Third International Edgar Allan Poe Conference: The Bicentennial, sponsored by the Poe Studies Association in October 2009. Scholars from fifteen countries and from across the United States came to Philadelphia to present talks on Poe's writing and life. The work in this collection was chosen to demonstrate Poe's continuing influence on authors from China, England, Japan, Portugal, and Russia, as well as American authors William Faulkner, Harriet Jacobs, Herman Melville, Joyce Carol Oates, and Mary Oliver.

No other American writer has had such a profound impact on the arts as well as on the popular imagination in the United States and abroad as Edgar Allan Poe, despite Rufus Griswold's nefarious "Memoir" or sometimes precisely because of its lurid portrayal of Poe, the man, and Poe, the author:

> [There is] scarcely any virtue in either his life or his writings. . . . His realm was on the shadowy confines of human experience, among the abodes of crime, gloom, and horror. . . . when Poe attempted the illustration of the profounder operations of the mind . . . he frequently failed entirely . . . [his poetry] evince[s] little genuine feeling. . . . He was not remarkably original in invention . . . his criticisms were guided by no sense of duty. . . . Irascible, envious . . . varnished over with a cold repellant synicism, his passions vented themselves into sneer. There seemed to him no moral susceptibility. [1]

Such devastating overviews of Poe's work by critics such as Rufus Griswold and Henry James, who have judged Poe's excesses as unpalatable, juvenile, or immoral and his bravado as undeserved, ironically have effectively promoted Poe's work and reputation. His influence on writers, visual artists, musicians, and even dancers demonstrates his ever-present and continuing influence. Such influence, clearly, calls into question Alexis de Tocqueville's 1835 claim in *Democracy in America* that "America has not as yet had any great writers."[2]

Poe and his work have survived bitter criticism and utter dismissal partly because his work reflects important aspects of the American psyche: the will to challenge convention in all its demands, the ability to innovate, and the audacity to attempt originality. This collection bolsters that claim and provides the reader with insights into Poe's continuing influence both in the United States and abroad. The Poe Studies Association international conference itself, along with the dozens of other bicentennial celebrations around the globe in 2009, provided strong evidence that Poe's work will continue to provoke interest and attract readers and critics nationally and internationally for centuries to come.

At the conference in Philadelphia, Japan was well represented. Kasai Kiyoshi, prominent mystery novel writer, gave a talk about how Poe's work and ideas have influenced and continue to influence his own writing. An interview with Mr. Kasai is included in this collection. In addition, three chapters on Japan's twentieth-century fiction writer, Edogawa Rampo, reinforce the great influence Poe's work has had on Japan's literary scene. For readers unfamiliar with Edwardo Rampo, an overview of his work appears below from the opening remarks by Takayuki Tatsumi, president of the Poe Society of Japan, who chaired a panel at the conference devoted to Poe and Rampo:

> The revival of Edogawa Rampo (1894–1965) in Japan coincided with bicentennial celebrations of Edgar Allan Poe. Poe exemplified American Romanticism, while Rampo survived Japanese Modernism. As is well known, the five ideographs for "Edogawa Rampo" (江戸川乱歩) were carefully selected to mimic the pronunciation of "Edgar Allan Poe," but in Japanese, they rather decadently suggest one "staggering drunkenly along the Edo River."
>
> From childhood on, Rampo had imbibed the best of western popular fiction. In 1914, as a student of economics at Waseda University in Tokyo, Rampo first encountered and seriously read Anglo-American detective stories by Poe, Sir Arthur Conan Doyle, and G. K. Chesterton, which fatefully determined his literary tastes. Rampo would go on to found modern Japanese detective fiction, and in doing so, pay homage to, and even surpass at times, the original works of his foreign and Japanese literary precursors.
>
> Rampo's very first work gives us a gentleman-thief reminiscent of Dupin, the prototype for the later Phantom. This first published story, "Nisen Doka" ("The Two-Sen Copper Coin," 1923), succeeded also in further complicating the cryptogrammic tradition that Poe, the father of world detective fiction, had inaugurated with "The Gold Bug" (1843). While it is true that Poe's arabesque, grotesque, and ratiocinative tales exerted great influence upon Rampo's Ero-Gro-Nonsense detective fiction, it is also true that Rampo's powerful and creative misreadings of his precursor compel us today to reread

the earlier tradition through the prism of his modern re-creations. So even though Poe fathered the genre of detective fiction, it was not until the twentieth century that it was truly established with an audience of its own and recognized on its own terms.

According to Kiyoshi Kasai, a major detective fiction writer and leading literary critic, the rise and popularity of the genre of detective fiction in the early twentieth century owes much to World War I; after all, it was this war's mass slaughter with so many anonymous deaths that reminded people to mark the significance of every individual's death (*Tantei Shosetsu Ron* [*A History of Japanese Detective Fiction*], 2 vols., Tokyo: Tokyo-Sogensha, 1998). Similarly, we find not only Romantic and individualistic tendencies within Modernist works of impersonality, but we also see anew how Modernist elements operate within hardcore Romantic writings. —Takayuki Tatsumi

The first of the three chapters on Rampo in this collection is by Seth Jacobowitz: "Pathologizing Modernity: The Grotesque in Poe and Rampo." Edogawa Rampo is the pen name of Hirai Tarō (1894–1965), and, according to Jacobowitz, the name Edogawa Rampo gestures not only toward a phonetic resonance with Edgar Allan Poe but a flâneur-like identity vis-à-vis the translated and globalized figure of Poe constructed by the Symbolist poets. As Jacobowitz explains, Edogawa Rampo was an iconic figure of twentieth century Japan and "has long been seen as a doppelganger to Poe both in terms of his intricately crafted detective stories and as a keen observer of what Baudelaire presciently dubbed 'modernité.' Indeed, Rampo quickly became one of the leading authors of the interwar period to distill the unsettling implications of mass society and its ills to a vast popular audience."

Jacobowitz's chapter compares Poe's use of "the grotesque and arabesque" with Rampo's contributions to the interwar aesthetic of "erotic grotesque nonsense" (ero guro nansensu). Rather than recuperate the stereotypical image of a consummately rational versus excessively Gothic Poe, the chapter reads the grotesque and arabesque in terms of a "productive hybridity" where one pattern unexpectedly emerges from another. When Poe and Rampo's thoughts on literary pattern are held up side by side, according to Jacobowitz, "it is evident that a powerful symmetry is at work. Much as the intermingled forms and decorative motifs of the grotesque and arabesque presented Poe with a conceptual framework for representing the cultural logic of antebellum America, so did the 'erotic grotesques' give Rampo a way to articulate the landscape of interwar Japan."

William O. Gardner, in his chapter, "Visionary Media in Edgar Allan Poe and Edogawa Rampo," uses Edogawa Rampo's essay "The Phantom Lord" (1936) to begin to build the bond between Poe and Rampo's understanding of how visual devices intrigued both authors. Edogawa Rampo inserts the lens, the projector, the screen, and other visual devices into a central position in his imaginative universe as Poe was similarly occupied with a wide range of visual and spatial media that informs Poe's work. The connection to painting, for example, is particularly strong: works such as "The Domain of Arnheim" and "The Island of the Fay" bear complex relationships to specific source paintings as well as broader traditions of landscape painting, while ekphrasis in such stories as "The Fall of the House of Usher" and "The Oval Portrait" is used to offer insights into the troubled mind of the painter within the tale or allegories on the nature of art itself. While Poe's Romanticism affords a central place for painting as a visionary and expressive art, Rampo displaces the visionary role of the artist with the mechanical work of lenses, mirrors, and other visual devices, as can be readily observed in such stories as "The Hell of Mirrors," "The Traveler with the Pasted Rag Picture," and "The Strange Tale of Panorama Island."

Yet, while the insertion of mechanical devices into Rampo's world might be expected to invoke twentieth-century objectivity or rationality, Gardner argues that these visualizing devices are, instead, imbued with the uncanny and the horrific. Moreover, far from invoking an exclusively twentieth-century progressivism, lenses and related visual technologies, for Rampo, are strongly connected with nostalgia and cultural memory. With reference to the above short stories as well as the essays "The Horrors of Film," "A Fascination with Lenses," and "Magic Lantern Shows," Gardner's chapter explores the meaning of visual technology for Rampo and its relationship to cultural memory as well as the media culture of Rampo's own time. Through this twentieth-century Pacific refraction, Gardner suggests new ways of thinking about the relationship of Poe to the visual culture of the nineteenth-century Atlantic world.

Mark Silver's chapter, "Poe's Shadow in Japan: Alternative Worlds and Failed Escapes in Edogawa Rampo's *Strange Tale of Panorama Island*," uses Poe's "The Domain of Arnheim" as an explicit point of departure for Rampo's novella *The Strange Tale of Panorama Island* (1926–1927). In the novella, Poe's work inspires Rampo's protagonist (Kôsuke Hitomi) to conceive an elaborate scheme for building an island utopia. Rampo's text, however, radically reconfigures the notion of the perfectly groomed but essentially natural landscape that Poe puts at the center of "The Domain of Arnheim." The visual splendors of the utopia conceived by Hitomi do not depend on improving nature but rather on replacing it more or less completely with simulacra of natural scenery undergirded by a vast system of behind-the-scenes machinery and gadgetry.

This emphasis on the marvels of technology in *The Strange Tale* reflects Rampo's own fascination with optical devices such as concave mirrors, lenses, telescopes, and the movie projector, as well as Japan's more general (and more angst-inducing) experience of rapid Westernization and modernization in the first decades of the twentieth century. By grafting elements of early Japanese machine-age culture onto Poe's concept of the enhanced natural landscape, Rampo turns his tale—which tellingly ends with the spectacular failure of Hitomi's project—into an implicit critique of Japanese modernity in the interwar period and of the cultural borrowing that characterized it.

As we move from Japan to China, we find Diane M. Smith's look at author Lu Xun's relationship to Poe in her chapter, "Lu Xun and Poe: Reading the Psyche." Smith begins her approach by centering on the protest in China's Tiennamen Square on May 4, 1919, that reinforced the belief that the future welfare of China would lie in a progressive agenda that would reject the stultifying dependence on tradition. The May 4th movement, as it came to be known, presented a challenge to nearly every aspect of Chinese culture—including literature—and spawned greater interest in the works of Western authors, including those by Edgar Allan Poe. Lu Xun and his brother, Zhou Zhouren, were instrumental in translating Poe's works for a Chinese audience. Lu Xun, hailed by Frederic Jameson as "China's greatest writer," set out to examine and to heal the national psyche through his literature. Influenced by Poe's investigation of the human psyche, Lu Xun used tropes of psychological disintegration and decay as a means of diagnosing the Chinese cultural psyche. Smith's chapter examines the similar structural and thematic elements in Poe's and Lu Xun's fiction. As the title of Lu Xun's first volume of stories, *A Call to Arms*, suggests, Lu Xun saw his fiction as a way to revitalize and challenge not only old Chinese literary forms but cultural traditions as well.

Moving further west across the continent to Russia, we find Alexandra Urakova's examination of the relationship between Poe and Gogol in her chapter, "'Breaking the Law of Silence': Rereading Poe's 'The Man of the Crowd' and Gogol's 'The Portrait.'" Taking the fact that both "The Portrait" by Gogol, translated and abridged, and a review of "*Tales*, by Edgar A. Poe" with the detailed summary of "The Man of the Crowd" were issued in two sequential volumes of *Blackwood's Edinburgh Magazine* (Oct. and Nov. 1847), Urakova examines the implications of having these two texts appear in the same cultural context and share the same reading audience. Urakova argues that the interconnections between these two works, although not so obvious as between "The Man of the Crowd" and "The Nevsky Prospekt" or between "The Portrait" and "The Oval Portrait," are by no means insignificant. According to Urakova,

> both Gogol and Poe turn to a Melmoth-inspired figure of an old man to represent city life and emblematize social evil. The old men are excluded, and at the same time included, in the social and economic relations sketched out as the circulation of crowds, money, commodities and energies. Their part in this circulation is different since it corresponds to two different axiological frameworks: one characteristic of an emerging modernity, the other referring to the more traditional Christian mode of sin and redemption.

Heading closer to the United States, we come to two chapters on Poe's influence in Portugal. The first, "'What Has Occurred That Has (Never) Occurred Before': A Case Study of the First Portuguese Detective Novel," by Isabel Oliveira Martins, does exactly as its title suggests: it traces the installments of "letters" by Eça de Queirós, Ramalho Ortigão, and Eduardo Coelho that comprise a piece called "The Mystery of the Road to Sintra." Martins argues that the detective in the letters is much like Poe's Dupin, that the narrator can be likened to the narrator of "The Murders in the Rue Morgue," Dupin's "assistant," and the gestures of verisimilitude are similar to those found in Poe's stories such as "MS. Found in a Bottle." The materialization of the detective story in the newspaper media shows the emergence in Portugal of a kind of writing that is the result of a mystifying game that has very tenuous borders between 'reality' and the fabulation needed to hold the reader's attention to help to solve a mystery.

The second chapter on Poe's influence in Portugal is by Margarida Vale de Gato, "'Around Reason Feeling'—Poe's Impact on Fernando Pessoa's Modernist Proposal;" it demonstrates that Poe's influence on Fernando Pessoa (1888–1935) began early in his life. The chapter traces the author's writing life and his poetic practice that helped move Portuguese literature into modernism through Poe's emphasis on rhythm, effect, and what Vale de Gato terms, "conflating reason and madness, while numbing the senses of physical reality through the rhythmic induction of rush and arousal."

As a bridge that links Poe's international influence to his impact on American writers, we have a set of poems by Charles Cantalupo entitled "Poe in Place." The first poem, "Poe in Massawa," is set in Massawa, Eritrea—certainly not a place Poe would have ever found himself, except in his imagination. Nonetheless, Poe's presence was felt there when Cantalupo photographed Haile Selassie's abandoned palace on the Red Sea and saw that he had inadvertently captured a perched raven on an exposed beam in the ruins. The poem uses this image of the raven and the structural form of "The Haunted Palace" as links to Poe. The other three poems take Poe's residences in Philadelphia, Fordam, and Baltimore as their prompts and conflate what might have been in the 1800s with what is now, filtered through on-site visits and reading Poe's letters and poems.

Next comes a chapter by Poet Laureate Daniel Hoffman, "Ligeia—Not Me! Three Women Writers Respond to Poe." Hoffman provides an overview of three contemporary women authors (two from the United States—Joyce Carol Oates and Mary Oliver—and one from England—Angela Carter) who respond to Poe's work in dramatically different ways. As Hoffman summarizes: "Each approaches Poe from a different point in his life and the life of his works: Carter is fascinated by Poe's birth and infancy; Oates by his last days and death; and Oliver by the lasting effect of his writings, we might say, his 'afterlife.'"

Shoko Itoh begins her chapter, "Gothic Windows in Poe's Narrative Spaces," with a quote by Joyce Carol Oates—"Who has not been influenced by Poe?" Itoh demonstrates how Poe's sense of the Gothic influenced William Faulkner's work, especially in relation to the physical settings, particularly houses and even more specifically, windows. She looks, particularly, at how both authors' works pay specific attention to the auditory associations with Gothic windows.

The last chapter in the collection, "Poe's Progeny: Varieties of Detection in Key American Literary Texts, 1841–1861," by John Gruesser brings us back to Poe's influence on nineteenth-century American authors. Gruesser argues that Poe's creation of the detective genre influenced *The Scarlet Letter*, *Benito Cereno*, and *Incidents in the Life of a Slave Girl*. He examines the detection strategies in "Hawthorne's fascination with the intersections between morality and psychology, Melville's biting critique of white Americans' willful obtuseness in matters of race, and Jacobs' efforts to create a hybrid text that reworks both the conventions of the African American slave narrative and elements from various Anglo American fictional genres."

Overall, the chapters in this collection complement and extend a project begun by Lois Vines's 1999 *Poe Abroad* (University of Iowa Press). At the end of her introduction, Vines acknowledges that, "*Poe Abroad* begs a second volume" (4); this volume, in part, answers that call. *Poe's Pervasive Influence*, however, also extends Vines' project by taking a wider perspective on Poe's influence, adding essays on American authors whose work directly echoes Poe's practice.

NOTES

1. Rufus Wilmot Griswold, "Edgar A. Poe," *The Prose Writers of America* (4th edition) (New York: Parry & McMillan, 1856). http://www.eapoe.org/papers/misc1827/1851pwa.htm. Accessed June 2011.

2. Alexis de Tocqueville, *Democracy in America* (London: Saunders and Otley, 1835). http://xroads.virginia.edu/~HYPER/DETOC/1_ch15.htm. Accessed June 2011.

Chapter One

Pathologizing Modernity:
The Grotesque in Poe and Rampo

Seth Jacobowitz

At the affective level, we are accustomed to think of the grotesque within a text as that which produces the effects of awe and terror or perhaps even revulsion. Often equated with or subsumed within a constellation of related terms such as the uncanny, the fantastic, the monstrous and the Gothic, the grotesque is typically regarded in the works of Edgar Allan Poe and Edogawa Rampo (1894–1965) as antithetical to the deductive and ratiocinative tendencies of their detective fiction. Nonetheless, both authors effected a compound version of the grotesque—"the grotesque and arabesque" derived from German Romanticism for Poe and for Rampo from the catchphrase "erotic-grotesque-nonsense" (*ero-guro-nansensu*)—which, in the manner of an essential clue, points toward the resolution of this apparent contradiction with a genre whose hallmarks are inference, observation and analysis of the forensic traces of modern life.

When I first began to consider these two authors in a comparative framework, I had a fairly straightforward idea in mind, namely, to see how their respective, combinatory approaches to the grotesque captured the cultural logic for their distinct eras (doubtlessly our historical moment is an outgrowth of theirs and has its own share of postmodern mutations). However, no sooner did I entertain what this project might reveal about antebellum America or interwar Japan than a presuppositional doubt intruded and overtook my original intention. Do our everyday assumptions accurately capture the semantic and historical range of the term? More pertinently, what might lie on the other side of an investigation of the grotesque if we cease to think of it strictly as a descriptive or atmospheric element and come to regard it as a signifying process in its own right? Indeed, what if the grotesque in Poe and

Rampo's oeuvres could be conceived from the outset not as the opposition of the monstrous or fanciful to the ratiocinative and scientific but rather their conjoining? As I argue in this essay, the grotesque as a mode of doubling and pattern-making is used by Poe and Rampo to represent the pathologies inherent in modernity that foreclose upon collective renewal and social order. This, in turn, threatens to transform our fundamental understanding of the term.

In keeping with these objectives, I have organized this essay into three sections. The first section returns to the archeological discovery of the grotesque during the Renaissance from the ruins of Roman antiquity and then examines a theorization of the grotesque by Bakhtin and others in a larger continuum that includes medieval European folk rituals and festivities such as Carnival. The second section explores several parallel uses of the grotesque in Poe's "The Murders in the Rue Morgue" and Rampo's *Strange Tale of Panorama Island* that reflect continuities and ruptures from its discursive origins. In particular, the motif of colonial terror in both texts underscores the shift from celebrating the supernatural and transcendental aspects of the grotesque toward the dispassionate observation of a violent alienation of social relations. The third section provides a close reading of the interlocking architectural and narratological structures of the grotesque in Poe's short story "William Wilson" (1839) and Rampo's novella *Stalker in the Attic* (*Yaneura no sanposha*, 1926) demonstrating that the subversion, or even perversion, of the grotesque is, itself, symptomatic of the pathologies of modernity.

EXCAVATION AND INTERPRETATION OF THE GROTESQUE

Conventional accounts of the grotesque invariably trace back to the Renaissance-era discovery of whimsical frescoes in the remains of Nero's *Domus Aurea*, which was buried in the fall of Rome a millennium earlier. These fanciful designs, in which human, semihuman and animal figures alternate with flowers, plants and purely geometric forms, came as a profound shock to classical notions of order, symmetry and logic. In *On the Grotesque: Strategies of Contradiction in Art and Literature* (1982), Geoffrey Harpham aptly notes that the word "grotesque" derives from "*grottesche*" in keeping with the subterranean caves in which they were discovered. It is a misnomer whose closest Latin equivalent is the sepulchral *crypta* or crypt. The origins of the grotesque, or at least its etymology, thus simultaneously "gathers into itself suggestions of the underground, of burial, and of secrecy"[1] in the traditional archeological sense and in a Foucauldian sense of rupture with the foundations of classical Western culture. In principle, then, the grotesque emerges from the broken shell of antiquity as a peculiarly modern construct, always already a deviant from established conventions of good form. Insofar as it is defined by one form arising from another, the grotesque would henceforth continue to prove particularly well suited to hybridity and modulation. It is also an apt metaphor for the return of repressed or unconscious drives, though as we shall see, studies of the medieval grotesque have, at best, an ambivalent relationship to psychoanalysis.

In keeping with these categorical ambiguities, Harpham introduces the reader to conflicting views of the grotesque in Wolfgang Kayser's *The Grotesque in Art and Literature* (1957) and Mikhail Bakhtin's *Rabelais and His World* (1965). Where Kayser ranges over the shifting nuances of the grotesque across the centuries from Renaissance to modernism, Bakhtin specifically invokes medieval tales, folk laughter and the masked rituals of Carnival as essential sources of communal revitalization and maintenance of social balance despite feudal (or later capitalist) inequities. Although Bakhtin's ascendance in the ensuing decades has overshadowed Kayser to the point of obscurity, it is worth citing his definition of the grotesque, which carries frighteningly relativistic, and therefore in some ways proto-modern, qualities:

> By the word *grottesco* the Renaissance, which used it to designate a specific ornamental style suggested by antiquity, understood not only something ominous and sinister in the face of a world totally different from the familiar one—a world in which the realm of inanimate things is no longer separated from those of plants, animals, and human beings, and where the laws of statics, symmetry, and proportion are no longer valid. This meaning ensues from a synonym for grotesque which came into usage during the sixteenth century: the dreams of painters (*sogni dei pittori*).[2]

These metaphysical uncertainties, coupled with a challenge to classical good form, constituted a powerful aesthetic statement that diversified and disseminated across continental Europe.[3] By the eighteenth century, however, some of this immediacy appears to have been lost. It was used interchangeably with the arabesque by the German Romantics, from whom Poe concocted his own variations and distinctions on the theme. Other contemporaneous offshoots are suggestive as well. Kayser notes that the grotesque "was somewhat extended in its application to certain *chinoiseries* which the eighteenth century related to the grotesque because of the fusion of spheres, the monstrous nature of ingredients, and the subversion of order and proportion which characterizes them."[4] While it is beyond the scope of this essay to explore in detail, we would be wholly justified in extending the polymorphous franchise of the grotesque to include the *japonaiseries* of the mid-nineteenth century with their fantastical subject matter, off-center or flat compositions, bold use of line and raw color without shading, and so on. The connection is further borne out when we consider that Symbolists such as Baudelaire and Mallarmé were simultaneously translating Poe into French even as they experimented with the alternatingly bizarre and pleasing effects from Japanese woodblock prints.[5] In this regard the cultural gulf separating Poe and Rampo (or East and West) proves rather smaller than we might imagine.

Beyond this point, Kayser's interpretation of Poe's contributions to the grotesque amounts to something like the free reign of the Romantic imagination, or perhaps, retrospectively, the synesthesia of the Symbolists. In a passage on Hoffmann's "The Sandman" (1816) that parenthetically draws in Poe, but inexplicably sidesteps any mention of Freud's essay on the uncanny, Kayser observes: "The distortion of all ingredients, the fusion of different realms, the coexistence of beautiful, bizarre, ghastly, and repulsive elements, the merger of the parts into a turbulent whole, the withdrawal into a phantasmagoric and nocturnal world (Poe used to speak of his 'daydreams')—all these features have here entered into the concept of the grotesque."[6] The grotesque thus seems to be a repository of an individual human imagination or psychology (Kayser gives no sign of Jung's collective unconscious, either) that incorporates dreams and the supernatural as part of its transcendence of prosaic reality. By the same token, it is this same alchemistic spirit, or what he calls Poe's "amazing talent for combination," that distinguishes his approach to detective fiction. Yet Kayser never takes the additional step of explaining this promising turn of phrase, or to reconcile a definition of the grotesque as *inherently* conducive to the seemingly contrary aims of the detective genre.

In contrast to Kayser, Bakhtin's point of departure is neither the ruins of Roman ornamental architecture nor the presumptive universality of psychoanalysis[7] but the seasonal rituals of Carnival tracing back at least to medieval times. Along with the lower classes' anarchic laughter as a buffer against the rigid hierarchies imposed by secular and clerical authorities, the annual festivities of Carnival achieve mastery over life and death in a social as well as biological sense. Where Kayser's grotesque belongs to an isolated aestheticism (i.e., the genius of Romanticism), Bakhtin's is resolutely materialist, corporeal, impersonal and utopian. Bakhtin insists that individual and community mirror one another's existence in Carnival:

> This festive organization of the crowd must be first of all concrete and sensual. Even the pressing throng, the physical contact of bodies, acquires a certain meaning. The individual feels that he is an indissoluble part of the collectivity, a member of the people's mass body. In this whole the individual body ceases to a certain extent to be itself; it is possible, so to say, to exchange bodies, to be renewed (through change of costume and mask). At the same time the people become aware of their sensual, material bodily unity and community.[8]

In other words, the individual is superseded by a ritual performance that affirms collective identity, the social rather than individual good. The prevailing order is temporarily suspended, even transgressed, during this time of exception so that it may paradoxically remain in force the rest of the calendar year.

Bakhtin's analysis of the grotesque in literature and the arts reminds us how the fecund and vulgar aspects of human existence (sexual intercourse, defecation, etc.), so often concealed or repressed from public display, come to the fore as a mapping onto our bodies and cultural landscapes: "The artistic logic of the grotesque image ignores the closed, smooth and impenetrable surface of the body and retains only its excrescences (sprouts, buds) and orifices, only that which leads beyond the body's limited space and into the body's depths. Mountains and abysses, such is the relief of the grotesque body; or speaking in architectural terms, towers and subterranean passages."[9] It is easy to read into this passage a comparison to the psychological and physical landscapes of Gothicism. But there is a critical difference—the Gothic organizes questions of heredity and property toward the narrowest of ideological ends: inheritance and succession, or dissolution. By contrast, according to Bakhtin, the horrors and profane excesses of the grotesque should lead toward social catharsis and rebalancing. The critical difference for Poe and Rampo, as we shall see below, is what happens when modernity short-circuits the potentially therapeutic powers of the grotesque.

COLONIAL TERROR

Eschewing American and creole equivalents such as New Orleans' Mardi Gras festival,[10] Poe insistently returns to the backdrop of European bacchanalia in such works as "William Wilson" (1839), "Masque of the Red Death" (1842) and "The Cask of Amontillado" (1846). He similarly gleans aspects of grotesque from daily life in the major European capitals in the crowded streets of London in "The Man of the Crowd" (1840) and Paris in "The Murders in the Rue Morgue" (1841). It is the latter in particular which expresses most clearly the alienating conditions of modern life deciphered from a pattern of anonymous, horrific and seemingly senseless criminal acts or behaviors.

For his part, Rampo makes ample use of early-twentieth-century Japan's panoply of festivals, street fairs, circuses and freak shows in, for instance, "The Daydream" (1925), "The Dancing Dwarf" (1926) and "The Carousel Goes Round" (*Mokuba wa mawaru*; untranslated, 1926). Rampo mostly stayed local to the environs of the old Edo/Tokyo downtown, especially Asakusa, where sundry traditional entertainments could be found alongside mass cultural offerings such as movie theaters and the Hanayashiki amusement park. Rampo's contemporary, Kawabata Yasunari, breathlessly captures Asakusa's carnal energies in his modernist novel *The Scarlet Gang of Asakusa* (1929–1930): "In Asakusa, everything is flung out in the raw. Desires dance naked. All races, all classes, all jumbled together forming a bottomless, endless current, flowing day and night, no beginning, no end. Asakusa is alive. . . . The masses converge on it, constantly. Their Asakusa is a foundry in which all the old models are regularly melted down to be cast into new ones."[11] In many respects, Asakusa would provide categorical fulfillment of the carnivalesque: it was the place where high, low and all points between congregate for refuge and pleasure-seeking. Yet Asakusa-as-foundry is not only carnal but industrial. Befitting its identity as a locus of entertainment industries (even if some were still in their infancy or cottage industry phases), it reminds us that modernity is perpetually in flux, an insatiable stoking of new desires and forms of consumption. The shunting away of desires from the communal to the individual, or from volkish authenticity to kitsch, would deprive the grotesque of its regenerative properties.

It is difficult to overstate the degree to which the grotesque in interwar Japan, phoneticized as *gurotesuku* rather than translated into Chinese characters, became a byword of the period on its own and as part of the floating signifier "erotic, grotesque, nonsense." Its frequent use in literature and journalism, including in a journal named *Grotesque* in the 1930s, simultaneously attested to a fascination and uneasiness with commodity fetishism, imperial expansion and the aftershocks of disruptive major events such as the Great Kantō Earthquake (1923) and the Great Depression (1929). While to some extent the eccentricities and pleasure-seeking ways of the Edo period (1603–1867) were re-invested with meaning in the late 1930s and 1940s, particularly as the authorities began to crack down on what were perceived as decadent Western ways, such nostalgia in no way betokened a viable possibility of return to the past.[12]

Poe's and Rampo's use of the grotesque, especially when interlaced with detective fiction, transforms the open bodies of Carnival into the wounded and murdered victims of modern life. At the same time, the certainties of the medieval worldview are replaced by one in which change is the only constant. It is not surprising, then, that Poe and Rampo alike do not focus on prescriptive solutions but case studies in a wide-ranging epidemiology. They adeptly register the recurring pattern of symptoms, if not precisely the causes or cures, for a society that no longer coheres.

"The Murders in the Rue Morgue" consists of three parts that sit uneasily side by side: a disquisition into the faculty of analysis is succeeded by the first-person account of an unnamed American narrator and how he made the acquaintance of the amateur detective C. Auguste Dupin, followed by the narrator's relating Dupin's deciphering of the double murder of a Parisian mother and daughter. Reflexive of the terms of its composition, the tale demands that the reader reflect upon the dual (or dueling) attributes of the grotesque and detective fiction. Analysis in the first part is distinguished from mere calculation: analysis requires "a host of observations and inferences"[13] as well as the ability to match one's mind with another's. Accordingly, no detail is sufficiently insignificant to escape notice and can be used to one's advantage.

Against this statement of consummate rationalism, the meeting of the narrator and Dupin trumps sense with sensibility. Homoerotic undertones prevail as the two encounter one another in a library in Montmartre, where they are both searching for the same rare volume of an unspecified book. A pair of Romantically inclined kindred spirits, they move in together, the narrator being a man of greater means than Dupin, whose family fortunes have waned due to equally unspecific circumstances. They share "a time-eaten and grotesque mansion, long deserted through superstitions into which we did not inquire, and tottering to its fall in a retired and desolate portion of the Faubourg St. Germain" (532). The grotesque mansion is left ambiguous and never mentioned again, an outward manifestation, perhaps, of Romantic sentiment and/or Gothic atmospherics. The two men are inseparable, taking nocturnal rambles together "arm in arm" through the city (*flâneurie*) and sharing their love of literature, dreams, and new scientific theories. This includes, ultimately, criminal forensics, when Dupin introduces the as-yet unsolved murder of two women reported in the newspaper. From this point forward, the story is solely concerned with how Dupin deduces the identity of the culprit. At the very least, however, the relationship between the narrator and Dupin and its setting imply coexistences that lie beyond the scope of analysis. One mystery will be solved while another, rife with suggestive detail, paradoxically remains.

Through careful observance of the evidence and his immense erudition, Dupin realizes that the murders were not committed by any man (or woman) but an escaped orangutan.[14] The animal, which got loose from its master, a sailor, finds its way into the apartment of a mother and daughter. Mimicking the behavior of its master, it tries to shave one of the women. When it cuts her unintentionally, the orangutan becomes enraged and kills both, stuffing one of them in the chimney to hide the evidence. It is an example of a civilizing act gone horribly wrong by a tropical monster (or, in the hands of less nuanced writers than Poe, subhuman races) whose very presence signals a social body under invasion.

As Kayser notes, the results of this gruesome incident are described by Dupin himself as "grotesqueries."[15] Yet unlike its mention earlier in the narrative, I would maintain this is best understood in a distinctly modern sense. Dupin's forensic decoding of the crime scene is a prime example of how detective fiction transforms fear and mystery into dispassionate mastery of the facts. According to popular interpretation, the genre indulges the reader in a thrilling view of disorder and mayhem in a society of ever-increasing size and complexity, followed by the assertion of control and re-establishment of the status quo. In this instance, the revelation of the killer does not truly restore society to order. Rather, it points to the porousness of trade and exchange where, along with tropical fruits and other sundry improvements to daily life, colonial terrors come home to roost in the imperial metropolis. Surely more worrying than the isolated case of an animal of superhuman strength and unpredictable temperament on the loose, it betrays the failure to inoculate against multiplying, unexpected dangers. At the risk of overstating the obvious, I might add that the murders are solved, but to no avail, since the murderer is not human, and therefore not subject to prosecution or punishment. The crimes are nonsensical acts that not only fall outside the bounds of reason but outside human law.

The colonial terrors of the grotesque also appear in Rampo's novel, *A Strange Tale of Panorama Island* (1927). The protagonist, Hitomi Hirosuke, is a penniless hack writer scraping by in Tokyo when he learns of the recent death of a former classmate, the scion of an industrialist family, to whom he bears an uncanny likeness. Having dreamt his whole life of having the financial resources to build his own utopian republic to satisfy his personal tastes, the writer devises and succeeds in carrying out a plan to pass himself off as the genuine article to the dead man's family. Within a year of assuming his new identity, he harnesses the deceased's considerable capital to transform a deserted island off the coast of Japan into the so-called Panorama Island.

It is a veritable colonial project, a prescient and telescoped version of what was to come in Manchukuo, as the puppet state of Manchuria under Japanese imperial domination was called from 1931 until the end of WWII. As Mark Driscoll has recently argued in *Absolute Erotic, Absolute Grotesque: The Living, Dead and Undead in Japan's Imperialism, 1895–1945*,

> The main feature of Hitomi's own private Manchukuo is having successfully recruited unemployed actresses, actors, and other bored and depressed beautiful people to experience the "ultimate curiosity" and willingly suicide themselves into statues or surgically hybridize with animals à la *The Island of Dr. Moreau*. After installing this capitalist second nature, Hitomi takes his seat in the middle of the island to enjoy the visual pleasure of watching the panoramas (using lights and movement to simulate cinematic "dissolves" and "fades"), which is said to surpass even the most lavish of Hollywood spectacles. He is apprehended in the end, but not before his "obscene production" has elicited the "heights of curiosity" in consumers thanks to his nihilistically "playing games with death and life."[16]

The crucial features of the modern grotesque should be self-evident. The island's extreme makeover into an amusement park and visual spectacle has no folk value or even much to offer in the way of subversive laughs. With the exception of Hitomi Hirosuke, whose name suggests the word play of "one who sees the world wide-eyed" befitting the viewer of panoramic vistas,[17] the island's new labor force and habitués are mere pawns or playthings not unlike the anonymous courtiers in Poe's "Masque of the Red Death." A living bestiary and machinery, these characters possess no subjective agency of their own, existing solely for the pleasure of the island's self-styled emperor.

When the openness of individual or communal bodies generates no means of escape, there is only gore, terror and dehumanizing alienation. In short, *Panorama Island* delivers the spectacle of uncompromising exploitation in eerie anticipation of the horrors to come in Japan's sprawling East Asian and Pacific empire. Given this self-centered perversion of the grotesque, it is almost to be expected that when Hitomi is unmasked by amateur detective Akechi Kogoro, Rampo's equivalent number to Dupin, he chooses to go out in a blaze of glory, exploding himself over the fantasy landscape rather than submit to another's sovereignty. This uncompromising attitude also fore-shadows the futile endgame of the Pacific War.

THE STALKER IN WILLIAM WILSON'S ATTIC

In grandiose and self-aggrandizing fashion, the opening lines of "William Wilson" are rife with the visionary and decadent extremes of Romanticism on the cusp of its metamorphosis into Symbolism, an event in which Poe, as we already noted, played a pivotal, posthumous role. William Wilson is an ordinary boy sent to school in a gloomy corner of southern England who finds that his name is shared by another student in his class. William Wilson is neither one's real name—the narrator uses it to stand in for any sort of common name that guarantees its namesake the disagreeable reality of being mistaken for another. As the narrative unfolds, we learn by degrees that the other Wilson increasingly and uncannily resembles him in all respects; in effect, a perfect body double who seems to exist solely to torment him. The other boy is a strangely liminal figure, almost a shadow from the outset. As time goes on, this other William Wilson begins to mimic the protagonist in unbearable ways, threatening to overtake his very sense of self-identity. Both to avoid his oppressor and the perils of the very sort of life-and-death strug-gle for unitary identity their antagonism foreshadows, the protagonist quits the school and roams the earth in self-imposed exile. Embarking on a life of debauchery and vice, he is haunted by this oppressive double no matter where he turns until their final, fatal confrontation in the conclusion. In this respect, "William Wilson" anticipates nearly all of the basic themes in Rampo's *oeuvre* including *Panorama Island* and "Stalker in the Attic": the ennui-ridden dilettante who finds himself only in the thrill of crime; the use of doppelgangers, doubles, and mirror-images; the carnivalesque and disguise (including pseudonyms);[18] and voyeurism and stalking, culminating in murder.

William Wilson is an assumed name that demands to be read literally. Will I am, will's son: the same testament to hereditary character echoing Dupin's history is voiced in the narrator's self-introduction, "I am the descendant of a race whose imaginative and easily excitable temperament has at all times rendered them remarkable" (427). The exceptionalism of the original, if pseudonymic, Wilson is ironically undercut by the existence of his unwanted twin. Suitably enough, the doubling of the protagonist recalls the near-synonymous interchangeability of the grotesque and arabesque: they become a pair of intertwined terms about intertwining.

In the encounter between William Wilson and his shadowy twin as well, the architecture of the school plays an essential part. There is, to be certain, a fair amount of Gothic imagery in "William Wilson," not only in terms of the heavy stone and timber labyrinthine design of the schoolhouse itself, but insofar as it amounts to the physical manifestation of the interior psychological state of the protagonist. Nevertheless, Wilson's fascination and confusion in relating its parts goes back to the pattern-making of the grotesque:

> But the house!—how quaint an old building was this!—to me how veritably a palace of enchantment! There was really no end to its windings—to its incomprehensible subdivisions. It was difficult, at any given time, to say with certainty upon which of its two stories one happened to be. From each room to every other there were sure to be found three or four steps either in ascent or descent. Then the lateral branches were innumerable—inconceivable—and so returning in upon themselves, that our most exact ideas in regard to the whole mansion were not very far different from those with which we pondered upon infinity. During the five years of my residence here, I was never able to ascertain with precision, in what remote locality lay the little sleeping apartment assigned to myself and some eighteen or twenty other scholars. (429)

Wilson's schoolhouse is a model of the grotesque with its bizarre proportions, branches that fold back in upon themselves, and hidden recesses. Within the schoolhouse is the school-room, where the pattern further repeats upon itself and is inlaid with a kind of graffiti in the protagonist's self-described inner sanctum (a graffiti, by the way, which should recall to cognoscenti the markings left behind in the *grottesches* of the *Domus Aurea* by such illustrious amateur diggers and tourists as Rafael and Michelangelo, Casanova and de Sade):

The school-room was the largest in the house—I could not help thinking, in the world. It was very long, narrow, and dismally low, with pointed Gothic windows and a ceiling of oak. In a remote and terror-inspiring angle was a square enclosure of eight or ten feet, comprising the *sanctum*, "during hours," of our principal, the Reverend Dr. Bransby. . . . Interspersed about the room, crossing and recrossing in endless irregularity, were innumerable benches and desks, black, ancient, and time-worn, piled desperately with much-bethumbed books, and so beseamed with initial letters, names at full length, *grotesque figures*, and other multiplied efforts of the knife, as to have entirely lost what little of original form might have been their portion in days long departed. (429–30; emphasis added)

In its layers and stores of knowledge, it signals identities lost and overlapping like a palimpsest, another suggestive dimension of the grotesque as pattern. Absent the story's violent terminus, it is perhaps the purest vision of converging or conjoining of names, partial and whole, with the grounds (or desk, benches, etc.) upon which they rest. The very same honeycombed rooms of the school also provide the location for the uncanny encounter between the two William Wilsons: a closet of sorts where the protagonist discovers the other sleeping, his features having become identical in every way to his own. So begins the protagonist's descent into a life of debauchery and profligacy as he attempts to rid himself of the accursed other, who seems to haunt him no matter how far and wide he travels through the capitals of Europe.

The grotesque shifts abruptly in the finale from Wilson's personal attempts to disguise and hide himself away to an altogether different sort of masquerade, Carnival, the ritual in which symbolic costumes and disguises at once *conceal and reveal* the body politic.[19] How appropriate, then, that so many of Poe's murders occur on the occasion of licensed and licentious excess, in which self ecstatically becomes other! The twist comes when self and other already mirror one another, as when the Grim Reaper in the "Masque of the Red Death" comes disguised as itself, or Wilson encounters his doppelgänger at a masquerade ball one fateful night in contemporary Rome. Incited by the mirrored reflection of his antagonist to commit murder, he finds: *"You have conquered, and I yield. Yet, henceforward art thou also dead—dead to the World, to Heaven and to Hope! In me didst thou exist— and, in my death, see by this image, which is thine own, how utterly thou hast murdered thyself"* (448).

We might recall what Bakhtin has to say about doubling or mirroring as a function of the grotesque, "We have already sufficiently stressed the fact that the grotesque imagery constructs what we might call a double body. In the endless chain of bodily life it retains the parts in which one link joins the other, in which the life of one body is born from the death of the preceding, older one."[20] In its portrayal of what we would call today a split personality disorder, "William Wilson" is nothing less than a perverse short-circuiting of the medieval ritual by madness, or at best, modern solipsism. The autonomy of the individual is not restored by this act of violence; Wilson's attempts to liberate himself from himself result in (double) suicide.

The architectural and psychological motifs of "William Wilson" strongly anticipate Rampo's "Stalker in the Attic," whose protagonist, Goda Saburō, similarly finds fascination in the hidden, inner recesses of a Tokyo boarding house. It is there he spies upon his fellow boarders through knotholes in the ceiling boards and after much rumination in his own closet, he will eventually murder one of them by dropping a lethal morphine solution into the victim's unsuspecting mouth from above. In this he is both lured and caught in the trap of Rampo's detective hero, Akechi Kogorō, who effectively serves as a double to the protagonist and his crime but only for the purposes of exposing him, not preventing the murder or rehabilitating the criminal he, in fact, helps to create. Akechi, in fact, regards him as an experimental subject of abnormal psychology.

The erotic-grotesque in Rampo's era depended upon stimulation from new forms of modernist and mass culture entertainments, to say nothing of surrendering to hardcore libidinal urges rendered timeless in the broader category of the grotesque. Consistent with the masked debaucheries and role playing associated with Carnival, the protagonist indulges in cross-dressing and homoerotic provocation (at minimum) in the back alleys and movie shacks of Asakusa. He further finds his antidote to the oppressive boredom of his daily life in "books by Poe, Hoffman, and Gaboriau, jumbled in amongst a slew of other detective novels."[21]

Eventually Saburō tires of endless rehearsals to a life of crime that he is simply too cowardly to put into practice. It is quite by accident that he discovers the brave new world of the attic one day while he lies in the closet of the room, where he hides himself away from his fellow boarders. In contrast to the spectacular, artificial vistas of *A Strange Tale of Panorama Island*, the attic presents an otherworldly appearance with its tiny pores of light from the rooms below and the roof above, a sort of voyeur's paradise. His observations of others unawares are at once bizarre and comical, as he is privy to sights otherwise invisible to the public: tracking the love affairs of a promiscuous female art student, the fetishist who licks away the stains on his suit and so on. Finally he comes upon a knothole directly above the sleeping body—and mouth—of the disagreeable dental school graduate Endō. Saburō hardly knows the other boarder, and his decision to kill him is not out of malice, but opportunity. In one of his postwar essays on Anglo-American detective fiction, Rampo recalls an obscure short story by a British novelist about a dentist who uses his profession to murderous advantage: "While the dentist is treating a fellow he holds a grudge against, he sticks the barrel of a concealed pistol into the patient's mouth and pulls the trigger. The patient has his eyes tightly shut and his mouth wide open. It is the perfect crime."[22] In this case there is an ironic reversal, as it is the would-be dentist, asleep, who is murdered with poison dropped into his gaping mouth.

> While Saburō was staring at Endō's face a strange thought occurred to him. If he were to spit down the hole, wouldn't it land right in Endo's wide-open mouth? It was as if Endō's mouth had been custom-made to lie smack dab under the knothole. Saburō had weird tastes, so he took the drawstring out of the Western-style underpants he wore beneath his tights and dangled it from the top of the knothole. He put the drawstring to his eye and looked down at it as though it were the sight of a rifle to see if he was right. It was an amazing coincidence. The drawstring, the knothole and Endō's mouth lined up perfectly. In other words, he knew if he spit down the hole it would definitely land in Endō's mouth. [23]

The homoerotic tensions in this passage notwithstanding, it occurs to Saburō later that night to murder Endō by stealing a bottle of morphine from Endō's room and dripping a lethal dosage of the solution into his open mouth. He is initially able to get away with the perfect crime, as it appears to the police and fellow boarders as though Endō has committed suicide. In the end, however, he is caught by Akechi, who becomes suspicious when he learns of an alarm clock set the night before by the would-be suicide and when he notices Saburō's sudden aversion to smoking. It turns out Saburō accidentally dropped the morphine bottle down the hole into Endō's tobacco pouch and this, subconsciously, causes his change in behavior. Akechi even throws in a missing button he falsely claims Saburō unknowingly lost in the attic and which was unique to him: a forensic game of cat-and-mouse in which the latter further gives himself away. Akechi abandons the scene at this point, knowing he has effectively signed Saburō's death warrant, since the other will either give himself up or take his own life now that his crime has been revealed.

As we see with "William Wilson," architecture and narrative in "Stalker in the Attic" mirror one another as a distortion of the medieval grotesque. Wilson's desperation to vanquish his adversary, to rid himself of his own shadow, runs the labyrinth of the school, and even of the world, but his final encounter in Carnival ends in *sui caedere*, literally killing oneself. This pathological state is more than matched by Goda Saburō's escalation from playing at crime on the streets of carnivalesque Asakusa to hiding away in the attic of the boarding house, where otherworldly lighting and endless possibilities for voyeurism holds out only the thinnest margins of social connectedness. Saburō's sociopathic murder of Endō, while less obviously fraught with circularity than Wilson's, nevertheless inexorably leads to his own death sentence when Akechi forces his confession, which involves the stagecraft of hanging upside down in the closet as if he were Endō's body double. By the same token, the trail of clues, real and imagined, that Akechi finds in the attic do nothing to explain away the senselessness of the crime. Unmoored from its original meaning of organic and social renewal, the grotesque can now be seen as conducive to the aims of detective fiction insofar as it, too, is now implicated in the pathologies of modernity.

NOTES

1. Geoffrey Harpham, *On the Grotesque: Strategies of Contradiction in Art and Literature*. Princeton: Princeton University Press, 1982, 27.
2. Wolfgang Kayser, *The Grotesque in Art and Literature*. Trans. Ulrich Weisstein. New York: Columbia University Press, 1981, 21.
3. See, for instance, Marina Warner, *Monsters of Our Own Making: The Peculiar Pleasures of Fear*. Lexington: University of Kentucky Press, 1998, 248–249, on the northward spread of the grotesque from Italy, and the range of artistic expression it occasioned by Hieronymous Bosch, Pieter Bruegel the Elder and others.
4. Kayser, 29.
5. Regarding the Symbolists' use of Japonisme, see Jan Walsh Hokenson, *Japan, France, and East-West Aesthetics: French Literature, 1867–2000*. Madison, NJ: Farleigh Dickson University Press, 2004.
6. Kayser, 79.
7. In keeping with his views of the carnivalesque as an integral part of the medieval world order, Bakhtin explicitly rejects what he sees as Freudianism's absurd claims for the bourgeois domestic order to represent the universal human psychic condition. He also ridicules the notion that Freud had access to the depths of the unconscious when in fact, at all times, his information was obtained from the utterances of the speaking subject, i.e., the patient.
8. Pam Morris, ed. *The Bakhtin Reader: Selected Writings of Bakhtin, Medvedev, Voloshinov*. New York: Edwin Arnold, 1994, 225.
9. Morris, 234.
10. American and creole expressions of the grotesque were a subject of deep interest to Lafcadio Hearn in the 1870s and 1880s before he departed for Japan and began to adapt and record its rich repository of folk tales, superstitions and ghost stories into English.
11. Yasunari Kawabata, *Scarlet Gang of Asakusa*. Trans. Alisa Freedman. Berkeley: University of California Press, 2005, 30.
12. Kuki Shūzō's *The Structure of Iki* (1930), for instance, distilled such nostalgia through the filter of Heideggerian philosophy. Besides Rampo, Akutagawa Ryūnosuke, Kawabata Yasunari, Tanizaki Junichirō and many other interwar writers likewise drew inspiration from the grotesqueries of Edo or earlier times, but did not, or rather could not, cease to be aware of their own modernity.
13. Edgar Allan Poe, *Tales and Sketches, Vol. 1: 1831–1842*. Ed. Thomas O. Mabbott. Urbana: University of Illinois Press, 2000, 530. Further references to Poe's tales are from this edition and noted parenthetically.
14. The latter is one of the many possibilities that Rampo, in one of his postwar catalogs of the conventions of the detective fiction genre, files under the heading, "the killer that is not human." See Edogawa Rampo, *The Edogawa Rampo Reader*. Trans. and ed. Seth Jacobowitz. Fukuoka: Kurodahan Press, 2008, 203.
15. Kayser, 80.
16. Mark Driscoll, *Absolute Erotic, Absolute Grotesque: The Living, Dead, and Undead in Japan's Imperialism, 1895–1945*. Durham: Duke University Press, 2010, 211–212.
17. The last name Hitomi is homophonous with the Japanese word for the pupil of the eye, while the first name Hirosuke suggests wideness or broadness. In short, then, a man of panoramic vision.

18. It is tempting to see in the name William Wilson a parallel to Rampo himself: if one were to translate William Wilson into a generic-sounding Japanese equivalent, Hirai Tarō, Rampo's actual name, would surely suffice. Hirai's choice to assume the literary persona of a Poe-like doppelgänger was in no sense a parasitic move along the lines of the shadowy "William Wilson" nor a clumsy attempt at homage but a brilliant recognition of the productive possibilities that could be had by building upon the essential meaning of the grotesque.

19. See Frances Connolly's discussion of Bakhtin and the relation of the grotesque to the carnivalesque in her "Introduction" to *Modern Art and the Grotesque*. Ed. Frances Connolly. Cambridge: Cambridge University Press, 2003, 8–11.

20. Morris, 318.

21. *The Edogawa Rampo Reader*, 45.

22. *The Edogawa Rampo Reader*, 211.

23. *The Edogawa Rampo Reader*, 58.

Chapter Two

Visionary Media in Edgar Allan Poe and Edogawa Rampo

William O. Gardner

In his essay "The Phantom Lord" (1936), Japanese author Edogawa Rampo (1894–1965) describes the literary author as a lord over of a "land of dreams" and proposes a clear division between the dream world of fiction and the world of actual events. Indeed, Rampo paraphrases the narrator of Poe's "Berenice" with the following: "for me the daylight world is but an illusion; the dreams of night are real."[1] Furthermore, regarding Rampo's detective fiction, he claims that "there is no relationship whatsoever between real events and my detective stories. They occupy completely different worlds" (151). In its privileging of the imagination, Rampo's essay seems to be a guileless restatement of Romantic aesthetics. His writings as a whole, however, reveal a fascination with the materiality of media that destabilizes the very division between reality and dream, a division that his essay ostensibly supports; this seeming contradiction generates the effects of unease, horror, and thrill that distinguish Rampo's work. Moreover, the fascination for media expressed in Rampo's writings provides an intriguing viewpoint from which to reconsider the role of media in the work of his trans-Pacific literary predecessor, Edgar Allan Poe.

The paradoxical role of media is embedded within Rampo's "Phantom Lord" essay itself, as the author describes his fascination with the material components of the print medium, which impelled him to collect his own set of moveable type as a boy. Yet the fascination of this typeset is two-fold: it excites the young Rampo as a medium or bridge to "the land of dreams," but it also appeals to him in its very physicality. He expands on this recollection in a later essay:

> I accumulated several thousand pieces of #4 type. Not yet stained with ink, their silver color was beautiful to behold. I would play with them one by one like little soldiers made of lead, then carefully put them back . . . in their handmade cases. The secret to reaching the land of dreams was hidden away in those rows of little lead bricks" ("My Love for the Printed Word," 1937). (164)

Later, he writes of how he and his playmates would hand-press their own literary magazine:

> One of the boys rolled the glossy ink over the silvery type, while another carefully laid out the paper. I would carefully grasp the handle of the printing press and firmly apply the press to the paper. It was great fun to slowly peel away the paper and examine the results. . . . In this way I began a relationship with printing type itself. It was a secret pact between us that has continued throughout my life. (164–65)

Whether consciously or unconsciously, in his description of his fascination with the conversion point between the materiality of media and the author's imagination, Rampo returns to an important theme of his literary predecessor Edgar Allan Poe. Unlike the fascination for the material tools of the print medium expressed by Rampo, however, in the case of Poe, we can often observe a preoccupation with the artifacts of the manuscript-based culture, the continued eclipse of which Poe had occasion to witness in the midst of the quickly developing print industry in antebellum America. As Kevin J. Hayes observes, "Though Edgar Allan Poe recognized print media as the cultural location where he would make his fame, he never forgot the literary traditions attached to manuscript culture."[2] Evidence of this recurrent fascination with the *technics* of manuscript culture include the two-part article, "Autography," published in the *Southern Literary Messenger* in 1836, which consists of commentaries on printed facsimiles of prominent authors' penned signatures (as well as wittily fictionalized samples of their correspondence); the repeated images of inscription, letters, and manuscripts in his other fictional works; and even the title of the literary magazine that was the culmination of Poe's ambitions as an editor, the *Stylus*.

In this essay, I will highlight some of the references to print media, visual media, and optic devices in Edogawa Rampo's work and discuss how they reconfigure, often with baroque excess, important themes in the works of Edgar Allan Poe, suggesting a writerly affinity that transcends the generic interest in mystery and horror that ostensibly links the Japanese master of popular fiction with his nineteenth century namesake. My goal is not to show the "influence" of one writer upon the other but rather to show that a similar interest in written and visual media links the authors across the temporal and spatial abyss that separates them and to consider how each author addresses his own time and place through an exploration of medial effects.

RAMPO'S "THE HUMAN CHAIR," TACTILITY, AND INSCRIPTION

Edogawa Rampo's fascination with the borders between tactile materiality and the works of the imagination is evident in one of his most famous short stories, "The Human Chair." In this work, a hideously ugly Japanese crafts-man designs a plush, Western-style chair in which he is capable of conceal-ing himself. At first, he uses this invention only to infiltrate a luxury hotel and commit theft, but he soon becomes besotted with the illicit thrill of being sat upon by beautiful, and otherwise inaccessible, women. The story, with the exception of a brief framing introduction, takes the form of a letter from the craftsman to Yoshiko, a beautiful and sophisticated female author, who has acquired the chair. After describing the genesis of his invention, the craftsman confesses his mad love for Yoshiko, whom he has "known" through the medium of the chair, and the reader experiences Yoshiko's hor-ror and disgust while reading the confession in the place of the addressee. In a twist ending, Yoshiko then receives a second letter, claiming that the previ-ous letter was just a work of fiction, designed to impress her with the letter-writer's skill and imagination as an author.

Interestingly, the disavowal of the "human chair" episode as a "harmless" fiction does not decrease the implications of the violation committed by the letter writer. On the contrary, the revelation that the first letter may have been a mere "prank" only intensifies the sense of psychological violence, in part because of an eerie doubling between the letter writer's two roles of furniture maker and amateur author, which are, in turn, doubles for Rampo's role as professional author or literary craftsman. The most salient commonality is the status of the chair, letter, or printed text as medium for the author's illicit imagination. The chair, a marvelous product of craft, is the medium through which the craftsman is able to have physical contact with the woman; it is a point of conversion between the craftsman's pornographic imagination—burning from the start with all sorts of "impudent, luscious, and luxurious 'dreams'"[3]—and the material realm and the existence of the Other. Similar-ly, the letter that passes from the craftsman, revealed to be "merely" an amateur author, is a similar point of conversion from the realm of the imagi-nation to the material. As described in the text, the arrival of the second letter, marked by the familiar and unpleasant "handwritten scrawl" (*fude-guse*) of the sender—the physical traces of the author's presence—elicits Yoshiko's horror and disgust.[4]

The uncanny traces of the author in this conversion point of imagination and materiality are what link the chair, the letter, and the printing process as described in Rampo's aforementioned essays. Although the printed text seemingly no longer contains the traces of the author's bodily presence, Rampo's essays on his fascination with the printed word reestablish this direct link (or "secret pact" in his own words) between the body of the author and the materiality of the medium, which has been obscured by mass manufacturing and impersonal systems of distribution. Rampo's essays call the reader's attention to the materiality of the "lead bricks" of printer's type and the glossy ink applied to paper, which are capable of converting the author's private realm of imagination into a seductively material artifact. Similarly, the reader of Rampo's "Human Chair," rhetorically placed into the position of the addressee of the two letters, is compelled to share the horror of psychological violence directed at Yoshiko—in the form of the handwritten letter for Yoshiko, or the printed text for Rampo's readers—at the ambiguous conversion point between imagination and materiality. That is, although the reader of Rampo's text does not actually witness the unnerving "handwritten scrawl" of the letter/fiction writer (nor do they experience the tactile sensation of sitting on the furniture master's "human chair"), still they are placed in the uncomfortable parallel position with Yoshiko as the recipient of his messages, through the craft of the *printed word* rather than the chair or the handwritten letter.

RAMPO, POE, AND LENS MANIA

The conversion point between dream and materiality is also what seems to fascinate Rampo with lenses and other visual media.[5] For example, in the essay "A Passion for Lenses" (1937), he describes the experience of holing himself up in his darkened upstairs room as a boy when light through an aperture turned the darkened room into a camera obscura; he then takes a magnifying glass to project a ray of light bouncing off the tatami mats onto the ceiling.

> The woven strands of rushes that formed the surface of the tatami appeared as wide as the boards in the ceiling. . . . They were projected all too clearly like a terrible nightmare or the drug-induced visions of an opium fiend. Even though I knew it was a play of the lens, I felt particularly upset. I suppose most people

would feel it odd to feel frightened. But I was overwhelmed by its reality. It was so shocking that from that day onward, my view of things changed completely. It was a turning point in my life. (149)

Similarly, in his essay "The Horrors of Film" (1926), Rampo describes with wonder and terror the sensation of seeing close-ups (or *ôutsushi,* "large projections," in Japanese) of silent film stars' faces, transformed through magnification into strange lunar landscapes. "Even a face as smooth as a newborn's appears distorted and bizarre: the kind of thing you might spy through a telescope on the surface of the moon" (137). Most terrifying is when a strip of celluloid first becomes stuck and then catches fire in the projector, consuming the frozen face of an actress with black spots and red flames (138–39). Here, as with the gigantic tatami fibers appearing on the ceiling in his essay on lenses, the terror seems to arise in large part from the mixing of different ontological layers. The flames engulfing the physical medium of the celluloid film seem to consume the fictional "content" of the film, which, itself, bears an uncanny indexical relationship to the physical world: projected out of scale and the natural time-space continuum to become an alien landscape, at once fantastic and bearing a searing reality.

In his introduction to *The Edogawa Rampo Reader,* Seth Jacobowitz notes the similarity between the cinematic terrors described in "The Horror of Film" and the surreal world of Rampo's prose-poem-like story, "The Martian Canals" (1927). In this visionary tale, the narrator describes himself wandering lost in a dark wood, until he encounters a clear pool of water in the middle of the forest. The narrator then finds his own body transformed into that of his voluptuous female lover, and, as if compelled by a mysterious outside force, s/he swims to a rock at the center of the pool, and performs a wild erotic dance, climaxed by tearing at her own body with her fingernails, until her skin is furrowed with red channels like the canals of Mars named in the story's title. Jacobowitz reasonably proposes a cinematic interpretation to this story, in which the pool is the "silver screen upon which the man's subconscious desires are violently and inexplicably projected."[6]

While I agree with the connection between this story and visual media, I would argue that the pool should rather be viewed as a lens at the center of the forest, which gathers the desire of the forest and the entire cosmos of the tale, as a lens gathers light, onto a focal point, the rock, where the protagonist is reconstituted as an image. The comparison with the protagonist's skin to the canals of Mars, the marks of a fantastical extraterrestrial civilization extrapolated through nineteenth-century observations of Mars through telescopes, further connects the reconstituted protagonist's existence to optic regimes or at least the ambiguous interface between human desire and imagination and technologically aided observation.[7] It is fascinating that this story does not figure the landscape as a fantastic "projection" of the individual subject's imagination, as would the more common Romantic trope of the lamp as discussed by M. H. Abrams,[8] but, rather, the subject him/herself is constituted or focalized out of the landscape, which has already been thoroughly permeated with the subject's psychology.

The sense in which the cosmos of Rampo's story is infused with a powerful, sexualized life force, which reconstitutes the subject in a process of focalization, suggests that this story could be read as a kitschy parody or perverse homage to Edgar Allan Poe's 1841 prose-poem-like short story, "The Island of the Fay," originally designed to accompany an engraving by the same name in *Graham's Magazine*.[9] The prologue to Poe's story proposes that the earth's "dark valleys," "grey rocks," waters, forests, and mountains, are "themselves but the colossal members of one vast and animate and sentient whole."[10] The general scheme of the two stories is similar, in that they involve a narrator-protagonist in the midst of "lonely journeying" through a dismal forest before encountering an enchanted pool or rivulet and island therein. In Poe's story, it is the apparitional Fay who seems to embody the life-force of the "animate and sentient" cosmos and whose circuits around the island in a canoe mirror those of the heavenly bodies, whose "cycle within cycle without end," revealed by man's "telescopes" and "mathematical investigations," are described in the prologue (601). Thus, Rampo's "Canals of Mars" exhumes the half-buried metaphor of a telescopic lens formed by the "mirror-like" and "glassy" rivulet in Poe's earlier tale (602), while substituting Rampo's signature "erotic grotesque" elements for Poe's transcendent (or, perhaps, sardonically faux-transcendent) vision.[11]

An examination of Poe's works reveals both a fascination with optical perception and effects as well as a fundamental ambivalence regarding telescopes and other optical instruments, which is connected with the author's constant troubling of the boundary between scientific, rationalist discourse and empirical evidence at one extreme, and the Romantic imagination and madness on the other. For example, even without introducing a more complicated optical instrument than a study window, Poe's short story, "The Sphinx," plays with issues of perspective and the relationship between optical "evidence" and the imagination and mental state of the individual subject. In this story, the protagonist, fleeing a cholera epidemic in New York, takes refuge in the home of a cultured friend on the banks of the Hudson. Fearing the epidemic and his own death, he immerses himself in his host's books and fevered meditations on the subject of omens and portents, only to be treated to a vision, upon looking up from his volume, of a huge monster descending a distant hill by the river banks. At the end of this story, however, his host reveals to him that the "monster" is, in fact, a death-head's moth suspended from a spider web in front of the study's window.

A similar play on perspective, connected by the shared motif of the death-head's insect, is found in the popular story "The Gold Bug," in which a telescope, commonly a device for observing large and distant heavenly objects, is employed in a certain fixed position to find a minute object: a skull in a tree, one of whose eye-sockets will reveal the position of a buried treasure. Indeed, "The Gold Bug" and "The Sphinx" could be seen as paired stories: while the former's central character, William Legrand, appears at first to be merely an eccentric and possibly mad recluse, his mastery over the set of optical inversions and decodings necessary to uncover the buried treasure reveals him to be a genius of ratiocination comparable to Poe's famous detective C. Auguste Dupin. The lack of mastery or comprehension of optical proportions and effects, on the other hand, leads the protagonist of "The Sphinx" to comically mistake the death-head's moth for a distant monster, unlike his more rationally masterful host. However, if the interpretation of William S. Marks is correct, in fact, the story may have an ironic twist: the confidently rational host may be equally unperceiving as the protagonist of "The Sphinx" for failing to realize that all is actually not well—that the monstrous "bug" of the cholera epidemic has in fact appeared in his home through the person of the protagonist, whose apprehension of the "death's-head" monster may be at least poetically true. [12]

OPTICS, SPECTACLE, AND POPULAR CULTURE

Numerous scholars of media and visual culture have pointed out how optical instruments, developed as the tools of rational, precise scientific observation from the Renaissance and Enlightenment onward, have been quickly adopted into popular media spectacles that indulge the fantastic, the erotic, and the irrational. For example, in *The Female Thermometer: 18th Century Culture and the Invention of the Uncanny,* Terry Castle explores how the phantasmagorical magic lantern shows featuring ghosts and demons conjured by means of the latest optical tricks in eighteenth-century Europe contributed at once to the demystification of ghosts and the spectralization of human psychology. Furthermore, she argues that in the following century, "Edgar Allan Poe . . . in his supernatural tales, used the phantasmagoria figure precisely as a way of destabilizing the ordinary boundaries between inside and outside, mind and world, illusion and reality." [13]

Similarly, in his study *The Lens Within the Heart: The Western Scientific Gaze and Popular Imagery in Later Edo Japan,* Timon Screech shows how, even before Japan's full opening to the West in the Meiji Period, tools of enhanced visual observation and visualization were seen as defining aspects of Western science and culture, on the one hand, and quickly incorporated into the carnivalesque and erotic popular culture of the Japanese "floating world," on the other. As is made clear in Rampo's nostalgic essay on the *utsushi-e* or Japanese-style magic lantern shows of his boyhood, the connection between optical technology and fantastic, dream-like fictional realms has its own roots in Japanese entertainment culture as well as its precedents in the West.[14] Yet while it may be rooted in the premodern, Rampo's media consciousness is also thoroughly connected to his Modernist generation of Japanese authors, who actively responded to the rise of a new popular culture, which included both cinema and mass-produced, mass-marketed print literature.[15]

In diverse writings from his tales and reportage to his quasi-scientific extended essay *Eureka,* Poe was constantly questioning and renegotiating the role of imagination, rationality, and empirical science in an age of scientific discovery and the popularization of both literature and scientific knowledge. The ambivalent and often ironic appearance of media of inscription and observation in his tales, from the stylus to the telescope, is emblematic of this tension between imagination and empiricism. Arguably, the ultimate expression of his ambivalence was his investment in the literary and journalistic phenomenon of the *hoax* and its debunking. As Linda Walsh summarizes, "scientifically educated beyond many of his peers and a pioneer in at least two genres that showcase scientific epistemologies—science fiction and detective fiction—he [Poe] embodies the tensions between the arts and sciences in the Jacksonian era. His hoaxes were public acts meant to call attention to these tensions, as they were written on science-related topics and carefully crafted and presented in popular news media for particular reading audiences"[16]

A century later, Edogawa Rampo reworked these preoccupations of Poe through visually excessive imaginative works that at times approached a campy pastiche of the American writer, while simultaneously exploring his personal obsessions with media: obsessions which coincidentally placed Rampo at the cutting edge of the visual, multimedia turn in modern Japanese culture during the 1920s and 1930s. During these decades, Rampo undoubtedly found Poe's ambivalent fascination with the technics of inscription and observation, empiricism and imagination, to be a compelling precedent to his own situation in a cosmopolitan but culturally anxious Japan, which in the span of a single generation had assimilated both the technology of the movie projector and the transnational dream-world of the cinema. Nevertheless, despite their shared preoccupations, we can detect a relative, if not absolute, difference in the two authors' employment of the trope of media within their works. Poe's works featuring media of inscription and observation tend to pivot on the ironic reversibility or indecipherability between imagination/ madness and empiricism/rationality. In extending this trope in his own works, however, Rampo draws attention not merely to the reversibility or ambiguity between the fictional and real, but to the very *traces of materiality* discovered within overtly imaginative and fictional worlds. It is these traces of the real, or traces of mediation itself, which lend Rampo's works their particularly timely and disturbing appeal.

NOTES

1. Edogawa Rampo, *The Edogawa Rampo* Reader, ed. and trans. Seth Jacobowitz (Fukuoka: Kurodahan Press, 2008), 152, 232. Further references will be from this edition and noted parenthetically.

2. Kevin J. Hayes, *Poe and the Printed Word* (Cambridge: Cambridge University Press, 2000), 29. On the subject of Poe, the print industry, and manuscript culture, see also Jonathan Elmer, *Reading at the Social Limit: Affect, Mass Culture, and Edgar Allan Poe* (Stanford: Stanford University Press, 1995), 37–47; and Meredith L. McGill, *American Lecture and the Culture of Reprinting, 1834–1853* (Philadelphia: University of Pennsylvania Press, 2003), 141–86.

3. Edogawa Rampo, *Edogawa Rampo zenshû [Collected works of Edogawa Rampo], Vol. 1* (Tokyo: Kôbunsha, 2004), 609.

4. Edogawa, *Edogawa Rampo zenshû,* 630; for an English translation, see *Japanese Tales of Mystery and* Imagination, trans. James B. Harris (Boston: Tuttle, 1956), 22–23. Matsuyama Iwao discusses tactility and the privileging of the haptic over the optic in "The Human Chair" in his study *Rampo to Tôkyô [Rampo and Tokyo]* (Tokyo: Chikuma shobô, 1994), 36–43.

5. Visual media and optical devices feature prominently in many Rampo stories such as "The Hell of Mirrors," "The Traveler With the Pasted Rag Picture," and "The Strange Tale of Panorama Island," and have been the subjects of fascinating studies by Hirano, Igarashi, and Looser. See Yoshihiko Hirano, *Hofuman to Rampo: Ningyô to kôgaku kikai no eros [Hoffman and Rampo: The Eros of Dolls and Optical Devices]* (Tokyo: Misuzu shobô, 2007); Yoshikuni Igarashi, "Edogawa Rampo and the Excess of Vision: An Ocular Critique of Modernity in1920s Japan," *Positions* 13.2 (Fall 2005): 299–327; Thomas Looser, "From Edogawa to Miyazaki: Cinematic and *Anime*-ic Architectures of Early and Late Twentieth-century Japan," *Japan Forum* 14.2 (September 2002): 297–331.

6. Seth Jacobowitz, "Translator's Introduction," in *The Edogawa Rampo Reader (*Fukuoka: Kurodahan Press, 2008), xxxiv.

7. The map of Mars's surface published by Italian astronomer Giovanni Schiaparelli (1835–1910) in 1878 identified "canali" or channels across the surface, which were mistranslated as "canals" and touched off decades of speculation about a canal-building alien civilization on Mars, led by such figures as Camille Flammarion (1842–1925) and Percival Lowell (1855–1916). For further discussion, see Robert Markley, *Dying Planet: Mars in Science and the Imagination* (Durham: Duke University Press, 2005); Eric S. Rabkin, *Mars: A Tour of the Human Imagination* (Westport, Conn.: Praeger Publishers, 2005); and William Sheehan, *The Planet Mars: A History of Observation and Discovery* (Tuscon: University of Arizona Press, 1996).

8. See M. H. Abrams, *The Mirror and The Lamp: Romantic Theory and the Critical Tradition* (London and New York: Oxford University Press, 1971), 52–67.

9. For a discussion of the origins of this short story, see F. DeWolfe Miller, "The Basis for Poe's 'The Island of the Fay,'" *American Literature* 14.2 (May 1942): 135–40.

10. Edgar Allan Poe, *Collected Works of Edgar Allan Poe, Volume* II, ed. Thomas Ollive Mabbott (Cambridge: The Belknap Press of Harvard University Press, 1969), 600. Further references to Poe's stories will be from this edition and noted parenthetically.

11. Kent Ljungquist interprets Poe's story as a "parody of certain attitudes and literary conventions found in Romantic nature poetry" and "an arch adaptation of the Romantic prospect piece" (151). Kent Ljungquist, "Poe's 'The Island of the Fay': The Passing of Fairyland," in *The Naiad Voice: Essays on Poe's Satiric Hoaxing*, ed. Dennis W. Eddings (Port Washington: Associated Faculty Press, 1983), 151.

12. William S. Marks III, "The Art of Corrective Vision in Poe's 'The Sphinx,'" *Pacific Coast Philology* 22.1/2 (Nov. 1987): 46–50. For discussions of the questions of perception and optics in Poe's work, see also James W. Gargano, "The Distorted Perception of Poe's Comic Narrators," *Topic* 16 (1976): 23–34, and William J. Scheick, "An Intrinsic Luminosity: Poe's Use of Platonic and Newtonian Optics," *The Southern Literary Journal* 24.2 (Spring 1992): 90–105.

13. Terry Castle, *The Female Thermometer: 18th Century Culture and the Invention of the Uncanny* (New York: Oxford University Press, 1995), 160.

14. Edogawa Rampo, *Edogawa Rampo zuihitsusen [A Selection from the Essays of Edogawa Rampo]*, ed. Kida Junichirô (Tokyo: Chikuma shobô, 1994): 197–200.

15. For a discussion of Modernist and avant-garde writers' responses to the growth of mass-marketed literature and visual media, see William O. Gardner, *Advertising Tower: Japanese Modernism and Modernity in the 1920s* (Cambridge: Harvard University Asia Center Publications, 2007); for a look at detective fiction, including the work of Edogawa Rampo with regard to 1920s- and 1930s-era discourses of modernity in Japan, see Sari Kawana, *Murder Most Modern: Detective Fiction and Japanese Culture* (Minneapolis: University of Minnesota Press, 2008).

16. Lynda Walsh, *Sins Against Science: The Scientific Media Hoaxes of Poe, Twain, and Others* (Albany: State University of New York Press, 2006), 51. The hoax stories that Walsh discusses include "Hans Phaall—A Tale" (1835), "The Balloon Hoax" (1844), "The Facts in the Case of M. Valdemar" (1845), and "Von Kempelen and His Discovery" (1849).

Chapter Three

Poe's Shadow in Japan: Alternative Worlds and Failed Escapes in Edogawa Rampo's *The Strange Tale of Panorama Island*

Mark Silver

Edogawa Rampo's novella-length work *The Strange Tale of Panorama Island* (Panorama-tô kidan, 1927) is typical of much of the fiction he wrote with Poe in mind, both in the problems it poses concerning cross-cultural textual borrowing and in its ambivalent representation of Japanese modernization. But if it is no more than typical in its engagement with Poe, it is unusual for the directness with which it addresses the possible meanings of that engagement.

The great reach of the shadow that Poe casts across this work by his Japanese namesake becomes apparent in the *Tale*'s first chapter, where Rampo explicitly cites Poe's story "The Domain of Arnheim" as an inspiration for his own main character's quest to build an island utopia.[1] In Rampo's hands, however, Poe's narrative lines are redrawn so that the romantic quest at the center of "The Domain of Arnheim"—the quest to create a vast, perfectly composed garden—becomes a fantasy of escape from modern Japanese life. This life, as Rampo's text represents it, is defined by several interrelated things: a wearying humdrumness, a sense of alienation engendered by the urban environment, the constraints of economic necessity imposed by modern capitalism, and a certain cultural ambiguity or doubleness that is connected with Japanese Westernization. In Rampo's text, moreover, escape from these things proves illusory: Western modernity, as it has reshaped

Japan, is not only sufficiently alienating to prompt a fantasy of escape. Its infiltration of the Japanese imagination is also sufficiently deep to dictate the very form such fantasizing takes, thereby rendering escape all but impossible. In Rampo's work, would-be escape from doubleness itself entails doubleness, and the physical structures of his alternative world lie in ruin at the tale's end. Where "The Domain of Arnheim" finishes on a high note, with a vision of physics-defying levitation, Rampo's work ends with deflation, disappointment, and a return to the grim banality and the limitations of ordinary life. Rampo's explicit positioning of *The Strange Tale of Panorama Island* within Poe's shadow thus seems to underline the same power of Western cultural influence that his text suggests is partly responsible for engendering the fantasy of escape in the first place. This coincidence between the circumstances of Rampo's own literary production and the circumstances of his character's fantasy suggests that the tale may be read as an enactment of the very failure of escape that Rampo portrays within his fictional world.

The basic plots of Poe's and Rampo's works are similar. In both works we meet the protagonist and learn of his obsession with the art of landscaping, we learn how he acquires the money to realize his obsession, and we are given a tour of the resulting utopia. In Poe's sketch, the gifted visionary Ellison, discovering that he has inherited a fortune of stupendous size, takes great pains to locate the perfect site for a colossal, landscaped park, and then spends the fortune creating it. The park is in every respect an improvement of nature: every vista, every rocky ledge, and the disposition of every blade of grass in its precincts has been premeditated and composed to absolute perfection. The latter half of the sketch consists of one long exquisitely wrought description of the approach to Arnheim and of the vision awaiting one behind its gate, ending with this virtuosic set-piece:

> [One sees] . . . a dream-like intermingling to the eye of tall slender Eastern trees—bosky shrubberies—flocks of golden and crimson birds—lily-fringed lakes—meadows of violets, tulips, poppies, hyacinths, and tuberoses—long intertangled lines of silver streamlets—and, upspringing confusedly from amid all, a mass of semi-Gothic, semi-Saracenic architecture, sustaining itself as if by miracle in mid-air, glittering in the red sunlight with a hundred oriels, minarets, and pinnacles; and seeming the phantom handiwork, conjointly, of the Sylphs, of the Fairies, of the Genii, and of the Gnomes.[2]

The protagonist of Rampo's story is a struggling writer named Hitomi Hirosuke. Missing what may be a note of irony in the peroration of Poe's story (irony which, if present, would suggest that such a revision of nature as Ellison seeks would result in an abomination rather than a paradise), Hitomi is inspired by "The Domain of Arnheim" to build a utopian landscape of his own. A large fortune comes within his reach when Hitomi hears that a wealthy business magnate and former classmate has recently died. As is often the case in Rampo's longer works in what came to be known as the genre of *ero-guro-nansensu* (literally, "erotic, grotesque, nonsense"), convenient coincidence helps the plot along. It so happens (and here Rampo nods at Poe's story "William Wilson") that Hitomi and this classmate, who is named Komoda, resembled each other so uncannily as to be frequently mistaken for twins. Hitomi boldly takes advantage of this resemblance to falsely assume Komoda's identity. He fakes a suicide at sea, finds the place where Komoda is buried, and messily transfers his double's decomposing body to the coffin in the adjacent grave. Hitomi fixes Komoda's grave to look as though Komoda clawed himself to its surface, and then lies at the roadside waiting to be discovered. Based on his reading of Poe's "Premature Burial" (a full paragraph of which Rampo quotes in Japanese translation), Hitomi anticipates that when he is discovered the doctors will mistake him for Komoda, believing that the latter had been buried alive after suffering an attack of catalepsy.

This ruse is a success, and Hitomi soon masters all of his double's affairs. His greatest worry is Chiyoko, the beautiful young wife that comes with his new identity. Fearful that she will detect his imposture, he resists the powerful temptation to share her bed. Having established himself in Komoda's place, Hitomi buys an island off the nearby coast and spends huge sums building his utopian landscape, which he calls "Panorama Island." As we learn later, this paradise consists of multiple intersecting and overlapping diorama-like spaces. (Hitomi sometimes calls them scenes [*keshiki*] and sometimes calls them worlds [*sekai*].) These spaces house stunning vistas, mostly of nature, that seem impossibly vast given the relatively small area of the island. All goes well with his project until Hitomi, unable to hold his desire in check, sleeps with the beautiful Chiyoko. The next morning, he senses that she has detected his impersonation and decides he must kill her. Hitomi lures Chiyoko to Panorama Island, shows her its wonders, and then, as the two bathe together in a hot spring, he strangles her. He cleverly disposes of her corpse, and it seems he is safe.

Disaster strikes when Hitomi's island community is infiltrated by a spy in the employ of one of Chiyoko's relatives; noticing a black hair stuck to the surface of a white concrete pillar, he is led to discover Chiyoko's corpse encased inside. Confronted with this evidence of his crime, Hitomi confesses to his impersonation but requests thirty minutes of freedom. The mad artist then seals his own fate, by packing himself into one of the fireworks scheduled, by standing order, to be shot off at dusk. As the story ends, the fireworks explode, sending off showers of stars, and with them Hitomi's bloody limbs and tissues splatter down on the still unfinished island, which over time then lapses into a sort of industrial wasteland "over-run with weeds, its peculiar huge iron-reinforced concrete pillars gradually losing their original form in the course of their exposure to the rain and wind."[3]

Among the many arresting elements in Rampo's story, its varied enactments of failed escape and its fixation on the trope of guilty, abortive imposture are especially prominent and suggestive. Hitomi's motivation for building the island and the fantasies enacted there are specific enough to encode considerable detail about just which elements of early twentieth-century Japanese urban life Rampo imagined his readers found most alienating. Hitomi is driven to build his island in large measure because of his longing to escape the limits of normalcy, to find something beyond the numbing round of everyday routine. He is, we learn early in the story, "completely bored with the world" and "has no desire to hold down a job and live out an ordinary life" (12). It is clear that one of the main attractions for Hitomi of a realm such as Arnheim lies in its otherworldly magnificence, so it is ironic that the utopia he actually creates should prove to be so heavily anchored in the very world he hopes to escape.

In Poe's highly visual story, particular emphasis falls on the splendor of Ellison's finished park and its approach as they appear to the visitor. The text contains hints that the landscape has been exquisitely shaped and groomed: it has in it a "weird symmetry," a "thrilling uniformity," and a "wizard propriety" (866). But at no time are we privy to the details of the labor that has gone into this landscape's making, or to how such things as the levitation of the "semi-Gothic, semi-Saracenic" architecture at the sketch's close have been engineered. The narrative, in fact, continually reverts to the notion that whatever labor has been expended is not that of men at all, but of "a new race of fairies, laborious, tasteful, magnificent, and fastidious" (867), or that it is, as the closing lines assert, "a phantom handiwork, conjointly, of the Sylphs, of the Fairies, of the Genii, and of the Gnomes" (870).

The final parts of Rampo's tale offer a similarly virtuosic piling up of visual pleasures. But as Hitomi guides Chiyoko around his island, Rampo repeatedly interpolates explanations into his descriptions—explanations of how its astonishing scenery has been created and of the infrastructure beneath it. The effect is rather like that of the magician who insists on telling you how the trick he has just performed was accomplished. These explanations continually reground the splendors of the island paradise in the realm of mere optical and sensory illusion: "If I told you the true extent [of the huge forest we just passed through]," Hitomi tells Chiyoko, "there is no way you would believe me." He continues:

> That's how small it is. That road follows a series of curves that have been laid down with such skill that they are undetectable, so that one is actually going over the same ground repeatedly without realizing it. The stands of cedars that extended so far on either side of us that you couldn't see the end of them were not all uniformly big in the way that you believed. The farthest ones were actually seedlings that were only about six feet high. It's not that difficult to adjust the lighting so that you can't tell such things. (58)

Similar tricks of perspective, scene-making, and lighting also turn out to account for a staircase that seemed to reach into the very clouds and for the apparently limitless expanse of a wide open grassy plain (59). Where Poe presents us with a seamless vision of splendid surfaces, then, Rampo repeatedly draws our attention to visual tricks, to constraints on our perception, and to the scaffolding behind the surfaces we are shown.

One can certainly find varied precedents for such visual play in premodern Japanese culture, especially in the realm of traditional garden design. Edo-period *kaiyû* (or "stroll") style gardens, for example, are based on designs meant to delight viewers walking through them with the transformations of scenery effected simply by rounding a bend in a path. Several classic Japanese primers setting forth traditional principles of garden design contain exhortations to use tricks of perspective to deepen the viewer's pleasure. For example the treatise *Illustrations for Designing Mountain, Water, and Hillside Field Landscapes*, a so-called "secret transmission text" (*hidensho*) dating from the fifteenth century or earlier and attributed to the priest Zôen, impresses upon the reader such rules as this: "you must make the stream valley appear to extend on and on, while at the same time you must reduce it to a small size." The captions to its illustrations likewise resort frequently to the principle of miniaturization; as one such explanatory caption says, "In a garden like this, the scenery of an immense ocean stretching out before a single mountain is reduced to small size."[4] The allied concept of "borrowed scenery" (*shakkei*), ascendant in the Muromachi and Edo periods, similarly increases the sense of scale in a garden beyond its actual size by incorporating views of faraway things (such as mountains visible in the distance) into the landscaping.[5]

Such domestic traditions may have played a role in shaping Rampo's basic sense of the playful possibilities inherent in the art of landscaping. One might point as well to other stories by Poe, such as "The Sphinx," which memorably grants a central place to a mistake of vision, as a possible inspiration for Rampo's engagement in *The Strange Tale of Panorama Island* with tricks of perspective.

But the shifts in emphasis we see in Rampo's treatment of the materials he has borrowed from Poe—and indeed the very title of his tale—are probably more directly traceable to the legacy he has claimed from a phenomenon that was geographically and temporally closer to him, that of the so-called *panorama-kan* or "panorama buildings" that enjoyed a vogue in the entertainment districts of Tokyo and Osaka following the first Sino-Japanese war (1894–95).[6] These were cylindrical buildings that used a combination of painted scenery on the interior walls, three-dimensional models, and tricks of perspective and lighting to create the illusion that one was looking at a naval battle, say, or a wide plain in Manchuria, against a nearly limitless horizon of either water or land. Hitomi's utopia, then, does not consist of artfully created landscapes, as Poe's domain does; rather, it is an artfully created simulacrum of landscapes, where almost nothing stands up to scrutiny. The narrative's continual re-grounding of the island's splendors in the realm of mere optical trickery suggests that this story is not about transcendence of the ordinary, but about the ultimate impossibility of such transcendence, a point that is further underlined by the failure of Hitomi's imposture and by the lapse of the island into an industrial wasteland of dilapidated concrete pillars.

Among the other elements of modern life that Panorama Island initially offers escape from are the unforgiving regime of capitalism (it is, notably, his lack of money and the necessity of taking on translation work that are set up as the biggest obstacles to Hitomi's plan to build a utopia) and the alienation that the urban environment engenders in its inhabitants. Recalling the thrill he felt as a child upon entering a local panorama building, Rampo's character observes:

> Outside the panorama building, there were trains running, hustlers hawking their goods at outdoor stalls, retail storefronts lining the street; day after day the city-dwellers passed each other by in never-ending streams. My own house was visible there too, almost lost among the mass of storefronts. But once you entered the panorama building, all those things disappeared entirely, and the wide open plains of Manchuria extended all the way to the distant horizon . . . there was one world outside the building, and another inside it. . . . Outside the Panorama Building, there were, to be sure, the city streets one was so accustomed to seeing on a daily basis. But inside the building, no matter which direction one looked in, there was no sign of them. (57)

The world that Hitomi creates once he has seized Komoda's fortune celebrates a similar impulse toward pastoralism. It is a realm where there are no streets, or crowds of strangers, or storefronts obscuring one's home, and where there is no evident need of money.

Indeed, the particular diorama-like spaces that Hitomi creates on the island are all (with one exception that proves the rule) scenes of naturally occurring landscapes, as opposed to anything drawn from the urban, visibly man-made environment. Hitomi guides Chiyoko through an underwater seascape, through a gorge with sublimely high walls, through a labyrinthine woods, past an inky, still pond in a forest glade, over wide open plains, past hillsides covered in flowers, and ultimately to the hot spring where he strangles her. The cumulative effect of these landscapes is to emphasize the attractions of such natural environments as retreats from the urban life that Hitomi remembers relegating to the unseen exterior of the panorama building in the Tokyo neighborhood of his childhood. Many of the scenes of island life further hold out the possibility of return to an Edenic state: all of the attendants living on the island (the majority of whom seem to be nubile women) have thrown off, or been directed to throw off, the trammels of clothing in order to frolic in the nude, and at one moment dozens of couples that can be seen chasing each other on a wide lawn are described as "playing at Adam and Eve" (64).

If, then, one is willing to accept its illusions, the island does seem to function plausibly, at least for a time, as a utopic escape from the pressures of modern urban life. But only for a time. The wealthy Komoda's fortune is not in the end so large as to completely obviate the worry about money that initially hampered Hitomi's designs; Hitomi confesses just before he commits suicide that funds for the project are on the verge of running out even before the island has been completed (80). What is more, the apparent escape Panorama Island offers from the conditions of modern life is continually undercut by the island's subtle replication of many of the very things that are emblematic of that life. The white concrete and iron reinforcing bars that figure so prominently in the construction of the island, for example, are the same materials that dominated early-twentieth century Japanese urban architecture (especially in the reconstruction of Tokyo after the Great Kantô earthquake of 1923). This similarity raises the possibility that the island and its mammoth construction project might be read metonymically, as the island-nation of Japan itself, with its own modernizing makeover. Alternatively, Hitomi's purchase and transformation of the island might be read as an act of colonization, in which case Panorama Island would stand not for Japan, but for its imperial periphery (Taiwan, the Korean peninsula, and Manchuria). Additional authority for this reading comes from the servile roles assigned to the islanders in Hitomi's utopia, including a group of a dozen or so nude women who carry Hitomi and Chiyoko around on their shoulders wherever they are bid. Also noteworthy in this connection is the apparent popularity with visitors to actual panorama buildings of scenes of Japanese imperial conquest. (As we have seen, the landscape that Hitomi calls to memory from childhood visits to his local panorama building is one of a wide open plain in Manchuria—which was then under the de facto rulership of a Japanese railway company and which would eventually become a Japanese puppet state.)

In either case, the island's dioramic combination of, as Hitomi puts it, "multiple worlds overlapping a single space," together with his assertion that such overlap may be likened to "the double exposure of a movie" (*eiga no nijuu-yaki-tsuke*), highlights a multiplicity and a doubleness that are fitting metaphors for the overlapping of cultures, languages, and technologies that characterized both the increasingly cosmopolitan Japan of the 1920s (thanks to what we might loosely call the overlay of Westernization on Japanese culture) and the spaces of Japan's overseas colonies (thanks to their overlay of Japanization on what we might loosely call their native culture). Such metaphors resonate as well with what William Gardner, among others, has referred to as the "double colonial situation of Japan," that is "the historical incursion of Western cultural and geopolitical power onto Japan, and the simultaneous projection of Japanese culture and power in Asia and the Pacific."[7]

The vision of utopia embodied by Panorama Island is additionally characterized by a notably paradoxical relationship to modern technology. In spite of the preference Rampo's protagonist shows for pastoral scenes of nature, there is one world on the island, "the machine kingdom," that not only hints at the difficulty of escaping machine-age culture, but indeed holds out the possibility of machines overrunning humans completely. In this world, a vast complex of machines accomplishing no practical purpose stretches from horizon to horizon, pulsing with automated movements, "moaning," "chewing one anothers' gears with black teeth," and "dancing like they have gone mad." And, as Hitomi is quick to point out, "unlike the situation in machine halls at world expos, there are no engineers or commentators to control or explain" these sinister machines (60). There are also hints sprinkled through the text that the entire island is powered by electric generators, most of which are deep underground, but at least one of which is loud enough to conveniently drown out the screams Chiyoko emits just before she is strangled, allowing Hitomi to kill her unremarked (70).[8] While most of the island seems, then, to promise a latter-day Eden, that promise is undercut by the machines in the garden, whether they be the symbolically threatening machines of the machine kingdom, or the functional, behind-the-scenes machines providing electric power and coincidentally enabling the violent murder of Chiyoko.

The fantasy of escape embodied in Rampo's island is, then, persistently haunted by the likelihood of its failure. Banal reality, the dictates of economic necessity, and the persistent traces of modernization, colonialism, and machine-age culture all conspire to ensure this. But the thing that finally proves decisive in the failure of Hitomi's project is his own status as an impostor, the doubleness that his escape entails. Hitomi fears continually that Komoda's young widow Chiyoko will discover him as a fraud. Virtually every time he encounters Chiyoko, he fears that she knows his game and is merely playing along with him: "Chiyoko must know her husband's every habit and the special features of every inch of his body," he thinks in one of these moments. "So if there were some part of him that differed in the slightest from [her husband], his mask would immediately be ripped off, and with that his scheme would fail" (38). This is in fact exactly what happens, given that it is the necessity of killing Chiyoko and concealing her corpse that ultimately doom Hitomi. There is, in other words, a conspicuous similarity between the optical illusions on Panorama Island, with their overlapping dioramic spaces, and the fraudulent identity of their maker. Neither is what it appears to be, and neither deception is sustainable. This similarity is high-lighted in the text by Hitomi's suicide, which leaves his own body parts spread over what he has made.

Hitomi's spectacular suicide thus becomes an eloquent expression of cog-nitive dissonance in the face of Japan's own, locally inflected, version of modernity. That modernity is represented here as both sufficiently alienating to engender a longing to escape it, and sufficiently tenacious to shape and infiltrate the very fantasies by which one would hope to effect that escape, thereby rendering escape all but impossible. Artistically speaking, Rampo's novella itself is an expression of this same cognitive double-bind, since its citation of Poe at its two most crucial junctures (the moment where Hitomi is struck with his obsession for utopias and the moment where he conceives his plan to make Komoda look like a victim of premature burial) seems to subordinate large chunks of the storyline of *Panorama Island* to Poe's liter-ary precedents. Through its citation of Poe, then, Rampo's text could be said to act out Japan's position as an island on the cultural periphery, as the overburdened recipient of the very cultural influences that have prompted the novella's fantasy of escape in the first place.

Such a reading raises the question of whether this enactment of the situa-tion of the "influenced," or the "cultural subordinate," is symptomatic or strategic—that is, whether Rampo the author has been more or less unwit-tingly constrained in his imagination of alternative worlds to creating a simu-lated version of Poe that willy-nilly replicates the very conditions it means to escape, or whether the tale is an ironic *representation* of the so-called "cultu-ral subordinate's" position in the shadow of his predecessors, all of which is framed by the text. So many of Rampo's writings are about various enact-ments of the desire for transformation (what Rampo called *henshin-ganbô* in an essay by that same name), and so many of them employ blatant pastiche, that it becomes tempting to read him as a figure who embodies the possibility of escaping from the self to revel in an essentially postmodern, boundary-crossing fluidity of cultural identity.[9] Such a reading is certainly attractive, but there is little if anything in *The Strange Tale of Panorama Island* to support it definitively. Indeed, given how frequently the new identities that Rampo's characters adopt are revealed as fraudulent (*Panorama Island* being a case in point), and how dire the consequences of these failed impersona-tions tend to be, Rampo may well have more to tell us about the fixity of our identities, and about the relative powerlessness he seems to have perceived in his position *vis-à-vis* the Western literary precedents represented for him by Poe, than about the potential for transcending these things.

NOTES

1. Edogawa Rampo, "Panorama-tô kidan [The Strange Tale of Panorama Island]," in *Edogawa Rampo Zenshû* (Tokyo: Kodansha, 1978), 3:12.

2. Edgar Allan Poe, "The Domain of Arnheim," in *Edgar Allan Poe: Poetry and Tales* (New York: Library of America, 1984), 869–870. All subsequent references to "The Domain of Arnheim" refer to this edition and are given in the main text.

3. *Edogawa Rampo Zenshû* (Tokyo: Kodansha, 1978), 10. All subsequent references to "The Strange Tale of Panorama Island" refer to this edition and are given in the main text.

4. This text is known in Japanese as *Senzui narabi ni yagyô no zu.* For an English translation, see David A. Slawson, *Secret Teachings in the Art of Japanese Gardens* (Kodansha International, 1987), from which the two quotations are taken (108, 109). A brief discussion in Japanese of this text and its putative author may be found in Saitô Tadakazu, *Nihon teien no mikata* [How to View Japanese Gardens] (Tokyo: JTB Kyanbukkusu, 1999), 78–79.

5. For several examples illustrated with photographs, see Marc P. Keane, *Japanese Garden Design* (Rutland, Vermont: Charles E. Tuttle, 1996), 140–141.

6. For a discussion in Japanese, see Kaneko Tsutomu, "Kaiki naru jinkô fûkei [Strange Artificial Scenery]," *Kokubungaku: kaishaku to kanshô* 59, no. 12 (December 1994).

7. William Gardner, *Advertising Tower: Japanese Modernism and Modernity in the 1920s* (Cambridge: Harvard East Asian Monographs, 2006), 69.

8. Other hints include a reference to the powerful electric lights that illuminate the undersea landscape (46) and to an underground source of electricity for the "machine world" itself (60).

9. Rampo's essay "Henshin ganbô" (1954) is translated as "A Desire for Transformation" in Seth Jacobowitz, *The Edogawa Rampo Reader* (Fukuoka: Kurodahan Press, 2008), 213–219.

The opinions presented in this essay are those of the author alone, and do not represent the official views of the National Endowment for the Humanities or the United States Government.

Chapter Four

Interview with Kiyoshi Kasai

Barbara Cantalupo

Barbara Cantalupo: First, I would like to thank you for taking the time to be interviewed this afternoon with the help of Seth Jacobowitz, Mark Silver, and Takayuki Tatsumi as translators. I will base my initial interview questions on the talk you just gave at the Bicentennial Conference, "The Crowd of Poe and Benjamin," since I cannot read Japanese, and, therefore, could not read your novel that is imagined as Dupin's "fourth case": *Gunshu no Akuma (The Devil of the Crowd: Dupin's Fourth Incident)* [Tokyo: Kodansha, 1996]. However, I'm most interested in understanding the influence Poe's work has had on yours. So, to begin: in grounding your discussion of the three Dupin tales on Walter Benjamin's observation that "the original social content of the detective story lies in the disappearance of the traces of the individual within the city crowd," you characterize the first two tales as deriving from the Gothic horror tradition with adventure as backdrop. "The Mystery of Marie Roget" provides a prototype for modernity in that the criminal disappears within the crowd. With that as the ground, you characterize "The Purloined Letter" as a "giant leap" . . .

Kiyoshi Kasai: To interrupt—in my opinion, "Marie Roget" and "The Purloined Letter" are actually similar since they both have the characteristic of some individual trace disappearing among a crowd of similar things—humans, in one case, a letter in the other.

BC: Okay. But how do I understand, then, the idea of the "giant leap"? I'm trying to understand that . . .

KK: Formalistically, the idea is the same, but the giant leap is moving from humans to objects.

BC: So, in your novel, do you collapse the two, or do you extend this idea of the giant leap?

KK: The setting of my novel takes place during the reign of Napoleon III when a new form of leadership arose, not based on the stratification of the classes but by considering the populace as a mass or *Gunshu* (an undifferentiated mass). The novel takes place in 1848, actually during a six-month period from February to the fall of that year. An uprising occurs in February, and the peasants and the middle-class join together, but the government oppresses this movement and many people die.

BC: So to get to the very basics for our readers, is the plot based on a crime of some sort? Is Dupin an outsider? How is he positioned in regard to the masses?

KK: I'll explain the opening part of the novel that is set in February 1848. Charles, the main character, acts as narrator and goes looking for a particular newspaper reporter. He looks for him in the midst of a crowd that's demonstrating in the streets. On one side are the demonstrators, and on the other side of the street is the army. Charles sees the newspaper reporter from behind, and he calls out to him. And just at that moment some unknown third man shoots the newspaper reporter, so Charles becomes a witness of this shooting. That single shot sets off the army, and they start shooting at the crowd. This incident is based on a historical incident on the Boulevard Saint-Germain.

BC: Ahhh . . .

KK: The actual provocation for this single shot is unknown, but I used it as a way to set up the plot. So the narrator goes to Dupin and describes what he's seen to try to discern the possible identification of this mysterious gunman who shot the newspaper reporter.

BC: Is the Dupin character a composite of Poe's Dupin and yours, is it someone without a particular identity related to Poe's character, or is he someone we would recognize as the same Dupin of Poe's tales?

KK: I've made a composite of all the representations of similar Dupin characters that have emerged since Poe's Dupin, but I've not gone against the basic characteristics of Poe's Dupin. I have added George Sand's characteristics to my Dupin. Did you know that George Sand's real name is Aurore Dupin?

BC: Ahhh . . . no, I didn't realize that. So your Dupin has some of George Sand's characteristics? And, then, how much of you is in your Dupin? What I mean by this is that in some ways Dupin's character traits emerge in ways that we can recognize as Poe-like rhetorical strategies—Dupin's disdain for rationality without intuition, his unorthodox phenomenological methodology, his ability to identify with psychologies so unlike his own, his mysteriousness, reclusiveness—so, in that way, of all the characters that Poe created, Dupin seems the most like the figure of the writer than any other. So, in the end, I guess I'm asking: with your Dupin, how like you is he?

KK: Well, I have added some aspects to his character that you might not recognize at first, among them Dupin's participation in the uprising. Also, the reader finds out that Charles (aka Baudelaire) plays a kind of Watson to Dupin's Holmes, and since Charles is the narrator, there is some inevitable association with me.

BC: In this respect, you argue that the detective story is a deviation from the realm of modern novels; neither the detective nor the criminal is given a realistic interiority or emotions. It's not that these aspects are not depicted but that the character of the detective must not be allowed to possess interiority or emotion. Is this true of the main character—of course, it's not clear to me whether the narrator or Dupin is the main character . . . ?

KK: Dupin is the main character. It's not that the characters in the detective tale do not have an interiority; it's simply that that interiority is not given to the reader. It was quite difficult to decide whether it's better to simply eliminate the interiority of these characters completely or to write with the idea that they have it, but it's not expressed. In this regard, literature before WWI and after is quite different.

BC: Does this difference apply, as well, to the structure of your novel? Is it, then, non-linear, what we would consider postmodern?

KK: Yes. But, since this is a detective novel, as is often the case with detective novels, the story is told nonchronologically. So, for example, with "Murders in the Rue Morgue," if one were to lay out all the events that are implied by the narrative in chronological order, you would start with something like the discovery of the ourang-outang in Borneo and narrate the rest of events from there. But, in fact, the narrative doesn't begin there . . . in that sense, the detective novel genre, itself, is a postmodern genre, and an artificial genre, also.

BC: If we could return, again, to the idea of how an author is present in the work he does . . .

KK: The Dupin that I have portrayed participates in the February uprising on the republican side. That side loses, and a new government drawing on the lineage of the house of Olean in July 1848 emerges. So Dupin, who is a republicanist, feels great disappointment, and he loses all interest in politics. So he takes refuge in his Saint-Germain house, closes the blinds, and goes into a funk. He retreats into a bookish existence. So the premise that one who suffers political disappointment then retreats into an intellectual life is based on my personal experience.

BC: Is there any sense in your novel, then, of Dupin's feeling a sense of accomplishment in solving a mystery, or is the character so jaded that it's simply a momentary distraction from his funk?

KK: The criminal in this story turns out to be Napoleon III's younger brother, a member of the aristocracy. The mystery is solved, but politically there's no satisfaction for Dupin. Moderne is the criminal, but the regime that Dupin was supporting does not succeed, even after this crime is solved. Charles (Baudelaire), politically speaking, is ineffective at the end of the novel. Although Charles is politically effective, he uses words to protest the regime. *Flowers of Evil*, itself, has a political implication by subtly criticizing the Second Empire.

BC: Does literature, then, in your opinion, have a role in politics? If so, how?

KK: For me politics is politics, and literature is literature.

BC: So it's more important, then, for you—as for Poe—to separate literature from politics. To quote Poe directly from his "Philosophy of Composition": "Now the object Truth, or the satisfaction of the intellect, and the object Passion, or the excitement of the heart, are, although attainable to a certain extent in poetry, far more readily attainable in prose. Truth, in fact, demands a precision, and Passion, a homeliness (the truly passionate will comprehend me), which are absolutely antagonistic to that Beauty which, I maintain, is the excitement or pleasurable elevation of the soul." Politics, then, is part of another arena altogether . . . even if the setting of the novel is embedded in a political struggle?

KK: There's really no point in putting overt political statements into novels, but a well written work of art, such as the *Flowers of Evil*, can have a political effect. There's a political dimension of even art for art's sake . . . politics is implicit in every artwork . . .

BC: Would you explain this idea further?

KK: There's a very close connection, for example, in the advent of mass death in war and the changes in the novel. After the advent of the detective form in "Murders in the Rue Morgue," the French writer Émile Gaboriau (1832–1873) inherits that form, and in England, we see something similar happening with Arthur Conan Doyle (1859–1930). They seem to have inherited this format of logical puzzle-solving from Poe.

World War I intervenes and changes this form in England and in the U.S. So we have Agatha Christie in England and Dorothy Sayers, and in the U.S., we have S. S. Van Dine, Ellery Queen, and others. In the 1920s and 1930s, both in England and America, we see a real efflorescence of the puzzle-solving genre. So I gave some thought to the question of why this happened at that time. In the course of the four years of World War I, over seven million people were killed. People of the countries who suffered from this experience, Germans, English, Americans, and French, in particular, came out of this with a new view of the world and a new way of looking at humanity. If one simplifies a bit, one can say that the nineteenth-century person had died.

Survivors, looking at the heaps of corpses lying around them, lying like garbage, wondered whether individuality might have been lost, interiority may also have gone. In France and Germany, one sees as a result of this, the rising of Dadaism with the idea that nineteenth-century forms were no longer adequate. But in the case of England, the detective novel was written in great numbers, perhaps fulfilling the same role Dadaism and Surrealism performed in France and Germany.

BC: There seems to be more of a sense of security with the detective novel since you have something that needs to be solved, and it gets solved while with Surrealism there is no trajectory that leads to a solution . . .

KK: In the detective novel, a single person dies, and the criminal, in order to murder that person, thinks of a number of different schemes . . . There are cases of the so-called remote control mysteries . . . cases where the murder occurs over a distance employing an alibi, and other variations of many kinds. And in this case, the victim is a single person and treated as a single person in contrast with the many faceless victims of the war.

BC: It matters, then, how this person has been murdered . . . his individual person is of importance . . .

KK: Yes. It's full of meaning . . .

BC: Unlike the masses of bodies . . . The detective story, in this regard it's reassuring . . .

KK: In a sort of parallel that matches the criminal's investing a lot of thought in the commitment of the crime, we find the detective who also uses his ratiocinative powers in figuring out the crime, and he thereby invests it with further meaning.

BC: In that way, it's possible to consider this process a political statement that insists on the value of the individual as a human being . . .

KK: Yes . . . So a fiction that invests meaning in the deaths of individuals might stand as a kind of resistance against mass death and warfare. It's my theory that this might explain the efflorescence of detective fiction after World War I that occurred in both the U.S. and England. In other words, the revival of detective fiction in a postmodern world emerges from the consciousness of the horror of war's dehumanizing results. And this is what prompted me to write this Benjaminist rewriting of Poe's detective: *The Devil of the Crowd: Dupin's Fourth Incident.*

Chapter Five

Lu Xun and Poe: Reading the Psyche

Diane M. Smith

On May 4, 1919, three thousand college students gathered in Beijing's Tiananmen Square to protest the Versailles Peace Treaty, which granted Japan territorial control over areas leased by Germany in China's Shandong province. Earlier in the century, the failed Republican revolution of 1911 had lent force to the belief, voiced by intellectuals, that China's salvation would be dependent upon the nation's willingness to embrace new avenues of thought. The student protestors in Tiananmen Square in 1919 gave this progressive agenda new impetus and a name: the May Fourth movement. Blaming the stagnant and authoritarian weight of Chinese tradition for China's susceptibility to foreign imperialism and warlord politics, the May Fourth generation looked to the West. In "The New Culture Movement Revisited," Arif Dirlik characterizes this generation as one that "sought liberation in ideas . . . [and was possessed] by a euphoric revolutionary eclecticism that had the power to imagine a basic unity in diverse ideas so long as they appeared progressive, democratic and scientific."[1] Their call for sweeping change embraced nearly every aspect of Chinese culture including literature, with literary periodicals such as *New Youth*, founded in 1915, advocating the use of the vernacular in place of classical Chinese. "The reform of writing was not an end in itself (at least not to everyone)," Dirlik explains, "but rather a means to purge the hegemony of old ideas and make new ideas accessible to larger numbers of people."[2] In their eagerness for fresh perspectives, Chinese writers turned to works of Edgar Allan Poe.

In their essay "Poe in China," Sheng Ning and Donald Stauffer document the special interest in the works of Poe in China during the 1920s. "It is no exaggeration to say," Ning and Stauffer observe, "that [during this period] almost all the leading [Chinese] writers . . . in one way or another, showed some interest in Poe."[3] Chinese author Lu Xun (1881–1936) and his brother

51

Zhou Zuoren had introduced Poe to Chinese readers with "The Story of a Jade Bug," a translation by Zhou Zuoren of Poe's "The Gold Bug," a copy of which, with Japanese annotations, Lu Xun had discovered in 1903 while a student in Japan.[4] In 1909, the brothers' two volume *Tales from Abroad*, which included Zhou Zuoren's translation of Poe's *Silence*, was published in Tokyo. Lois Vines attributes the increased interest among the Chinese in Western authors, in part, to the reprinting of *Tales from Abroad* in 1920 and subsequently in 1924.[5] Numerous Chinese authors undertook translations of Poe's works; there were several translations of "The Tell-Tale Heart" and "The Raven," the title of the poem becoming "The Song of the Owl" in one version.[6]

Categorizing different aspects of Poe's impact upon Chinese writers during this period, Ning and Stauffer conclude that the "most common kind of influence was his use of certain kinds of emotional effects and his psychological probing into people's minds."[7] For Lu Xun, heralded as "the soul of China,"[8] this "psychological probing" took on a distinctly political character. The tropes of psychological disintegration and decay that serve primarily as expressions of internal landscapes in Poe's fiction, for Lu Xun became a means of diagnosing a collective state, a cultural psyche. This paper will examine ways in which Lu Xun and Poe utilize common structural and thematic elements in their probing of the human psyche, which, for Lu Xun, becomes *A Call to Arms*.[9]

After seeing a slide depicting a group of his fellow countrymen as robust yet callous spectators at the execution of a Chinese man who had been accused of spying by the Japanese, Lu Xun, then a medical student in Japan, decided that a doctor of the soul was what his people truly needed, and he turned from the study of medicine to literature. In his preface to his first volume of stories, Lu Xun describes the realization that he had come to as a result of viewing the slides:

> After this experience I felt that the practice of medicine was nothing urgent . . . since no matter *how* healthy or strong the bodies of a weak-spirited citizenry might be, they'd still be fit for nothing better than to serve as victims or onlookers at such ridiculous spectacles. . . .The most important thing to be done was to transform their *spirits*, and of course the best way to effect a spiritual transformation—or so I thought at the time—would be through literature and art.[10]

In his first published story "Diary of a Madman,"[11] which appeared in *New Youth* in 1918, Lu Xun draws upon a device familiar to readers of Poe: the destabilized narrator. Like the narrator of Poe's "The Tell-Tale Heart," Lu Xun's narrator ostensibly suffers from acute paranoia. He feels threatened by passersby, his neighbors, even his older brother and the doctor whom his brother has called in to examine him, all of whom he suspects of being cannibals eyeing him as their next meal. He observes "a savage glint" (33) in the doctor's eyes, "a murderous gleam" (39) in his older brother's eyes, "murderous looks" (37) in children's eyes, and is disturbed by the "white and hard" (32) eyes of a steamed fish. In her discussion of Poe's "The Oval Portrait," Sylvie Richards points to the "familiar psychoanalytic equation: to look at = to devour," quoting the writings of Otto Fenichel: "Very often sadistic impulses enter into the instinctual aim of looking: one wished to *destroy* something by means of looking at it, or else the act of looking itself has already acquired the significance of a modified form of destruction."[12] Both Poe and Lu Xun draw upon this equation as a means of expressing psychic threats.

From the one-eyed feline in "The Black Cat" to the "divine orbs"[13] of Ligeia and the "eye-like windows" (126) of the Usher mansion, the eye holds a privileged place in Poe's signifying system. In a philosophical reading of "Ligeia" as "a story that retells Locke's fables of the wandering soul,"[14] Joan Dayan proposes that "Ligeia's eyes lead us . . . to the critical meditation on doubling and identity."[15] These issues are reconfigured in "The Tell-Tale Heart," when the narrator perceives the victim's eye as that of a vulture circling and threatening to devour its prey. Charles May underscores the auditory connection between "eye" and the first person pronoun: "when the narrator says he must destroy the 'eye,' he means he must destroy the 'I' . . . by killing the old man the narrator fulfills his desire to destroy himself."[16] In her discussion of "To Helen"(1848), Dayan finds "something less than ideal or sanctifying about these eyes. . . . For the observing poet, 'the fair sex' and the 'romance' she bears can only be experienced here as fragment. Her distillation into nothing but eyes will be repeated at the end of 'For Annie.'"[17] The process is reenacted in "The Oval Portrait," where the woman is distilled into a portrait by means of the artist's eyes. His eyes, Sylvie L. F. Richards explains, "become the sadistic weapons for the transference of life from the young woman to the canvas. The painter continues to work, to draw out the life of his subject, disregarding the pain he is causing."[18] Through the "sadistic impulse of looking," Richards concludes, the painter of "The Oval Portrait" achieves the "depersonification of the woman," who "becomes the artist's palette."[19]

This psychic link between "to see" and "to devour" is a recurrent trope in Lu Xun's first volume of stories. In his mock anti-heroic epic, "Ah Q—The Real Story" (1921), the title character functions as a type of Chinese everyman, who embodies the vicious traits of the society that victimizes him. "It is clear that Lu Xun's portrait of Ah Q is a fictional fleshing-out of the able-bodied Chinese spy in the news slide incident," Lee observes. "He is, in short, a body without an interior self, a face in the crowd, and the crowd's summary mirror-image."[20] In the closing chapter, Ah Q experiences a partial awakening or epiphany as he watches the eyes of the crowd awaiting the spectacle of his execution for a theft for which he had become the scapegoat. He recalls having once encountered a hungry wolf, the eyes of which, "ferocious and timid at the same time" (170), had terrified him. The eyes of the assembled crowd appear even more terrifying: "Sharp and dull at the same time, these eyes had already devoured his words and now sought to tear into something beyond mere flesh and bone. Neither closing in nor dropping back by so much as half a step, they stalked him with persistent tenacity. And then they all merged into a single set of fangs that ripped and tore at Ah Q's soul" (170–72).

In his comments on Lu Xun's fiction in the context of third-world literature, Fredric Jameson proposes that in this literature "psychology, or more specifically, libidinal investment, is to be read in primarily political and social terms."[21] He notes, for example, that "classical sex manuals are at one with the texts that reveal the dynamics of political forces."[22] Jameson designates the "libidinal center" of Lu Xun's "Diary of a Madman" as "the oral stage," and points to "Lu Xun's mobilization of it for the dramatization of an essentially social nightmare—something which in a western writer would be consigned to the realm of the merely private obsession, the vertical dimension of the personal trauma."[23] Lu Xun chooses the highly subjective form of the diary to convey this "social nightmare." When Lu Xun's madman seeks an explanation for the attitudes of people toward him, he can come up with only one, the fact that "twenty years ago, [he] trampled on the account books kept by Mr. Antiquity" (30). Ever since this time, he worries, "it's hard to say what they'll do" (32). The challenge to tradition represented by the attack upon Mr. Antiquity's account books clearly aligns the madman, whom Lee identifies as "an artistic version of Lu Xun's inner voice,"[24] with May Fourth iconoclasm. The madman is able to penetrate through the façade of Confucian virtues to the cannibalistic nature of his society. Seeking further clarification of his perceptions from history books, he finds the words "BENEVOLENCE, RIGHTEOUSNESS, AND MORALITY" on every page masking the message "EAT PEOPLE!" (32), written between the lines of the entire volume.

Poe's madman claims to have acute senses that enable him to hear "all things in the heaven and in the earth" (187), including the heartbeat of his dead victim. The self-reflexive nature of the narrator's perceptions is readily apparent throughout the tale, manifesting itself "above all" (187) through the sense of hearing: "I knew the sound well" (188). In Lu Xun's fictional world, madness becomes a vehicle of privileged cognition into the outer world of social and political realities. Lee comments upon the repeated references to the presence or absence of moonlight throughout "Diary of a Madman": "The recurring image of the moon gives rise symbolically to a double meaning of both lunacy (in its Western connotation) and enlightenment (in its Chinese etymological implication). Thus it is precisely the Madman's growing insanity that provides the basis for an unusual process of cognition which leads to his final realization of the true nature of his society and culture."[25]

In his preface to *A Call to Arms*, Lu Xun employs the metaphor of the iron house to describe the repressive nature of Chinese culture and society in the early twentieth century as well as his inner doubts about the role of the writer in such a culture:

> Suppose there were an iron room with no windows or doors, a room it would be virtually impossible to break out of. And suppose you had some people inside that room who were sound asleep. Before long they would all suffocate. In other words, they would slip peacefully from a deep slumber into oblivion, spared the anguish of being conscious of their impending doom. Now let's say that *you* came along and stirred up a big racket that awakened some of the lighter sleepers. In that case they would go to a certain death fully conscious of what was going to happen to them. Would you say that you had done those people a favor? (27)

Lu Xun's reliance on metaphorical landscapes and lyrical tableaux to probe what he viewed as the spiritual sickness of the Chinese people is a technique Poe repeatedly uses to portray the troubled psyche. Poe's Egaeus speaks of "gloomy, gray, hereditary halls" and the "gray ruins of [his]memory" (97). When Roderick Usher's "cadaverous complexion" shocks his childhood friend, Usher reveals that the "*physique*" of the family mansion, with its "gray walls and turrets, and of the dim tarn into which they all looked down," has had an effect on his spirit (131). Similarly, the gray complexions of characters in Lu Xun's fictional world, especially those of children, reflect the psychic impact of the iron house. Lu Xun's madman is able to perceive the shadow of the iron house in the "iron grey" faces of young people and even children. When he confronts a young man of "about twenty or so" with the question: "Is this business of eating people right?" the young man's response ranges from avoidance to denial. Finally, "his face . . . gray like a slab of iron," he says, "It's always been that way" and takes refuge in silence. "It must be because his mom and dad taught him to be that way," the madman concludes. "And he's probably already passed it on to his own son. No wonder that even the children give me murderous looks" (37). His final desperate cry, "Save the children" (41) is that of a drowning man.[26] The preface, written in classical Chinese in contrast to the vernacular of the diary, the mode popularized by the New Culture movement, shows that his worst fears have been realized. He has been eaten, reabsorbed into the cannibalistic culture, and now, "sound and fit again," a nameless functionary in the system, he "awaits an "official appointment" (29).

Lee characterizes Lu Xun's fiction as a product of two conflicting tendencies, "public didacticism and personal lyricism."[27] If the didactic impulse in "Diary of a Madman" politicizes the trope of madness that we see in "The Tell-Tale Heart" and many other works by Poe, the lyricism embedded in later stories such as "Medicine" (1919) politicizes the narrative of death and loss familiar to Poe's readers. Central to this process is Poe's most well-known emblem, the bird of ill omen.

In "Medicine," the parents of a sick boy pay an executioner for a mantou, a large steamed bread roll, which has been soaked in human blood, in the hope that it will cure their son of tuberculosis. Lu Xun, like Poe, was no stranger to the disease. In his essay, "Father's Illness," Lu Xun gives a moving account of his own boyhood experiences with traditional cures which doctors prescribed for his father, who eventually died of tuberculosis. The family struggled to raise money to pay the fees of doctors whose prescriptions required them to find "sugar-cane which had seen three years of frost" or "a pair of crickets . . . an original pair, from the same burrow,"[28] while the father's health continued to decline. After coughing up blood, his father was given a drink of ink by one physician "based upon the desperate logic," von Kowallis explains, that "'black blocks out red.'"[29] This experience led Lu Xun to embrace the study of Western medicine in Japan. "My dream was a beautiful one," he wrote in the preface to his first volume of stories, "after graduation, I'd go home and alleviate the suffering of all those unfortunates who had been victimized like my father" (23).

The ominous sounds of the young boy's coughs in "Medicine" continue to punctuate the narrative as Kang, the executioner, who later joins other customers at the parents' teahouse, loudly announces in a self-congratulatory tone: "Guaranteed cure! Guaranteed! When you eat it when it's warm like that, a mantou soaked in human blood is a guaranteed cure for any kind of T.B. there ever was" (54). The blood, the reader learns from Kang's harangue, is that of executed revolutionary Xia. While in jail, Xia had tried to convert his jailer, Kang sarcastically reports, by telling the jailer that "the Great Manchu Empire belongs to all of us," only to receive "savage blows." Xia's reply, "Pitiful, pitiful," is dismissed as "crazy talk" by the tearoom's patrons (55).

In the final section of the story, the mothers of both the now dead child and the executed Xia encounter one another when they visit their sons' graves, which lie on adjoining plots. Seeing Xia's grave adorned with a wreath of red and white flowers, his mother is convinced that it is her son who placed the flowers there to protest his execution. She calls upon her dead son to communicate with her through the crow perched on a nearby tree by making it alight on his grave mound. The crow is motionless: "Head pulled in, it stands straight as a writing brush on the branch, looking as though it were made of cast iron" (58). Then, after a single caw, it "crouches, spreads it wings, and then, straight as an arrow, flies away into the distance" (58).

In his "Philosophy of Composition," using "The Raven" as his model, Poe points to the need for "some amount of suggestiveness—some under current, however indefinite, of meaning" (553). The "suggestiveness" of the final two stanzas of the poem, he explains, is meant to "pervade all the narrative which has preceded them" and reveal the "emblematical" significance of the bird as "Mournful and Never-ending Remembrance" (554). In his grief over the loss of Lenore, Poe's narrator has immersed himself in solitude and books "of forgotten lore" and, as Benjamin F. Fisher suggests, "appears to be only too ready to perceive his surroundings, which represent his own mindset, as those of Gothic horror. . . . even admitting more than once that his own 'sad fancy,' rather than supernaturalism, motivates his reactions."[30] In the closing paragraphs of "Medicine," Lu Xun also employs the link between the black bird and the supernatural to suggest an "under current . . . of meaning." Xia's mother, grieving over the loss of her son, like the lover lamenting the loss of Lenore, looks to the bird as a messenger from beyond the grave. But Poe's poem ends with an image of immobility, "still is sitting, *still* is sitting" (103), the raven serving as an emblem of the internalized process of painful memory. In "Medicine," Lu Xun invokes the lyrical to convey the political, ending with the imagery of flight. At first motionless on a tree branch, the crow combines two seemingly conflicting images, its "cast iron" appearance echoing the iron house, and the writing brush suggesting the writer's task of liberating its inhabitants from superstition and other walls. The crow takes flight, ignoring the superstitious expectations of the grieving mother, perhaps tracing an escape route from the repressive iron house via revolution as Milena Doleželová-Velingerová has described.[31]

The recurring tropes of death and decay in Poe's and Lu Xun's works inevitably lead to a consideration of their portrayal of women. Lu Xun's vision of the cannibalistic nature of society informs several of Poe's tales about women, including, as suggested earlier, "The Oval Portrait." When the painter's young wife, "not more lovely than full of glee: All light and smiles and frolicsome as the young fawn" is gradually drained of her life by means of her husband's "pallet and brushes and other untoward instruments" (153), he refuses, in the words of Paula Kot, "to see that he cannibalizes his wife's vitality for his art."[32] Several layers of containment imprison the wife's spirit: her portrait, enclosed within a frame "richly gilded and filigreed in Moresque," is hidden within a niche of a room lying "in a remote turret" of the chateau, guarded like a fortress or iron house by "heavy shutters" and "armorial trophies" (151). Furthermore, her tale is enclosed within a frame tale of a badly wounded narrator whose valet has made "forcible entrance" (151) into the chateau and who reads of the genesis of her portrait from an account within a slim volume lying on the pillow of the bed. The breech made into the chateau by the narrator and his servant is paralleled by the breech made into the narrative structure by the lack of closure for the frame tale. As Kot notes, "Poe refuses to return the story back to the narrator."[33] Just as the woman's portrait overwhelms the narrator by its "absolute life-likeness of expression," leaving him "confounded" and "subdued" (152), her story also resists containment, reminding us of Cynthia Jordan's contention that Poe recognized "the need to tell not only the story of loss, but the second story as well: the story of recovery and restoration, 'the woman's story.'"[34]

"Poe was especially prolific in creating images of violently silenced women," Jordan explains, "their vocal apparatus the apparent target of their attackers, who, in the earlier stories, are the storytellers themselves."[35] Poe's long list of cannibalized women includes Berenice and Ligeia. Egaeus appropriates the perfect white teeth of Berenice as "des ideés" (103). In "Ligeia," the narrator's longing for his deceased first wife cannibalizes the life of his second wife, Rowena. Newly married to Rowena, he claims, "My memory flew back, (oh, with what intensity of regret!) to Ligeia, the beloved, the august, the beautiful, the entombed. I reveled in recollections of her purity, of her wisdom, of her lofty, her ethereal nature, of her passionate, her idolatrous love. Now, then, did my spirits fully and freely burn with more than all the fires of her own" (120). J. Gerald Kennedy, cautious about feminist rereadings of Poe's tales, draws upon evidence of Poe's tragic losses of key women in his life, emphasizing the narrator's childlike dependency on Ligeia and his feelings of abandonment after her death. His repressed resentment, Kennedy argues, is expressed through his "scheme of symbolic retribution"[36] in which Rowena figures as the victim. "The pattern of violence against women throughout Poe's fiction," Kennedy concludes, thus "repeatedly betrays the male protagonists' outrage at his own helplessness and insufficiency."[37] By cannibalizing the life of his new bride, the narrator succeeds only in producing a mummified version of his memory of Ligeia.

The cannibalization of women, Lu Xun recalls in "My Views on Chastity," was practiced during ancient times when "women were usually the chattels of men, who could kill them, eat them, or do what they pleased with them. After a man's death, there was naturally no objection to burying his women with his favorite treasures or weapons. By degrees, however, this practice of burying women alive stopped and the conception of chastity came into being."[38] Stories such as "New Year's Sacrifice" (1924) in *Wandering*, Lu Xun's second volume of fiction,[39] incriminate the intellectual class of failure to effect meaningful reform in China, especially for women, whom the traditional Confucian hierarchy relegated to the inferior position of yang.

The narrator of "New Year's Sacrifice" is an intellectual who has returned home to celebrate the New Year with his conservative Uncle Lu and family. During his stay, he recognizes a beggar on the street as Sister Xianglin. She looks to him, an educated man, for answers to fundamental human questions about the existence of the soul, hell, and the possibility of reunion with deceased relatives in an after-life. The narrator vacillates, eventually turning to the noncommittal response, "'I can't say for sure'" (223). Feeling vaguely anxious after she departs, the narrator shrugs off an underlying feeling of responsibility by reassuring himself that if "you conclude everything you say with a *can't say for sure*, you always remain comfortably free and clear no matter how things turn out" (224). Shortly after, he learns of Sister Xianglin's death and proceeds, like the narrator of Poe's "The Oval Portrait," to piece together "a portrait of her life" (227).

Widowed at a young age, Sister Xianglin is taken on as a servant in the Lu household where she becomes a conscientious worker. In accordance with tradition, having become the property of her mother-in-law after the death of her husband, she is later sold to a man from the hills, whom she is forced to marry after a struggle during which she deliberately hits her head against the corner of an incense table. When she later loses this second husband to disease and their son to a hungry wolf, she returns to her job in the Lu household. Because she was remarried after the death of her first husband, Lu, a neo-Confucian, will not allow her to take part in the preparation of the New Year's festivities for fear of evil influence. The scar on her head, the symbol of her resistance, becomes a mark of shame. Frightened by another servant's warning that she will be sawed in half in the after-life to satisfy her two warring ghost husbands, she uses her wages to donate a doorsill at the temple to expiate her "sin." When this does not cure her social ostracism, her spirit broken, she becomes a beggar.

In "My Views on Chastity," Lu Xun attacks the traditional belief that widows should remain chaste, which became institutionalized during the Ming dynasty (1368–1644). "[T]he chastity which is extolled today," he explains, "is for women only—men have no part in it" (138). The chaste woman "kills herself when her husband or fiancé dies . . . [or] manages to commit suicide when confronted by a ravisher, or meets her death while resisting. The more cruel her death, the greater glory she wins. If she is surprised and ravished but kills herself afterwards, there is bound to be talk" (138). "Only a society where each cares solely for himself and women must remain chaste while men are polygamous," he concludes, "could create such a perverted morality, which becomes more exacting and cruel with each passing day" (143).

Like the wife in Poe's "The Oval Portrait," the untutored Xianglin is, as Marston Anderson explains, "an essentially mute character: her rote repetitions of the at first "rather effective" account of her child's death end by making her a laughing stock." "The 'I' who narrates her story," Anderson adds, "is not in any direct sense responsible for her sufferings . . . but he has the power that she lacks to vocalize her grief, and has done so forcibly for the reader. Yet his failure to go a step further and use this power to grant meaning to her story makes him, the text implies, a guilty accomplice of the superstition-ridden society that has produced her tragedy."[40] Sister Xianglin is cannibalized by this society in much the same way that her son is devoured by the wolf. Yet, at the end of the story, the narrator, listening to the fireworks exploding in the air, experiences "a deep sense of well-being and [feels] wholly free of worldly cares" (241). The memory of Sister Xianglin, the sacrificial offering, has diminished to a "yellow patch of light the size of a human head—the glow of the oil lamp" (240), an illuminated portrait of cannibalism.

Commenting upon the narrative closure of "New Year's Sacrifice" and other stories by Lu Xun, Anderson points to "the narrator's sudden statement of his emotional response, a response that often seems incongruous to the events he has narrated." "These 'lyric' passages," she continues, "can only represent the cathartic moment in which the disappointed dream, the stubbornly enduring memory, the alien life-fragment is exorcized."[41] The pain expressed by Lenore's lover, who exclaims," "Take thy beak from out my heart" (101), is replaced in "New Year's Sacrifice" by imagery conveying forgetfulness and oblivion and, ultimately, reabsorption into the mindless and conformist mainstream. For Poe, there is no such cathartic moment. "Much of Edgar's career," Kenneth Silverman concludes, "may be understood as a sort of prolonged mourning, an artistic brooding-on and assemblage of the fantasies activated by an ever-living past."[42] "The emblematic meaning of the [raven] . . . *Mournful and Never-ending Remembrance* . . . can stand as the motto of almost everything he ever wrote."[43]

In his assessment of Lu Xun's fiction, Lee concludes that "[t]hough grounded in a Chinese reality, with elements drawn from his home milieu, the stories, when read together, present an allegory of a people told by an intensely subjective author. Underneath the realistic veneer of setting and character are to be found certain inner voices from the depth of a troubled psyche."[44] Both Poe and Lu Xun listened to these "inner voices." Their works explore the gray terrain of the human psyche, employing its ominous birds, cannibalizing eyes, and madmen as barometers of psychic states. Poe's tales, especially those of women, recent criticism suggests, succeed in transcending the level Jameson describes as "personal trauma" to become visions of a "social nightmare." Lu Xun, a political writer from the outset, devoted his career to awakening China's "light sleepers" to another nightmare, that of China's iron house. When the May Fourth generation opened a window to the West and Poe, it provided Lu Xun with "eye-like windows" capable of probing the psyche of a culture.

NOTES

1. Arif Dirlik, "The New Culture Movement Revisited: Anarchism and the Idea of Social Revolution in New Culture Thinking," *Modern China*, vol. II, no. 3 (July 1985): 253.

2. Ibid., 292.

3. Sheng Ning and Donald Barlow Stauffer, "Poe in China," in *Poe Abroad: Influence, Reputation, Affinities*, ed. Lois Davis Vines (Iowa City: University of Iowa Press, 1999), 149.

4. Ibid., 149-50.

5. Louis Vines, "Edgar Allan Poe: A Writer for the World," in *A Companion to Poe Studies*, ed. Eric W. Carlson (Westport: Greenwood Press, 1996), 532.

6. Ning and Stauffer, 151. The owl, Ning and Stauffer explain, is viewed by the Chinese as a "bird of omen" and was also "intended to remind Chinese readers of the classical poem bearing the same title" (151).

7. Ibid., 152-53.

8. Banners accompanying Lu Xun's funeral procession on the afternoon of October 22, 1936, according to Harriet C. Mills, bore this inscription. See Douwe W. Fokkema, "Lu Xun: The Impact of Russian Literature," in *Modern Chinese Literature: May Fourth Era*, Harvard East Asian Series, no. 89, ed. Merle Goldman (Cambridge: Harvard University Press, 1977), 189.

9. This is the translation, used by Leo Ou-fan Lee, of the title of Lu Xun's first volume of stories, published in 1923. Cf. the less militant tone of Lyell's translation in note 10.

10. Lu Xun, Preface, *Cheering from the Sidelines*, in *Diary of a Madman and Other Stories*, trans. William Lyell (Honolulu: University of Hawaii Press, 1990), 23-24. This edition is the source of further citations, given in the text, to this work and to Lu Xun's fiction. In "The Power of Mara Poetry," Lu Xun praises Byron, Shelley, and others for leading the way toward spiritual renewal by rebelling against the prevailing ethics of society. "The essay," Lee asserts, "can be read as a romantic manifesto in which Lu Xun proclaimed his new role as a writer." See Leo Ou-fan Lee, *Voices from the Iron House: A Study of Lu Xun* (Bloomington: Indiana University Press, 1987), 21.

11. The title, derived from Gogol's short story published in 1835, reflects the interest of Lu Xun and his brother in the literature of Eastern Europe, which they considered the mouthpiece of oppressed peoples. There has been much critical discussion of Lu Xun's "Diary of a Madman" in relation to its Russian predecessor. See Fokkema, 96-97.

12. Qtd. Sylvie L. F. Richards, "The Eye and the Portrait: The Fantastic in Poe, Hawthorne and Gogol," *Studies in Short Fiction* 20 (Fall 1983): 309.

13. Edgar A. Poe, "Ligeia," in *The Portable Edgar Allan Poe*, ed. J. Gerald Kennedy (New York: Penguin, 2006), 113. Further citations are from this edition and noted parenthetically in the text.

14. Joan Dayan, *Fables of Mind: An Inquiry into Poe's Fiction* (New York: Oxford University Press, 1987), 178.

15. Ibid., 180.

16. Charles May, *Edgar Allan Poe: A Study of the Short Fiction*, Twayne Studies in Short Fiction, no. 28 (Boston: G. K. Hall and Company, 1991), 78.

17. Joan Dayan, "Poe's Women: A Feminist Poe?" *Poe Studies/Dark Romanticism: History, Theory, Interpretation*, vol. 26, nos. 1-2 (June 1993): 6.

18. Sylvie L. F. Richards, "The Eye and the Portrait: The Fantastic in Poe, Hawthorne and Gogol" *Studies in Short Fiction* (Fall 1983): 309.

19. Ibid., 309.

20. Lee, *Voices from the Iron House*, 77.

21. Fredrick Jameson, "Third-World Literature in the Era of Multinational Capitalism," *Social Text*, no. 15 (Autumn 1986): 72.

22. Ibid., 72.

23. Ibid., 72.

24. Lee, *Voices*, 53.

25. Ibid., 54. Douwe Fokkema points out that "Chinese cultural history. . . provides instances of a respectful role for the madman, notably in the representation of the Taoist eccentrics" (96). However, "the Taoist outcast aspires after metaphysical values" Lu Xun's madman, Fokkema argues, is that of romantic literature in that he "present[s] an interpretation of the world" (96).

26. The influence of Western science upon Lu Xun and others of the May 4th generation is evident in the madman's use of the imagery of Darwinian evolution to stress that China's survival would be dependent upon the nation's willingness to break from its blind adherence to tradition: "If you don't change . . . a real human being's going to come along and eradicate the lot of you, just like a hunter getting rid of wolves—or reptiles!" (40). Lee finds "somewhat fragmented paraphrases" of both Darwin and Nietzsche in "Diary" (56).

27. Lee, *Voices*, 59.

28. Lu Xun, "My Father's Illness," *Silent China*, 399.

29. Jon Eugene von Kowallis, *The Lyrical Lu Xun: A Study of His Classical-Style Verse* (Honolulu: University of Hawai'i Press, 1995), 13.

30. Benjamin Fisher, *The Cambridge Introduction to Edgar Allan Poe*. (Cambridge: Cambridge University Press, 2008), 44.

31. See Milena Doleželová-Velingerová, "Lu Xun's 'Medicine," in *Modern Chinese Literature: May Fourth Era*, 221-31, for her discussion of the story's epilogue.

32. Paula Kot, "Painful Erasures: Excising the Wild Eye from 'The Oval Portrait,'" *Poe Studies/Dark Romanticism: History, Theory, Interpretation* vol. 28, nos. 1&2 (June/Dec. 1995): 2.

33. Ibid., 5.

34. Cynthia Jordan, "Poe's Re-Vision: The Recovery of the Second Story," *American Literature* 59 (1987): 19.

35. Ibid., 2.

36. J. Gerald Kennedy, "Poe, 'Ligeia,' and the Problem of Dying Women," in *New Essays on Poe's Major Tales*, ed. Kenneth Silverman (Cambridge: Cambridge University Press, 1993), 114.

37. Ibid., 126.

38. Lu Xun, "My Views on Chastity," *Silent China*, 142.

39. This translation of the title of the second volume, published in 1926, is used by Lee. Other translations include *Hesitation* and Lyell's *Wondering Where to Turn*.

40. Marston Anderson, "The Morality of Form: Lu Xun and the Modern Chinese Short Story," in *Lu Xun and His Legacy*, ed. Leo Ou-fan Lee (Berkeley: University of California Press, 1985), 41.

41. Ibid., 39-40.

42. Silverman, *New Essays*, 78.

43. Ibid., 240.

44. Lee, *Voices*, 59.

Chapter Six

"Breaking the Law of Silence": Rereading Poe's "The Man of the Crowd" and Gogol's "The Portrait"

Alexandra Urakova

Edgar Poe's books break the law of silence, which the wizard of "A Terrible Vengeance" could not break, when he asked the monk to pray for him, and the letters in the Bible became bloodstained.

—Haito Hazdanov, "Notes on Gogol, Poe, and Maupassant," 1929

If one thinks of Poe's counterpart in Russia, it would most likely be Nikolai Gogol, born in the same 1809, and representing "dark Romanticism" for Russian readers, among others. Parallels between the two authors range from fear of being buried alive, either fictional or personal, to flaneûr-like descriptions of city landscapes. Thematically linked tales, "The Portrait" (1842) and "The Oval Portrait" (1842), on the one hand, and "The Man of the Crowd" (1840) and "The Nevsky Prospect" (1833–1834), on the other hand, are traditionally paired. [1] By breaking the pairs and reading together "The Man of the Crowd" and "The Portrait" instead, I hope to challenge the usual course of comparative discussion. In these stories Poe and Gogol took a traditional folkloric figure, the old wanderer, and placed him on the mean streets of the modern city. Both overtly demonized social relations by making their old men stand for the vices of the city or the crowd, and yet developed a vision of city life with all its social controversy emphasized. These affinities, which, like Poe's purloined letter, have remained in full view but unnoticed, give us a rationale to cross-read the tales without forcing the comparison too far. However similar their understanding of literary convention, Poe's and Gogol's social and political backgrounds ultimately ensure that each author takes a strikingly different view of emerging modernity.

63

In his illuminating essay, "'Trust No Man': Poe, Douglass, and the Culture of Slavery," J. Gerald Kennedy suggested that Poe's *The Narrative of Arthur Gordon Pym* ought to be read alongside Douglass's *Narrative*, considering that both of them for about two years inhabited the same Baltimore neighborhood. More importantly, they belonged to the same social milieu, and their "very different books carry the imprint of a common culture pervaded by racial hostility and deception."[2] In the case of Poe and Gogol we can also speak of a certain, though altogether different, "neighborhood." Physically separated by the Atlantic, they shared the same publishing context and reading audience of *The Blackwood's Magazine* for 1847. "The Portrait," translated by Thomas B. Shaw, appeared in volume 62 for October; a review of Poe's tales, with "The Man of the Crowd" (extendedly resumed) being published in the adjoining November issue.[3]

At first sight "The Portrait," a tale about the fate of art in modern society, has little in common with Poe's story. A poor artist named Chartkov purchases a remarkable portrait of the old man at the picture show. The night that follows, he dreams of the old man stepping out of the canvas and collecting bags of gold coins right in front of him. One of the bags is accidentally discovered in the portrait's frame in the morning, and it not only helps Chartkov pay his debts, but furthers his career as a modern painter. Selling his art, he ultimately loses his artistic skills and tragically ends his life. As we learn from the second part of the tale, the old man in the portrait was a usurer whose money brought misfortune to the debtors while he was alive. He ordered a painting in his deathbed in hope that he would not die completely if his features were accurately reproduced. Eventually, the portrait appears again up for auction, is stolen, and therefore continues its fatal route.

Even from this brief summary, one can tell that the intricacy of the tale's framed plotting contrasts with the scarcity of "The Man of the Crowd's" narrative economy. And yet the common publishing context was not altogether accidental. The tales fulfilled conventions of a mid-nineteenth-century *Blackwood's* story and perfectly fitted its framework: each combined a fantastic plot with a modern setting and contained a moral message.[4] Paraphrasing Kennedy, we can perhaps speak about the imprint of common *literary* culture, both Gothic and Romantic, that allows us to establish the points of contact between these "very different" texts. Furthermore, the fact that a translation from Gogol and a long discussion of Poe's tale came out in consecutive numbers of the leading European journal shows that both authors were tapping into a similar Zeitgeist.

By the time the tales were written, the Gothic "evil fiend" or "villain" had already given way to the city outcast, whose occupation could have been as diverse as a usurer, an antiquarian, an old-clothes man, a criminal, or a beggar. One would think of the 1820s–1830s as a transition point from the mythic, folk-tale character of a malicious old man, a wizard, or a demon, to its more modern, realistically specified treatment, the one we observe, for example, in Balzac's *Gobseck* (1830) and *The Wild Ass's Skin* (1831). The uncanny aspect of old age haunting the nineteenth-century imagination from Coleridge's *The Rime of the Ancient Mariner* (1798) and Scott's *The Antiquary* (1816) to Dostoevsky's *Crime and Punishment* (1866) merges with another enduring and highly Romanticized literary myth, that of the Wandering Jew. The legend of Ahasver that inspired such classic examples of Gothic fiction as Charles Maturin's *Melmoth-the-Wanderer* (1820) recurs in various texts of the period. It echoes, for instance, in Balzac's *The Centenarian, or, The Two Beringhelds* (1824), a novel about a hundred-year-old sorcerer returning after his death, a character that itself can be seen as a bridge between Maturin's *Melmoth* and *The Antiquary* in Balzac's own *The Wild Ass's Skin*. A decade later the myth becomes modernized, urbanized, and politicized in Sue's *The Wandering Jew* (1844–1845). The wanderer is now part of the urban landscape as it will be further emblematized in Baudelaire's poem "The Seven Old Men" (1861): a flaneûr meets an uncanny old man and his six likenesses one Parisian morning; a stick adds "a finishing touch" to the man's ghostly portrait giving him "the clumsy gait" of a "three-legged Jew."[5]

The old wanderer on the city streets was already a topoi but not yet a cliché in mid-nineteenth-century fiction. Not surprisingly, Gogol's usurer, like Melmoth, is a ghostly wanderer passing from one purchaser to the other, in the form of the portrait. Merciless to his debtors and endowed with magic power, he shares some features with both Balzac's Gobseck and the Centenarian. The usurer is not Jewish as his occupation implies; but even though his origins are vaguely described as "southern" or "oriental" instead, they are still regarded as alien: "He went about in a voluminous Asiatic robe. His dark complexion bespoke his southern origin, but as to his nationality, whether he belonged to India, or Greece, or Persia, no one was certain." Complexion, dark blazing eyes, and heavy protruding eyebrows, make the old man "different from all the ash-colored inhabitants of the capital."[6] In "The Man of the Crowd," as in Balzac's *The Centenarian*,[7] a reader has a sense that the old man might hold a secret, but the reader never quite knows what that secret is. Balzac's sorcerer has "vigor and force decidedly not that of old men,"[8] and so does Poe's character: the *Blackwood's* reviewer even pointed at the improbability of his "pedestrian powers" as of those of his convalescent observer able "to keep upon his legs, running and walking, the whole of the night and of the next day."[9] Poe's wanderer, indeed, ceaselessly rushes about the city as the Wandering Jew ceaselessly rushes through the world, even though the route of the former is circumscribed by the limits of the maze-like cityscape.[10]

Both characters, Poe's and Gogol's, combine the cursed restlessness of the Wandering Jew with overtly demonic features. The narrator recollects that his first thought, upon seeing the old man's expression, was that

"Retszch, had he viewed it, would have greatly preferred it to his own pictural incarnations of the fiend."[11] There is a striking parallel to this commentary in Gogol's story: when the usurer requests the artist to paint his portrait the latter exclaims, "What could be better! He offers himself as the devil I'm painting in my picture" (553). Gogol's artist, like Poe's imaginary Retzsch, prefers the old man's "authentically" demonic appearance to a fantasy; cf.: "he couldn't help but say, 'That's who ought to be the model for the devil!'" (553). This fantastic touch adds to the social marginality implied by the occupation of one character and the alleged criminality of the other. Poe and Gogol independently capture the moment when the mystic becomes modern, their tales revealing the complex vision of social alienation. The usurer lives in Kolomna, the city outskirts. The "man of the crowd" is homeless. Socially alienated and demonic, both seductively stand outside society. Outcasts as they are, yet also endowed with supernatural energy, the old men represent the mysterious power of the crowd to take hold over a solitary walker and to get him involved in its restless and bustling routine.

Seen in this perspective, the story lines run in parallel. "The Man of the Crowd" opens with a scene in the hotel café: the narrator, a city flaneûr, watches "the tumultuous sea of human heads" (507) through the smoky glass of a large bow window. As Robert Byer persuasively suggests in his famous Marxist reading of the tale, this dramatic setting "might be likened to, though it inverts, the window gazing and endless appetency that define the perspective of the commodity shopper."[12] Here the viewer (the narrator) himself sits in the window while the viewed objects (the men and women of the crowd) are displayed to him "outside" in the street, where the viewer of the kaleidoscopic world of commodities would "naturally" place himself.

Gogol's narrative originates at the picture shop: like a café, it was a place that a mid-nineteenth-century flaneûr would have certainly spotted.[13] Moneyless, Chartkov enters the shop not to buy pictures but to examine human nature; he is eager to find out what sort of people wanted these productions. Further into "The Man of the Crowd," the narrator and the old man will also purposelessly walk "among the host of buyers and sellers" of the London bazaar (512). In "The Portrait," Chartkov will stroll along the pavement, leveling his eye-glass at the passersby. In the first edition of the story it says that he observed growing and flashing flows of people through huge windowpanes of his new studio at Nevsky Prospect while lying on the Turkish sofa.[14] And although Gogol leaves out the scene in the tale's revision, the studio remains at the junction of city life and art, the latter gradually losing its high destination and becoming a sellable commodity. Chartkov will paint his numerous models in a grotesquely depersonalized way, similar to how Poe's narrator describes the London crowd:

The uniform, lifeless, forever immaculate and, as it were, buttoned-up faces of the government officials, soldiers, and statesmen did not offer his brush adequate scope. . . . The only thing he saw before him was a uniform, a corsage, or a dress coat before which the artist is unmoved, and before which all imagination withers and dies. (538)

In these tales, we therefore encounter a vision of the city typical for modernity: each character feels superior to the crowd of either passersby or shop customers, alternating curiosity with detachment; however the city remains an obscure place where a casual purchase may turn fatal and a casual encounter is fraught with meaning. Chartkov discovers the portrait of the usurer amidst a heap of old, dusty paintings, torn canvases, and frames without gilding. Poe's narrator snatches the old man's face out of the picturesque crowd. Both get "arrested and absorbed" (511) by their discovery which leads to a purchase in the first case and to a pursuit in the second. No longer detached from the crowd, Poe's narrator becomes a part of it in the course of the old man's chase. The portrait pulls Chartkov out of the isolated life of a poor artist and makes him a man of society.

After meeting the old man, each character undergoes uncanny transformation. Driven by jealousy toward more talented painters, Chartkov eventually begins to purchase distinguished works of art and pitilessly destroy them. It says that he "devours" masterpieces with "the eyes of basilisk" (542). The eyes are the most striking feature of the old man's face: "They seemed to glare, glare out of the portrait, destroying its harmony with their unnatural liveliness" (513). Chartkov, with his "basilisk" stare, becomes the portrait's living incarnation: "It was as if that terrible demon which Pushkin has described had been reincarnated by him" (542). In Poe's story, the narrator shares the restlessness and idiosyncrasy with the stranger. He is forced to adjust himself to the old man's rhythm in the course of the pursuit; the mimetic doubling suggests vibes or "fluids" passing from one body to the other.[15]

Remarkably, both seducers seem indifferent to their victims. The usurer collects his bags of gold insensible to Chartkov's presence; Poe's old man never notices his pursuer even when they meet face to face at the end of the tale. The artist and the flaneûr are dragged out of their privacy not by the power of persuasion but by some external mysterious force emanating from the old men. The shift from rational or rhetorical persuasion to mystery and occult compulsion was certainly in the spirit of the time expressing contemporary anxiety about mesmerism and magnetism;[16] yet, as I will further argue, Gogol is more indebted to traditionally Gothic plotting than Poe, when rendering this subject.

The difference lies mainly in the nature of seduction. The usurer tempts Chartkov with gold, which the latter accepts and invests in his career of a modern painter. The economy of "The Portrait" is thus framed by a pact-with-a-devil conventional plot. At his deathbed Chartkov sees people surrounding him as horrible portraits. "The portrait was doubled, quadrupled before his eyes, and at last he imagined that all the walls were hung with these awful portraits, all fastening upon him their unmoving living eyes" (542). This Hoffman-inspired episode, indeed, represents the uncanny nature of the growing or expanding capital. The portrait stamps itself on faces as if they were coins, including Chartkov's own. Money is the absolute evil in Gogol's narrative and yet it can still be resisted by poverty, redemption, and sacrifice. The counterexample of Chartkov's downfall is given in the second part of the tale, in the example of the artist who painted the portrait. Repenting that he involuntarily brought evil in the world, he retires to the monastery, gives away his earthly possessions, and dedicates himself to God. As David Hermann observes, Gogol's second artist "follows the same path" as Chartkov "but manages to turn back where his predecessor had gone over the edge. The possession that undergoes him is the image of the evil he seeks to capture on his canvas; it is too a form of wealth, the soul of a moneylender, permeated for Gogol with the essence of cash."[17] It is not surprising that in the monastery, the artist excels in icon-painting; when his son Leon comes to visit him, the aged man is icon-like himself, cf.: "His face . . . shone with the light of heavenly joy" (559). What recommends the icon to Gogol is precisely its removal from the scene of capitalism and relations of exchange: icon is the antipode not only of the portrait but also of the coin.[18]

The old man's diamond, glimpsed through his ragged clothes, teases the narrator of "The Man of the Crowd" in a way altogether different from that of the portrait's glistening gold. Unlike Gogol's usurer, the old man has no money to give; and even though he does not beg, he is closer to the social type of the beggar as described by Jacques Derrida: "The beggar represents a purely receptive, expending, and consuming agency, an *apparently* useless mouth. . . . He consumes and destroys surplus-values."[19] The diamond-hilted dagger was absolutely commonplace to the Romantic literature of the day. However, it makes us seriously reconsider the story about a pact with a devil in Poe's tale: the "devil" does not offer any material benefits to the "victim"; the diamond functions merely as a sign of difference distinguishing the old man from the rest of the crowd. Such an anomalous flashing of wealth is what the pre-capitalist etiquette manual prescribed for aristocrats: even dressed as a peasant, the aristocrat should always allow a little bit of gold thread to peep through a rip in his burlap culottes.[20] Developing Byer's parallel between "the crowd's unhealthy vitality" and "the circulation of commodities" in Poe's tale, we may suggest that the old man stands for the object of luxury in the commodified world of the city. The irony is that he is economically inferior to other passersby as well as to the narrator, resident of a fancy hotel located in the center of London.

As Kevin Hayes has recently argued, the narrator reads the faces in the crowd "in much the same way as he reads newspaper advertisements," and this suggests that "virtually all city dwellers are walking advertisers, sandwichmen and sandwichwomen who sell whatever they have to sell to their fellow members of the urban public."[21] Conversely, the old man advertises something that cannot be easily defined and labeled:

> As I endeavored, during the brief minute of my original survey, to form some analysis of the meaning conveyed, there arose confusedly and paradoxically within my mind, the ideas of vast mental power, of caution, of penuriousness, of avarice, of coolness, of malice, of blood-thirstiness, of triumph, of merriment, of excessive terror, of intense—of supreme despair. I felt singularly aroused, startled, fascinated. "How wild a history," I said to myself, "is written within that bosom!" Then came a craving desire to keep the man in view—to know more of him. (511)

This fragment reveals how the surplus of meaning becomes transformed into the surplus of desire. Accordingly, the price the narrator pays for his involvement is not the loss of the soul (as it is undoubtedly Chartkov's case!) but the loss of energy. Wearied unto death by the end of the pursuit, the narrator finally becomes a consumer consumed by the crowd he desires to appropriate. The old man, to the contrary, ceaselessly restores his energy from the crowd's activity; that is why he *is* a man of the crowd, part of its attractions and phantoms. All this makes the moral of the tale equivocal. Labeling the old man as "the type and the genius of the deep crime," (515) the narrator compensates for his disappointment and exhaustion by a moral judgment, seeking substitution for the desire he ultimately has to abandon.

Replacing a soul-for-money exchange by the endless circuit of desire, Poe surpasses Romantic dualism of the demonic and the divine, and of the material and the spiritual, which is fundamental to the axiological structure of "The Portrait." The social world represented in "The Man of the Crowd" is arbitrary, self-mirrored, and somehow seamless; it lacks a binary system of meaning although it does not seem to propose any other. There are no absolute values in Poe's tale that, as in "The Portrait," could counterpoise the social evil. The evil itself is questionable, for we have no evident proofs of the old man's maliciousness apart from the narrator's opinion. Gogol's contemporary, the Russian critic Vissarion Belinsky, criticized "The Portrait" for being not "modern." "The idea of the tale would have been genuinely beautiful," he wrote, "had it been conceived *in the modern spirit*."[22] Belinsky found the tale faulty for using a traditional fantastic formula to convey the subject. One might suggest that "The Man of the Crowd," a "fantastic and peculiar tale" as Poe himself called it,[23] became one of the emblems of literary modernity due to the fluidity of its meaning.[24] Poe's model, objectifying contemporary market relations, is self-centered; it lacks transcendence that Gogol's tale, faithful to the Orthodox Christian system of belief, introduces in his tale as a counterforce.

And yet the differences between the models of social representation as discussed above appear to be more attenuated at the narrative level of the tales. To complicate the argument, I would like to focus on "the story of a story," to borrow Henry James's expression. The "history" of the old man, either narrated or silenced, indeed, plays a significant role in the narrative structure of each tale. As it was mentioned above, we learn about the moneylender, his misdemeanors, and his painter's successful resistance in the second part of "The Portrait." Storytelling takes place at the auction where two connoisseurs compete for the old man's portrait "which could not fail to attract attention of anyone who had any knowledge of art" (545). Suddenly a young man interrupts the bargain saying: "I, perhaps, have more right to this picture than anyone else" (545). The young man is Leon, himself a gifted artist and a son of the man who painted the moneylender. By telling the story he hopes to get the portrait back and destroy it, fulfilling his father's deathbed wish. Even the supreme work of art should be sacrificed if it misses its higher moral destination; this belief of Gogol, notoriously foreshadowing the fate of his own *The Dead Souls*, manifests itself already in "The Portrait."[25] But, ironically, by trying to get the old man's portrait, Leon gets involved in the bargain. He has to compete with the auction-buyers outbidding the item's already "incredible" price. The story itself becomes a currency of exchange. One cannot paint the moneylender nor tell his story harmlessly. First the portrait, and then the story, take on the power of his cursed money put into circulation. The narrator eventually serves the devil's purposes as the portrait is stolen, because the attention of the spectators is distracted. "Someone had succeeded in taking it away, taking advantage of the fact that the attention of the listeners was distracted by the story" (561).[26] "The Portrait's" narrative dynamics undermine, though by no means destroy, the dualistic structure of the tale's meaning as the act of telling becomes pervaded by commerce and, its high moral purpose notwithstanding, fails to break with the economic structure of circular exchange.

The old man's "wild history" in "The Man of the Crowd" is the ever elusive object of the narrator's desire: the relation of the latter to the story is that of a "book that doesn't permit itself to be read" (506). The narrator's own explanation of the book's "unreadability" is ethical when he speaks of men who die with despair of heart and convulsion of throat, on the account of the hideousness of mysteries which will not suffer themselves to be revealed. The story's content is dangerous; to remain safe it is better to leave it aside. But as Terrence Whalen reminds us, "information functions as commodity or, more precisely, as capital itself" both in society and in Poe's own "economic imagination."[27] Whalen shows that in "The Purloined Letter," for example, "by the instant logic of both the tale and the emerging relations of production, information would lose all value the instant it became common knowledge."[28] Dupin preserves the private affairs of the Queen as secret; the old man's mystery is likewise out of the reach of both the narrator and the narrative. The stranger's reluctance to share knowledge similarly gives him privilege over the narrator, endows him with power. But unlike the Queen's secret exchanged for a check, the old man's story is doomed to be buried with his keeper and therefore utterly wasted, lost. In "The Man of the Crowd" Poe offers a perverse way of escaping the economic pattern of the exchange relations. His tale opens up a sphere of privacy as a possibility of such escape. Louis Renza claims that "in Poe's mid-nineteenth century world, the 'public,' the highlighted site of accepted or contested values, was coming into existence as a special, alienated category of social experience, partly in the guise of the American capitalist marketplace and mass culture."[29] Defending privacy was therefore a kind of social protest, individual challenge, or revolt. Poe's "aggressive protest against a public complex," in Renza's words about "The Purloined Letter," is even more apparent in "The Man of the Crowd." Also, surpassing Romantic dualisms, Poe introduces a new set of binary oppositions to describe the modern urbanity: privacy and publicity, transparency and obscurity, consumption and waste.

The story told by Leon in "The Portrait" is above all a didactic message addressed to the public as Gogol's literary work itself was meant to be. The ambiguity lies in its delivery: the tale containing the "truth" comes in a fictional form; the storyteller has to entertain his reader to attract his attention, and eventually misses the target. As is well known, later in his career Gogol rejected fiction as such, and attempted to reach to his audience directly, particularly in "The Selected Passages from Letters to Friends" (1847). Poe obviously fulfilled different artistic goals. In "The Man of the Crowd," he indeed sacrifices the narrative interest for the novelty of effect. The reader does not get the old man's "history" that he would expect in the "framed" narrative, but instead enjoys the original turn of the plot. The "law of silence" remains unbroken, but the effect is achieved. While Gogol conceived literary craft primarily as public preaching, Poe rather saw it as a practice of privatizing the verbal matter through the novelty of combinations. It is therefore not so surprising that Poe and Gogol got dissimilar results starting from the same ground.

And still their casual encounter on the pages of the leading European literary magazine is, indeed, symbolic. Reading their texts together, we can follow the traces by which thematic and generic conventions borrowed from the storehouse of European Romantic tradition alter as they get an imprint of a radically different national, social, and cultural background. That difference may be summed up as follows: Gogol's view of contemporary society was somehow more traditional than Poe's and therefore more dependent on the binary oppositions of the good and the evil, the demonic and the divine. However, he was concerned with the over-spreading power of capitalist logic infecting even the act of telling a story, of delivering the truth. Poe, on the contrary, gives us a more modern view of social relations by transcending Gothic or Romantic dualism and posing private values as a means of resistance or escape.

NOTES

1. See, for example: Alexander Nikoljukin, *Vsaimosviasi literatur Rossii i SSHA* (Moskva: Nauka, 1987), 66–68; Mihail Yamploski, *Tkatch i visioner* (Moskva: Novoe Literaturnoe Obozrenie, 2007), 329–30; 427–28. The plots of the mentioned tales are, indeed, strikingly similar. "The Man of the Crowd" and "The Nevsky Prospect" open with a description of the city crowd. Poe's flaneûr pursues the old man. Gogol's young men chase pretty women, which leads to the tragic delusion in the one case and the amorous defeat in the other one. A gas-lit city landscape is dazzling and deceiving in both tales. "The Portrait" and "The Oval Portrait" are stories with a living portrait motif: the portraits preserve the "life" of the models in the picturesque form and strike observers by the lifelikeness of their expression.

2. J. Gerald Kennedy, "'Trust No Man': Poe, Douglass, and the Culture of Slavery," in *Romancing the Shadow: Poe and Race*, ed. J. Gerald Kennedy and Liliane Weissberg (New York: Oxford University Press, 2001), 226.

3. Thomas B. Shaw, "The Portrait. A Tale: Abridged from the Russian of Gógol," *Blackwood's Magazine* (Oct. 1847): 62; "American Library," *Blackwood's Magazine* (Nov. 1847): 62. "The Man of the Crowd" is the only one of Poe's *Tales* (Wiley and Putnam edition) apart from "The Conversation of Eiros and Charmione" discussed in the review at length; the review, as is well known, was the matter of Poe's pride.

4. The *Blackwood's* anonymous reviewer of "The Man of the Crowd" even accused Poe of sacrificing the plot's probability for the sake of "the moral truth": "In a picture of this kind, a moral idea is sought to be portrayed by imaginary incidents purposely exaggerated." Op. cit., 585.

5. Charles Baudelaire, "The Seven Old Men," in *Les Fleurs du Mal*, trans. Richard Howard (Boston: David R. Godine, 1982), 93.

6. Nikolai Gogol, *The Collected Tales and Plays*, ed. Leonard J. Kent (New York: Pantheon Books, 1964), 547. Further references to "The Portrait" will be from this edition and noted parenthetically.

7. Balzac's *Le Centenaire* was republished under the title *Le Sorcier* in 1837, an edition in which it was much more readily available. However, we do not know if Poe ever read Balzac, who is not mentioned anywhere in his work.

8. Honoré de Balzac, *The Centennarian, or, The Two Beringhelds*, trans. George Edgar Slusser (New York: Arno Press, 1976), 95.

9. Op. cit., 585

10. Steven Fink for the first time introduced the myth of the Wandering Jew in the discussion of "The Man of the Crowd" in Steven Fink, "Who is Poe's 'The Man of the Crowd'?" (paper presented at the Third International Edgar Allan Poe Conference: The Bicentennial, Philadelphia, PA, October 8–11, 2009).

11. Edgar Allan Poe, *Tales and Sketches*, vol. 1: 1831–1842, ed. Thomas Olive Mabbott (Chicago: University of Illinois, 2000), 511. Further references to "The Man of the Crowd" will be from this edition and noted parenthetically.

12. Robert H. Byer, "Mysteries of the City: A Reading of Poe's 'The Man of the Crowd,'" in *Ideology and Classic American Literature*, ed. Sacvan Bercovitch and Myra Jehlen (New York: Cambridge University Press, 1986), 221–46.

13. The beginning of Gogol's story repeats the beginning of Balzac's *The Wild Ass's Skin* whose character, penniless and desperate Raphaël, by chance enters an antiquarian shop that changes his life.

14. Nikolai Gogol, *Sobranie sochinenii*, vol. 3 (Moskva: Goslitizdat, 1952), 252.

15. See Byer describing affinities between the narrator and the old man, the narrator and the crowd in the terms of contagion. "Mysteries of the City," 241.

16. In the first edition of "The Portrait" the old man appears to Chartkov as a fiend and gives a long speech describing the benefits of their pact.

17. David Hermann, *Poverty of the Imagination: Nineteenth-Century Russian Literature about the Poor* (Evanston, IL: Northwestern University Press, 2001), 85.

18. The intermediary option suggested in the tale is the sublime devotion to art illustrated by the example of Leon, Chartkov's fellow-artist and the son of the artist who painted the portrait. Leon travels to Italy where he lives in poverty and perfects his skill. Still there is scarcely a distinction between preaching Christianity and preaching true art, as is evident in the artist's words to his son: "You have talent; do not destroy it, for it is the most priceless of God's gifts" (559). The logic of gift giving challenges the economic relations of exchange.

19. Jacques Derrida, *Given Time: I. Counterfeit Money*, trans. Peggy Kamuf (Chicago and London: Chicago University Press, 1992), 134.

20. I am thankful to Harold Veeser for this hint.

21. Kevin J. Hayes, "Visual Culture and the Word in Edgar Allan Poe's 'The Man of the Crowd,'" *Nineteenth-Century Literature* vol. 56, no. 4 (Mar. 2002): 445–65. The "reading" metaphor prevailing in Poe's tale is a frequent subject of critical discussion. Apart from Byer and Hayes, it is discussed, for example, in Amy Gilman, "Edgar Allan Poe Detecting the City," in *The Mythmaking Frame of Mind: Social Information and American Culture*, ed. James Gilbert, Amy Gilman, Donald M. Scott, and Joan W. Scott (Belmont: Wadsworth, 1993), 71–90; Stephen Rachman, "'Es lässt sich nicht schreiben': Plagiarism and 'The Man of the Crowd,'" in *The American Face of Edgar Allan Poe*, ed. Shawn Rosenheim and Stephen Rachman (Baltimore: Johns Hopkins University Press, 1995), 49–91.

22. Qt. in Nikolai Gogol, *Sobranie sochinenii*: V. 3 (Moskva: Goslitizdat, 1952), 305.

23. Edgar Allan Poe, *Essays and Reviews*, ed. G. R. Thompson (New York: Literary Classics of the United States, 1984), 872.

24. I rely on the concept of modernity as expressed in Zygmunt Bauman's *Liquid Modernity* (Cambridge: Polity Press, 2000), for example.

25. Gogol burned the manuscript of the second volume of *The Dead Souls* in 1845.

26. In the first redaction of the story the portrait is not stolen. The image of the old man miraculously disappears from the canvas replaced by a landscape scene. Gogol obviously wanted to stress the social aspect in the later version of the tale.

27. Terence Whalen, *Edgar Allan Poe and the Masses: The Political Economy on Literature in Antebellum America* (Princeton: Princeton University Press, 1999), 245–46.

28. Ibid., 245.

29. Louis Renza, *Edgar Allan Poe, Wallace Stevens, and the Poetics of American Privacy* (Baton Rouge: Louisiana State University Press, 2002), 7.

I am grateful to Tim Farrant for his insightful suggestions and generous advice on the subject of the essay. The essay was read by Steven Fink, Paul Hurh, and David Mills. I am thankful to the readers for their comments.

Chapter Seven

"What Has Occurred That Has (Never) Occurred Before": A Case Study of the First Portuguese Detective Story

Isabel Oliveira Martins

For almost the whole of the nineteenth century Portuguese culture and literature were peripheral and subsidiary to other cultural and literary systems. The historical and political context engendered by several circumstances, including the Napoleonic invasions (1807–1811), the subsequent rule by the British who had come to help fight the French and a period of civil war that lasted until nearly the end of the 1830s might explain this situation. This context left the Portuguese literary scene in a somewhat backward position. Nevertheless, as Maria Leonor Machado de Sousa points out, "many of the Portuguese intellectuals and writers who had chosen exile returned from France and England eager to share new aesthetic ideas and authors with others in their country."[1] Among these ideas were the Romantic ones which would, however, become so exaggeratedly overused that they would subsequently provoke a strong reaction toward the end of the nineteenth century.

Thus, from the mid-1860s to the mid-1880s, the cultural and literary scene in Portugal began to gradually change under the influence of a generation of writers—later called *A Geração de 70*, or the 70s Generation—who had had the opportunity to have contact with and were also open to different ideas coming from abroad. This generation included several writers such as Antero de Quental, maybe the most well-known poet of the group; Eça de Queirós, who would become one of Portugal's greatest nineteenth-century novelists; Ramalho Ortigão, who although he would not be as well-known as the rest still enjoys a place in our literary canon; and Teófilo Braga, who can be considered the first systematic historian of Portuguese literature.[2] These writers, albeit having a different self-consciousness about the contribution of

75

their literary production as agents of change, were experimenting with new modes of expression in which the affinities with Poe's work can be detected although most of the time these are not directly acknowledged by the authors.

For the public in general, translations were one of the main resources to discover and remain in touch with these new trends, particularly those that were published in periodicals that had gained general acceptance and were flourishing in the latter half of the nineteenth century. French was a language well known among the Portuguese cultural elite since they could not only speak it but even write in it. At the same time, in France, as Margarida Vale de Gato argues, there was also a growing interest in works from outside, particularly those in the English language. This was already noticeable in the eighteenth century but it reached a more decisive stage in the nineteenth century when the, until then, imitated classic models began to give way to an interchange with the "North," drawing closer to German culture and in opposition to the old "Midi" tradition as a way to modernize French literature.[3] This urge for renovation corresponded to a search for new discursive modes that could match the important historical and ideological turn that was taking place in nineteenth-century France. It was helped by the increased number of translations available, the result not only of the growth of a monolingual readership but also to allow for cultural openness and the wishes of the diaspora, both embedded in the revolutionary ideals of the Enlightenment.[4]

Thus it is not surprising that Poe's work rapidly became a focus of interest to French authors because the American writer seemed to condense what they were looking for, as Patrick Quinn, as well as Tieghem, argues, albeit pointing to different reasons:

> It was the discovery of Poe by Baudelaire that finally brought France into the mainstream of modern literature. For here was a writer who combined what the French could see and appreciate, a sense of form and a respect for the intellect, with . . . the ability to move as in dreams through the depths of the mind and to illuminate the kind of verities the reason knows not of.[5]

Even if Poe had already been appreciated and even translated by other French authors, it was nevertheless Baudelaire's translations of Poe's work, published between 1856 and 1865, that contributed to the American author's European reputation and which made him known in Portugal. In fact, between 1866 and 1867, Eça de Queirós, then a young writer starting his career, published a series of installments (*folhetins*) in the *Gazeta de Portugal* (*Portugal Gazette*) that were later collected under the title *Prosas Bárbaras* (*Barbarian Prose*). In the installment entitled "Poetas do Mal" (Poets of Evil), he critically analyzes, although in a very general way, Poe's work together with

that of Baudelaire and Flaubert. Even if Eça does not exactly praise Baudelaire's band, as he calls them, he is able to address what seem to be their most
important aspects. Remarking that they are "bored," Eça argues:

> [they] look for a new idea, one without order and bizarre, and they appear
> clothed in a new unordered and bizarre form. They know that the Arcadian
> mutations are worn out; that the old trees on which the classical liras were
> hung are now dry; . . . Thus the revolution in art professed by Baudelaire's
> band is not, as the common critic argues, the alteration in the use of rhymes,
> metric, or prose; it is the whole divine poem of modern societies which is torn
> to shreds. The new forms are the symptom of its dissolution. The spirits cannot
> breathe the modern air stuffed with materialism: they suffocate, they suffer,
> they moan and then, just as Heine has put into song, they ask for the jealousy,
> the dark violence, the tearing of the flesh, the thefts, the kisses between lips
> filled with blood. And then these books appear—"New Extraordinary Stories,"
> "Flowers of Evil," "Salammbô," etc. The first is by Edgar Poe; through those
> pages there passes the demon of perversity, now stiff and livid like a cypress,
> then jovial, noisy, merry, falling head over heels, displaying his torn clothes,
> laughing while he shows his rotten teeth, sinister and debauched like a street
> clown. Poe does not have Hoffman's vague enlightenment nor Darwin's cold
> imagination. Poe proclaims the reality of terrors and visions, reality. His book
> is the delirious epic of the nervous system. [6]

Eça's first influences were therefore connected to what was also new, or
thought of as new, in Portugal as Jaime Batalha Reis has testified: "The first
influences on Eça de Queirós—those that are more openly recognized in his
first works, the writers I personally know he liked—were primarily (Hein-
rich) Heine, Gérard de Nerval, Jules Michelet, and Charles Baudelaire; at a
distance, or at second hand, Shakespeare, Goethe, Hoffmann, Arnim, Poe,
and powerfully dominating all of these, Victor Hugo."[7] Although Eça would
later become the most important spokesman of realism, albeit a realism that
he considered had to be covered with the diaphanous mantle of fancy, in
those first years, roughly until 1872, he (along with other fellow-writers and
friends) was indeed experimenting with new forms of writing.

On Saturday, July 23, 1870, a Portuguese daily newspaper—*Diário de
Notícias*—announced on its front page under the heading "O mysterio da
estrada de Cintra" ("The Mystery of the Road to Sintra)" that it had just
received a singular piece of writing, an unsigned letter sent by post containing the beginning of an extraordinary narrative describing the kidnapping of
a physician and his friend that might be connected to a terrible murder. It also
added that, owing to the interest of the narrative, its "literary form" and the
crime it seemed to reveal, they felt compelled not to abridge it and so would
begin publishing it in the place of the *folhetim*; in other words, the place
where fiction used to be published. The next day, July 24, the paper began

publication of a series of letters that came to be known as the first Portuguese detective story, "O Mistério da Estrada de Sintra" ("The Mystery of the Road to Sintra"), which came out soon after in the form of a book.

The letters appeared as installments in the newspaper until September 27, and their varied authorship was always concealed because they were signed using different initials. The last letter revealed that the whole story was fictional and had been the ingenious creation of two young writers, Eça de Queirós and Ramalho Ortigão, in collusion with Eduardo Coelho, the editor of the newspaper at the time and a friend of both writers. This work has to be regarded as belonging to a period of experimentation for both authors. In fact, fourteen years later, in 1884, when the second edition appeared, Eça and Ramalho wrote a letter as a preface in which they explained how the idea had occurred to them—over a cup of coffee on a summer night—and how they had worked on it—one in Lisbon, the other in Leiria—"without method, without a plan, without a school, without documents, without a style, having recourse only to the 'crystal tower of Imagination,' . . . to their joy and audacity."[8]

Their main intention had been to innovate, to provoke, to shake up the literary and moral situation, wishing to wake up "in shouts" the mental inertia of Lisbon, which at the time was asleep and at the mercy of such authors as Ponson du Terrail or Octave Feuillet. Fourteen years later, they did not recognize themselves in it anymore since now both were writers who were no longer interested in sentimentalities but had devoted their work "to study humbly and patiently the clear realities of their street" (vii). They accepted its re-publication because the main intention was still valuable as a lesson to a new generation of writers—to innovate—and no author should be ashamed of something done with honesty. Finally, it was the celebration of a long friendship (vii–ix).

For two months, the letters were published every day except Monday, the day when the newspaper was not published, amounting to fifty-six install-ments: ten by a man named "Doutor***" (in one of these there was a short letter by José Viegas Ferraz); four by his friend F., a writer; two letters by Z., a "reader" who casts some doubts upon the veracity of the narrative; eighteen written by the *Mascarado* (*Masked Man Narrative*); eleven by A.M.C. (the first nine entitled "Revelações de A.M.C."/ "Revelations by A.M.C.," and the last two, the first of which was entitled "Continuam as revelações de A.M.C."/ "The Revelations of A.M.C. Continued" and the second "Con-cluem as revelações de A.M.C."/ "The Revelations of A.M.C. Concluded"); eleven by a "She," with the title "As Confissões d'Ela" ("Her Confessions"). On the last day, along with A.M.C.'s conclusions, there was "A última carta" ("The Last Letter") signed by Eça and Ramalho explaining the literary bluff.[9] Briefly, the narrative dealt with the accidental murder of Rytmel, a British captain, by his married lover, the Portuguese Countess of W., Luísa, who, possessed by jealousy, had given him an excessive dose of opium to make him sleep so that she could read what she thought were the letters of a new woman in the captain's life. In the end, she retires to a convent. The whole story, however, was told using multiple and fragmentary interventions and could only be reconstituted through the gathering of all the letters sent to the newspaper in a rather similar method to Dupin's concatenation of alleged "facts."[10]

The first nine installments corresponded to the doctor's account of the mysterious events that he and his friend F. had involuntarily become caught up in. He describes in great detail how, on the twentieth of July when returning from Sintra, they were kidnapped by a group of four masked men and taken blindfold in a carriage to a house where there was a man lying on a chaise longue. There he was asked to confirm that the man was dead and how death had occurred. In the meantime, he was able to capture some details of the room in which the corpse lay. The narrator presents his view of the facts in flashback after he has been freed by his persecutors and at a time when he does not know the whereabouts of his friend F. from whom he had been separated shortly after arriving at the house; he does not know either where the house in which he had been held is or who the men who kidnapped him were or even who exactly the dead man was and how he had died. Nevertheless, by the end of the doctor's extensive narration (1–31), the reader knows that a British man had died by ingesting too much opium (suicide or murder?), that there was a lady involved in the mystery, that the four masked men, particularly a tall one who was the doctor's main interlocutor, seemed to have honorable intentions and were not involved in the apparent murder. There was also another man involved who the doctor just names as A.M.C. and identifies as being a student of Medicine from Viseu. This man had suddenly entered the house, to which he had the key, carrying a hammer and nails. He also seemed to have more than significant knowledge about the strange death although he did not have anything to do with the other masked men. The doctor's narration ends in a cloud of mystery since he had been blindfolded again and led out of the house without any further explanations. Although there were several details that might lead an attentive reader to suspect being in the presence of a fictional narrative, an effective appeal was made to the narrator's credibility.

First of all, while describing all he had seen, the doctor uses a very similar method to that in the Dupin tales. In these, Dupin tries to solve crimes by using his sharp ability to observe small details, by paying attention to different testimonies and by the final concatenation of the collected facts. In the end, the crime is used to create a kind of brief and tense play in which imagination, observation and intelligence appeal to the reader's curiosity and observation skills which in turn allow the reader to enjoy the reading and to have the feeling they are participating in solving the crime. Although the doctor's narrative contains some absurd and unreliable observations,[11] other remarks have the powerful effect of verisimilitude because the "detectivesque" mode is used—for example, he notes how the masked men behaved, he describes the room in great detail (the objects, the disposition of the furniture), the position of the body, an exquisite embroidered handkerchief left lying on the floor, the smell of perfume, the elegant stationery and even the blond strand of hair, all of which have the ability to invoke real referents.

The reliability of the narrative or the illusion of truth also came from the very fact that the first-person narrator, writing in a troubled and confessional tone, felt himself helpless to explain what had happened (thereby in some ways quite similar to Poe's narrator in "The Murders in the Rue Morgue"). In fact, in his last letter, he even resorts to the expediency of asking the editor, who he argues will be in a better state of mind, and the readers at home to find a better approach to the hidden truth by analyzing his narrative and trying to come to the right conclusions through using a logical and inductive method.[12] In this way he is almost appealing to the analytic ability of a collective Dupin. Indeed, the fact that Poe's narrator remains nameless throughout allows the readers to project themselves in his place and stand by Dupin's side. Then again, the narration in the Portuguese story, very close in time to the alleged events, also adds a certain sense of truth—an effect that can be found in some of Poe's stories, particularly in "MS. Found in a Bottle."

Secondly, the medium used—the newspaper—asked for a credulous readership in the sense that the reader was directly invited to take part in the elaboration (or re-elaboration) of the story, again in a somewhat similar way to Poe's story. In addition, some parts of the doctor's narrative were cleverly interwoven with external remarks that contributed to its alleged credibility. For instance, on July 27, in the middle of the front page news, there was a short note, unsigned but presumably belonging to the newspaper editors, which reported that the third set of correspondence published that day contained new stimuli for the ever increasing curiosity created among the readers, and even though they had received many letters and verbal inquiries about the mystery, the newspaper could not answer them because they were also dependent on the person who was sending the letters and so they were "anxious spectators" as well.[13] In this way, by merging the authority of the newspaper with the space of the narrative, the "truthfulness" of the fictional text was consequently assured. Again, all these aspects are used in Poe's "The Murders in the Rue Morgue" in which the credibility of the story comes not only from the kind of narrator used but also because the whole story pretends to have originated in a case that had been reported in the *Gazette des Tribunaux*, a real newspaper "from which Dupin and his friend first learned of the Rue Morgue murders in later versions of the tale."[14]

In the Portuguese story, this potentially mystifying game is continued with the introduction of other narratives such as the ones by Z. The first letter by this character is preceded by an editor's note[15] stating that the letter had been received three days earlier but as it contained relevant material connected with the doctor's narrative it would be published before F.'s letters. Z. identifies himself as a reader of installments and one who had begun reading the story thinking it to be an ingeniously created "canard," a kind of story very similar to those created by American and French imaginative writers, and an even better example of what he calls the "roman-feuilleton."[16]

In this part of Z.'s letter, the falsehood of the doctor's narrative is clearly stated. When Z. indignantly tries to contradict the doctor's description of A.M.C. by stating that he knows someone with those initials and that that person could never have been involved in a murder since he knows him, and by supplying numerous details of A.M.C.'s life, including that of his being engaged to a lovely girl, he implicitly gives credibility to the doctor's narrative. Even so, Z.'s first letter establishes various doubts and contributes to another aspect of Eça and Ramalho's work: while constructing a sort of detective story, they were also criticizing the Portuguese literary scene and at the same time the public taste for exaggerated and sentimentalist kinds of fiction. Again, this double agenda was possible because of the medium used—the newspaper. In the interim, and once again, Z.'s limited and focalized point of view further contributes to the complexity of the plot.

Following Z.'s letter, the newspaper began publication of F.'s letter to the doctor that corresponds to four installments. Z. had left certain doubts about the doctor's narrative and his friend F. (who had been kept prisoner in the house but in another room) is able to "miraculously" send a letter through a Prussian citizen—Frederico Friedlann—who studied spirit phenomena and whom he is able to reach through a hole in the wall of the room which communicates with the other man's room in an adjoining house. F.'s detailed narrative has two objectives: first, because he is writing to his friend and through his limited observations, the story again acquires a certain degree of verisimilitude since he corroborates and enlarges on some of the doctor's comments such as the existence of a possible motive for the alleged crime— the existence of a large sum of money (£2,300) which he overhears being mentioned by one of the masked men. F. also believes he is in a place where gambling and Masonic rituals take place and that the masked men are involved in some kind of sordid affair. Secondly, the story becomes even more entangled and full of inconsistencies, which again are exposed by Z.'s second letter that follows the doctor's last letter (55–59).

The doctor's final letter, announced by the newspaper as having been sent together with the last part of F.'s narrative, described his last attempts to solve the mystery in which he had unwillingly become implicated. Having received F.'s letter by mail and being unable to find his friend or confirm any of the "facts" described, he declares that he will be out of the country when the newspaper publishes his letter. He also disagrees with F. about the character of the masked men, particularly of the Tall one, whom he considers to be a gentleman. He also reveals that one of them might well be a friend of F.'s and finishes his letter by pleading to A.M.C., whom he thinks holds the solution to the horrible mystery, to help. On the whole, a series of obvious incongruities is made apparent and if the reader has not already detected them, they are clearly denounced in Z.'s next letter (60–64). Z. deconstructs the doctor's narrative by putting forward a series of unanswered questions, but, once again, he contributes to the continuation of the bluff when he determinedly observes that everything has been done so that the doctor, whom he considers to be an accomplice to the crime, might escape and cover up the crime with the delirious inventions he has been sending to the newspaper, which in the end he asks the editor to erase. [17]

In a way similar to what happens in Poe's "The Murders in the Rue Morgue," this first nucleus of the narrative comes to an end without any effective solution to the mystery. Nevertheless, what can be considered as the second main part of this story follows a quite different pattern from Poe's story (in which Dupin, after gathering the facts, begins to solve the mystery). In the Portuguese story, the long participation of the Tall Masked Man begins on August 12 (65–124). He identifies himself as the cousin of Luísa, the Countess W., and claims that he is writing because she has asked him to rebut the inexcusable charges against him, his friends and the "good doctor," or else she would herself turn to the police. This contribution follows a very different pattern of discourse. The Masked Man tells the story of the love affair between Luísa and the British captain, Rytmel, from when it began three years earlier during a voyage to Malta until a few days prior to the events narrated in the preceding installments. He is also a first-person narrator but one that is well equipped to transmit what he has seen and heard in a somewhat interesting opposition to the previous narrators.

This also gives Eça de Queirós (the presumable author) the chance to parody (again) the readership's literary tastes since this very long narrative contains all imaginable Romantic commonplaces: sweeping and forbidden passions, a handsome, blond, brave, melancholic and delicate captain (Rytmel), disputed first between two women (Luísa, the sweet, blonde, frail and idealistic wife of a cold, trivial and dissolute man, very similar to Madame Bovary, and the very violent and passionate Cármen, the Cuban wife of a Spanish merchant who tries to kill Rytmel and then kills herself) and then a third party, Miss Shorn, a lovely young woman who could give the captain what Luísa could not—children and a respectable life. Add to all this the scenarios, the delineation of the situations—Malta, Gibraltar, India (from whence the captain had returned as a hero and whose brave accomplishments are also described) and a lover's attempt to escape by boat—the metaphorical play and the cultural references and the whole narrative becomes a masterfully achieved subversion of Romantic ideals.[18] However, at the end of the Masked Man's last installment, there is almost nothing new to be added to the main mystery. The reader only knows now that there is a forbidden love affair—although it has already been hinted at that it might end in tragedy. What emerges in this part of the narrative is a kind of similarity with Poe's minimization and manipulation of the public's mind.

Finally, what can be considered a third nucleus of the narrative— "A.M.C.'s Revelations" (125–150) and the two other parts containing more revelations and the conclusion (185–192) and "Her Confession" (151–184)—continues the ingenious mystifying game in which alleged facts are intermingled with paroxysms of illusion and also contains a new aspect: moralization. Very briefly, in this part A.M.C., a pragmatic, provincial man and an autodiegetic narrator, tries to convey the events he has witnessed and lived through in a manner that he announces is written in a form close to realism: "May these confidences written with the most conscientious scruple contain the lesson which is always at the heart of any truth."[19]

In his revelations, the reader learns how he met the Countess by chance and how he became her confidant and came to help her in solving the distressing situation in which she found herself. The first part of his narrative (nine installments) alternates between a description of his own moral values and how he has to overlook them since he recognizes in the Countess the pain of tragedy and also the explanation for some of the events that had been left unresolved in the doctor's narrative. Then he passes the word to the Countess so that she might explain the more obscure aspects related to the captain's death by announcing that her confession, in the form of a letter, might well be called "the official report of the autopsy of an adultery."[20] If one expects a confessional and restrained tone in her discourse, then one is disappointed as once again the authors continue their mystifying game because her narrative is rather disconcerting, alternating between the description of verisimilar situations and numerous others which are full of mundane and perplexing events since Eça even inserts one of his own literary creations—Carlos Fradique Mendes, the satanic poet—as a character with whom Luísa has a peculiar encounter during a reception at her house. Finally, however, everything is explained, including the accidental murder as a result of the Countess's imaginative and sentimental nature. It is then up to A.M.C. to conclude the narrative in which the reader learns that Luísa has retired to a convent, how they disposed of the captain's body and that all those involved in the case have decided that the lesson she has learned is enough of a punishment since the justice of men would just turn this affair into a scandalous and prejudicial crime.[21] He also states that they decided to tell the story, although omitting the names of the persons involved, so that society could discover them and absolve or condemn them (180).

A.M.C. further reveals that he is happily married to his Teresinha as well as the whereabouts of all the other characters. Moreover, he states with a double significance that F. is writing a book in collaboration with Fradique Mendes on the outskirts of Lisbon, lying under the trees on the grass—a book that would kick out and exterminate all the abortions that the dominant Portuguese literary schools have made by subjugating the inviolable freedom of the spirit (192). After his conclusion, the letter signed by Eça de Queirós and Ramalho Ortigão revealed the truth about what was the most accomplished literary bluff, and at least during the whole month of July 1870 one may suspect that there were still people who believed it to be a true account.

Although what is considered to be the first Portuguese detective story does not exactly correspond to Poe's model, it is nevertheless a production which has affinities not only with the Dupin tales but also with Poe's work in general. Actually, one could argue that in most of Poe's tales, whether telling stories that defy any kind of familiar experience or common sense or that pretend that some of the narrated events are not only verisimilar but even factual, the use of a first-person narrator is one of the most important resources to achieve that effect. In addition, Eça and Ramalho's story also has affinities with Poe's use of the periodical press. The Portuguese story was ironically successful because it was published in a mass media newspaper directed at the general public, without distinction of class, gender or cultural and economic status. In 1870, *Diário de Notícias* was in its sixth year of publication. It was one of the first popular newspapers available at a low price and using all the new advances in technology. It was also one of the first to rely on a higher circulation and on the income from publicity. Although primarily concerned with "objective" news and without political affiliation, the newspaper nevertheless had to correspond to a new kind of reader—one that wanted to be objectively informed but that began to ask for sensational news as well. There was a new mental attitude in these new readers who looked for a kind of emotional escape from the daily routine of their lives and who were prone to believe sensational reports. They therefore contributed to the huge success of the serials in which sentimental stories were published in installments and which were already hugely popular in France, engaging such writers as Alexander Dumas and Eugène Sue. Therefore, the authors of the first Portuguese "detective story," who were indeed aware of the reader's gullibility, played around with "what had (never) occurred before" and with what Poe had used in his detective fiction as well as in other works.

By means of a whole rhetorical and stylistic arsenal, together with the use of contextual conditions external to the text such as, for instance, the employment of pseudo-newspaper news related to the pseudo-actual facts, the transcription of documents (letters and diaries), the quotation of books presented as being written by the characters, they created a type of writing which is the result of a mystifying game in which there are very tenuous boundaries between "reality" and the necessary efabulation that is used to hold the reader's credulous attention (and help solve the mystery)—a game at which Poe was definitely the master.

NOTES

1. Maria Leonor Machado de Sousa, "Poe in Portugal," in *Poe Abroad: Influence, Reputation, Affinities*, ed. Louis David Vines (Iowa City: University of Iowa Press, 1999), 115.

2. Other figures usually connected to this group are: Jaime Batalha Reis, Guerra Junqueiro, Oliveira Martins and Guilherme de Azevedo.

3. Margarida Vale de Gato, "Edgar Allan Poe em Translação: Entre Textos e Sistemas, Visando as Rescritas na Lírica Moderna em Portugal (c. 1860–1900)," unpublished Ph.D. dissertation (Lisboa: Universidade de Lisboa, 2009), 170.

4. "À l'esthétique fermée du XVIIIème siècle succéda une esthétique ouverte, qui s'alimenta des sources étrangères à l'art pur, qui trouva sans fin autre chose que l'art, qui porta ses regards à la fois sur le monde extérieur, et sur les profondeurs mystérieuses du moi." Philippe Van Tieghem, *Les Grandes Doctrines Littéraires en France: De la Pléiade au Surréalisme* (Paris: PUF, 1965), 150.

5. Patrick F. Quinn, *The French Face of Edgar Poe* (Carbondale and Edwardsville: Southern Illinois University Press, 1957), 44.

6. Eça de Queirós, "Poetas do Mal," *Gazeta de Portugal* (Oct. 21, 1866). Later included in *Prosas Bárbaras*, first published in 1903, after Eça's death. NB: the Portuguese original is provided throughout. "Então como vão para uma ideia nova, desordenada e bizarra, aparecem vestidos com uma forma nova, desordenada e bizarra: eles sabem que as mutações arcádicas estão gastas: que as velhas árvores donde se dependuravam liras clássicas estão secas: que os caminhos trilhados pelas togas brancas de pregas hieráticas levam ao deserto. Assim esta revolução na arte feita pela banda Baudelaire não é, como diz a crítica ordinária, hemistíquios, prosas, rimas e medições que se alteram: é todo o poema divino das sociedades modernas que se vai aos farrapos. As formas novas são o sintoma da sua dissolução. Os espíritos não podem respirar o ar moderno pesado de materialismos: sufocam, sofrem, gemem; e então, como o aborrecido que cantou Henri Heine, pedem os ciúmes, as violências escuras, os rasgões da carne, os roubos, os beijos entre lábios tintos de sangue. Então aparecem estes livros—'As Novas Histórias Extraordinárias,' 'As Piores do Mal,' 'Salambô,' etc. O primeiro é de Edgar Põe; entre aquelas páginas passa o demónio da perversidade, ora hirto e lívido como os ciprestes, ora galhofeiro, jovial, ruidoso, às cambalhotas, mostrando os rasgões do fato, às risadas mostrando a podridão dos dentes, sinistro e debochado como um palhaço das esquinas. Põe não tem o vago iluminismo de Hoffmann, nem a fria imaginação de Darwin. Põe diz a realidade dos terrores e das visões, a realidade. O seu livro é a epopeia desvairada do sistema nervoso." Eça de Queirós, *Prosas Bárbaras* (Lisboa: Edição Livros do Brasil, 2001), 92. Further references will be from this edition.

7. Jaime Batalha Reis is one of his fellow writers and the one who wrote an introduction to the publication of the above-mentioned *Prosas Bárbaras*. "Assim as primeiras influências que actuaram em Eça de Queirós—aquelas que mais evidentemente se reconhecem nas suas primeiras criações literárias, os escritores de cuja frequentação eu posso dar testemunho – foram principalmente, Henrique Heine, Gerardo de Nerval, Júlio Michelet, Carlos Baudelaire, mais distantemente, ou mais em segunda mão, Shakespeare, Goethe, Hoffmann, Arnim, Põe, e, envolvendo tudo poderosamente, Vítor Hugo" (*Prosas Bárbaras*, 22).

8. "Para esse fim, sem plano, sem methodo, sem escola, sem documentos, sem estylo, recolhidos á simples 'torre de crystal da Imaginação,' desfechámos a improvisar este livro, um em Leiria, outro em Lisboa, cada um de nós com uma resma de papel, a sua alegria e a sua audacia." Eça de Queirós e Ramalho Ortigão, *O Mysterio da Estrada de Cintra* (Lisboa:

Livraria de Antonio Maria Pereira, Editor, 1894), v. All subsequent references to this work unless otherwise noted will be from this third edition and cited parenthetically in the text and in the endnotes. Again, an English translation of the text will be provided together with the Portuguese original.

9. Although there has been some controversy regarding the four-hand authorship, the general opinion is that Eça was the author of most of the installments, particularly the Doctor's letters, the (Tall) masked man narrative, "Her Confession," F.'s letter and Z.'s letters, leaving Ramalho Ortigão only with the parts dealing with A.M.C.'s narrative.

10. See "Plan of publication" at the end of this essay, which we hope will allow a better understanding of the complex structure of the narrative.

11. Among these somewhat absurd observations was, for instance, the doctor's conclusion that a specific kind of woman was involved in the mystery merely by observing a single strand of hair: "The woman was blonde, certainly fair-skinned, and short—'mignonne'—because the strand of hair was extremely thin, extraordinarily pure and its white root seemed to have been attached to the cranial tegument by a tenuous and delicately organized connection. Her character was probably sweet, humble, dedicated and loving because the hair had not that cutting harshness of the hair belonging to people with a violent, selfish and proud temperament. The owner of that hair must have simple and elegantly modest tastes, because of its perfume and also because it was not frizzled or capriciously rolled, as if once part of fancy hairstyles. And she might well have been educated in England or Germany because the extremity of the hair had been cut in a certain way, a common habit amongst northern women but one completely alien to southern women who prefer to wear their hair in its abundant natural state." / "A pessoa a quem elle pertencia era loura, clara de certo, pequena,—mignonne—, porque o fio de cabello era delgadissimo, extraordinariamente puro, e a sua raiz branca parecia prender-se aos tegumentos craneanos por uma ligação tenue, delicadamente organisada. O caracter d'essa pessoa devia ser doce, humilde, dedicado e amante, porque o cabello não tinha ao contacto aquella aspereza cortante que offerecem os cabellos pertencentes a pessoas de temperamento violento, altivo e egoista. Devia ter gostos simples, elegantemente modestos a dona de tal cabello, já pelo imperceptivel perfume d'elle, já porque não tinha vestigios de ter sido frisado, ou caprichosamente enrolado, domado em penteados phantasiosos. Teria sido talvez educada em Inglaterra ou na Allemanha, porque o cabello denotava na sua extremidade ter sido espontado, habito das mulheres do norte, completamente extranho ás meridionaes, que abandonam os seus cabelos á abundante espessura natural" (27).

12. "The Editor who judges with a cold mind and the readers who read this letter quietly at home will be better equipped to arrange the facts, to establish more correct deductions and be better able to get at the occult truth through induction and logic." / "O senhor redactor, que julga de animo frio, os leitores, que socegadamente, em sua casa, lêem esta carta, poderão melhor combinar, estabelecer deducções mais certas, e melhor approximar-se pela inducção e pela logica da verdade occulta (28)."

He had also done the same at the end of the previous deduction regarding the hair, when he states that "those were just conjectures, deductions of the imagination, which are neither scientific truths nor judicial proofs." / "Isto eram apenas conjecturas, deducções da phantasia, que nem constituem uma verdade scientifica, nem uma prova judicial" (27).

13. *Diário de Notícias*, Number 1662, 6th Year, Wednesday, (27 July, 1870):1. This note was not published in the publication of the letters as a book. There are other examples such as the one mentioned: On July 29th there was another note claiming that the newspaper was already in possession of the 5th letter and that same day, just after the doctor's 4th letter, there was a shorter one signed by a "José Viegas Ferraz" who claimed he might have some clues to the mystery because on twentieth July he had seen the carriage in which the doctor and his friend were taken. Again, this letter was not included in the book. *Diário de Notícias,* Number 1664, 6th Year, Friday (29 July, 1870): 1.

14. Richard Kopley, *Edgar Allan Poe and the Dupin Mysteries* (New York: Palgrave Mac-Millan, 2008), 36. Kopley also adds a very interesting approach to the significance of newspapers in "The Murders in the Rue Morgue" not only because he reveals new sources, particularly from *The Philadelphia Saturday News and Literary Gazette*, but also because he argues

that the significance of newspapers "reflects their significance in Poe's imagining this tale"—the use of elements external to the game—thus inviting "analysis of the mystery of its creation" (40–41).

15. This includes more information that appeared to validate the doctor's narrative: "Note from the *Diário de Notícias.*—In the original of the letter published yesterday there were some words written in pencil, which we only detected after printing the newspaper. Those words contained the following observations: *The masked man's photo was taken at the photo house Henriques Nunes, in Chagas Street, Lisbon. Maybe there one may get some information about the photographed subject.* Before we publish the long letter written by F. . . . , of which the first part was sent to us yesterday by the Doctor, it is our duty to make known another very important one, which we received by internal postage, being signed with the initial _Z._ and which has already been in our possession for three days. This letter, which is so closely connected to the sequence of events of this narrative, is the following: . . . " / "Nota do Diario de Noticias.—No original da carta publicada hontem havia algumas palavras a lapis, nas quaes só fizemos reparo depois de impresso o jornal. Essas palavras continham esta observação: A photographia do mascarado foi feita em casa de Henrique Nunes, rua das Chagas, Lisboa. Talvez ahi possa haver noticia do sujeito photographado. Antes de darmos á estampa a longa carta de F . . . , cuja primeira parte nos foi hontem enviada pelo medico, é dever nosso tornar conhecida uma outra importantissima que recebemos pela posta interna, assignada com a inicial _Z._, e que temos em nosso poder ha já tres dias. Esta carta, que tão estreitamente vem prender-se na historia dos successos que constituem o assumpto d'esta narrativa, é a seguinte: . . . " (32).

16. "This narrative attracted me and I followed it with the unconcerned curiosity that links one to an inventively fabricated *canard* or with a story very similar to *Thugs* or with some others of the same kind with which the imaginative vein of American and French fantasists has been every now and then arousing Europe's attention and having a huge success. The narrative in your periodical when compared to the others had the original merit of describing events that were taking place at the same time as they were read; the fact that the characters were anonymous and also that the main motive of the plot was so surreptitiously covered that none of the readers could use any proof to contest the veracity of the portentously Romanesque affair which the author of the narrative had suddenly remembered to toss into the middle of the honest, simple, humdrum and prosaic society in which we live. I thought I had found the most perfect example of the *roman feuilleton* when quite unexpectedly I find in the installment published today the initials of a man's name—A.M.C.—to which it was added that the person designated by these letters is a student of medicine and born in Viseu." / "Interessava-me essa narrativa e segui-a com a curiosidade despreoccupada que se liga a um *canard* fabricado com engenho, a um romance á similhança dos *Thugs* e de alguns outros do mesmo genero com que a veia imaginosa dos phantasistas francezes e americanos vem de quando em quando acordar a attenção da Europa para um successo estupendo. A narração do seu periodico tinha sobre as demais que tenho lido o mérito original de se passarem os successos ao tempo que se vão lendo, de serem anonymas as personagens e de estar tão secretamente encoberta a mola principal do enredo, que nenhum leitor poderia contestar com provas a veracidade do caso portentosamente romanesco, que o auctor da narrativa se lembrara de lançar de repente ao meio da sociedade prosaica, ramerraneira, simples e honesta em que vivemos. Ia-me parecendo ter diante de mim o ideal mais perfeito, o typo mais acabado do *roman feuilleton*, quando inesperadamente encontro no folhetim publicado hoje as iniciaes de um nome de homem—A.M.C.—accrescen-tando-se que a pessoa designada por estas lettras é estudante de medicina e natural de Vizeu" (33–34).

17. "The Mystery of the Road to Sintra is an invention; it is not a literary invention, as I thought at the beginning, but a criminal invention with a specific end. Here is what I could deduce about the motives of this invention: There is a crime, no doubt, that is clear. One of the accomplices is the doctor***. . . . This entire story is simulated, artificial, poorly invented! All those carriages that gallop mysteriously through the streets of Lisbon! All those masked men, smoking along the way, at dusk, those roads of romance where the carriages do not stop at any barrier and where, at dark, gentlemen gallop in whitish cloaks. It sounds like a romance from the times of Villele's [*sic*] ministry. . . . Deduction: the doctor was the accomplice to a crime; he knows that someone possesses that secret; he feels that it is going to be revealed, he fears the

police, there was some indiscretion; so, he wants to raise dust, to divert the investigation, to avert inquiries, to confuse, to obscure, to conceal and to puzzle and while he agitates the public he packs his bags, cowardly flees to France, after being the murderer here! What is my friend M.C.'s role in all this I do not know. I beg you, Mr. Editor, please sweep away these unbelievable inventions from the installment of your newspaper." / "O *Mysterio da Estrada de Cintra* é uma invenção: não uma invenção litteraria, como ao principio suppuz, mas uma invenção criminosa, com um fim determinado. Eis aqui o que pude deduzir sobre os motivos d'esta invenção: Ha um crime; é indubitavel; é claro. Um dos cumplices d'este crime é o doutor ***. . . . Ah! como toda esta historia é artificial, postiça, pobremente inventada! aquellas carruagens como galopam mysteriosamente pelas ruas de Lisboa! aquelles mascarados, fumando n'um caminho, ao crepusculo, aquellas estradas de romance, onde as carruagens passam sem parar nas barreiras, e onde galopam, ao escurecer, cavalleiros com capas alvadias! Parece um romance do tempo do ministerio Villele. . . . Deducção: o doutor *** foi cumplice d'um crime; sabe que ha alguem que possue esse segredo, pressente que tudo se vae espalhar, receia a policia, houve alguma indiscrição; por isso quer fazer poeira, desviar as pesquisas, transviar as indagações, confundir, obscurecer, rebuçar, enlear, e em quanto lança a perturbação no publico, faz as suas malas, vae ser cobarde para França, depois de ter sido assassino aqui! O que faz no meio de tudo isto o meu amigo M. C. ignoro-o. Senhor redactor, peço-lhe, varra depressa do folhetim do seu jornal essas inverosimeis invenções" (61–64).

18. The analysis of this aspect of the narrative has been particularly developed by Ofélia Paiva Monteiro in three essays published in *Revista Colóquio/Letras*. See "Um jogo humorístico com a verosimilhança romanesca. "O Mistério da Estrada de Sintra," Numbers 86, 97 and 98, respectively July 1985: 15–23, May 1987: 5–18 and July 1987: 38–51.

19. "May these confidences written with the most conscientious scruple contain the lesson which is always at the heart of any truth! The private existence of each one of us makes part of the great history of our times and of humanity. When revealed in its acts, there is no heart that will not countersign or contest the principles that rule the moral world. When the novel, which nowadays is a scientific form just beginning to babble, reaches maturity as the expression of truth, the Balzacs and Dickens will reconstitute on one single passion a whole character and with it the whole psychology of an era, just as the Cuviers can today rebuild an unknown animal by using just one of its bones." / "Possam estas confidencias, escriptas com o mais conscencioso escrupulo, conter a lição que existe sempre no fundo de uma verdade! A existencia intima de cada um de nós é uma parte integrante da grande historia do nosso tempo e da humanidade. Não ha coração que, desvendado nos seus actos, não offereça uma referenda ou uma contestação aos principios que regem o mundo moral. Quando o romance, que é hoje uma fórma scientifica apenas balbuciante, attingir o desenvolvimento que o espera como expressão da verdade, os Balzacs e os Dickens reconstituirão sobre uma só paixão um caracter completo e com elle toda a psychologia de uma época, assim como os Cuviers reconstituem ja hoje um animal desconhecido por meio d'um unico dos seus ossos" (125).

20. "The notebook which I sent to you, Mr. Editor, contains a copy of the long letter which she has addressed to her cousin. I give up the place which I have occupied in the columns of your periodical to allow publication of this document that might well be called—The official report of the autopsy of adultery. Afterwards I will report the destiny we gave to the corpse and what became of the countess." / "O caderno que lhe remetto encerra, senhor redactor, a copia da longa carta dirigida por ella a seu primo. Cedo o logar que estava occupando nas columnas do seu periodico á publicação d'este documento, que verdadeiramente se poderia chamar—O auto de autópsia de um adultério. Depois direi o destino que démos ao cadaver, e o fim que teve a condessa" (150).

21. "In jail and delivered unto the action of the courts it would make an interesting, scandalous and prejudicial criminal case. Restored to itself, it will be an example, a lesson." / "Encarcerada e entregue á acção dos tribunaes, seria uma causa-crime, interessante, escandalosa, prejudicial. Restituida a si mesma, será um exemplo, uma lição" (186).

Plan of publication in *Diário de Notícias - The Mystery of the Road to Sintra -*
Saturday, July 23, 1870 – announcement of the reception of the narrative
Sunday, 24 – Doctor***'s first letter
Tuesday, 26 – Doctor***'s second letter

Wednesday, 27 – Doctor***'s 3rd letter + short note about the letters
Thursday, 28 – Doctor***'s first part of the 4th letter
Friday, 29 – short note saying the newspaper is already in possession of the 5th letter + continuation of the 4th letter + a short letter from someone named João Viegas Ferraz
Saturday, 30 – Doctor***'s 5th letter
Sunday, 31 - continuation of the 5th letter
Tuesday, August 2 – Doctor***'s 6th letter
Wednesday, 3 – Doctor***'s 7th letter
Thursday, 4 – note by the editor + letter by Z.
Friday, 5 – first part of the 1st letter by F . . . to the Doctor
Saturday, 6 – second part of F.'s letter
Sunday, 7 – third part of F.'s letter
Tuesday, 9 – last part of F.'s letter
Wednesday, 10 – editor's short note + Doctor***'s last letter
Thursday, 11 – Z.'s second letter
Friday, 12 August – Thursday, 1 September - the (Tall) Masked Man narrative – 18 letters/ installments
Friday, 2 September – Sunday, 11 September - A.M.C.'s revelations – 9 letters/ installments
Tuesday, 13 September – Saturday, 24 September – Her confession – 11 letters/ installments + a short note by A.M.C. on the last day
Sunday, 25 September – A.M.C.'s revelations continued
Tuesday, 27 September – A.M. C.'s conclusions + last letter signed by Eça de Queirós and Ramalho Ortigão.

Chapter Eight

"Around Reason Feeling": Poe's Impact on Fernando Pessoa's Modernist Proposal

Margarida Vale de Gato

Fernando Pessoa (1888–1935), the Portuguese writer who took modernist depersonalization to the extreme of *heteronymy* (writing under different personae), read Poe in English. Pessoa lived in South Africa from 1896 to 1905, and it was there he penned his first literary projects in English. This should be underlined against claims such as T. S. Eliot's that French admiration for Poe stemmed from deficient English knowledge or insinuations like Harold Bloom's that claim that Poe always sounds better in translation.[1] Pessoa, whom Bloom ranked as the most representative poet of the twentieth century along with Pablo Neruda,[2] engaged with Poe in ways that cannot be dismissed so easily. Pessoa wrote in English the following appraisal: "Poe had genius, Poe had talent for he has great reasoning powers, and reasoning is the formal expression of talent."[3] As a contribution to the understanding of the extent of Poe's impact on the inception of Portuguese modernism, this essay focuses mainly on Fernando Pessoa's early English poetry under the name of Alexander Search.

Attaching great significance, in his biographical accounts, to his early immersion in English culture, Pessoa would register, at the age of 14, his readings of "E. A. Poe's poems—almost all."[4] These eventually led him to elect *The Choice Works of E. A. Poe* as one of the titles to be included in the Queen Victoria Memorial Prize, an academic award he won at the close of 1903. The profuse markings contained in that volume, along with Pessoa's many passing references to Poe in his published and unpublished notes and correspondence, his attempts in the genre of detective and reasoning short stories, and the three translations he famously published in 1924–25 of "The Raven," "Annabel Lee" and "Ulalume"—all these have prompted critical analysis of the Poe/Pessoa relationship.[5]

Pessoa's wealth of English poetry, however, has elicited little excitement from critics and readers alike who tend to consider that the modernist Pessoa was born with his Portuguese texts, especially after the publication of the first poems by his heteronymic personalities. If readers are understandably more attracted to the fully developed breadth of the Portuguese Pessoa and his avatars, criticism should rescue "the English" Pessoa, for, as Luísa Freire points out in *Entre Vozes, Entre Línguas* (*Between Voices and Languages*) Pessoa's move into a different language and cultural code at an age that coincided with his formal education was important to his later development of distinct poetical voices, not to mention the fact that his texts in English were already signed by different names, if not different persons: Professor Trochee, David Merrick, Charles Robert Anon, or Horace James Faber and his translator "Navas."[6]

Alexander Search, whose name is symbolic both of Pessoa's megalomaniac ambitions and of the reflexivity of the "artist as a young man," is the most-often found signature in the English poetry of 1903–1910. Giving vent to Pessoa's teenage fixation on decadence and morbidity, Alexander Search may be considered a pre-heteronym.[7] In 1905, two successive diary entries describe Alexander Search's productions as "pure Poesque" and "Poesque, complicated with Baudelaire and Rollinat style."[8] This evidence, along with a mere screening of some titles of the compositions ascribed to Search— "The Accursed Poet," "Dreams," "Insomnia," "The Unnatural and the Strange," "The Maiden," or the "Unconscious Corpse"—suffices to generate the hypothesis of Search as the Poesque persona of Pessoa. That this persona was also seminal to Pessoa's Modernist tenets is the argument I shall make, on the basis of two compositions of Search where Poe's "The Bells" functions as a genetic subtext: "Ode to the Sea" and "Insomnia." Those two pieces not only anticipate two of the most famous compositions in Pessoa's mature work—"Maritime Ode," by the naval engineer heteronym Álvaro de Campos, and "Autopsychography," by himself—but also herald important features of that work, which the Poe/Pessoa relationship may partially account for.

WORD-OBSESSIONS AND THE MONOTONE

"The Bells" is a poem included in Pessoa's list of a projected poetry selection of Poe in Portuguese, and among his papers we find an attempt at its translation. This knowledge has drawn George Monteiro's attention, in his seminal essay on Poe and Pessoa in 1988, to the possible resonances of Poe's "The Bells" in Fernando Pessoa's "Ó Sino da Minha Aldeia" (O Church bell of my village), which, along with the poem "Paúis" (Swamps), echoed "other bells" to form the dypthic "Twilight Impressions" and mark Pessoa's first published Portuguese verse, in 1914.[9] Monteiro's intuition, confirmed through the finding of earlier drafts where Pessoa insisted particularly on the onomatopoeic effect of the chiming of the bells ("tanger de sinos"), elicited subsequent essays drawing a host of other possible sources and bell-poems.[10] It is intriguing, though, that in this source-hunt none of the commentators has uncovered the existence of the previous Alexander Search's versions, which are in fact three, including a poem properly entitled "The Bells," from 1908, which I choose to leave out of this discussion, since it is rather self-evident and loses comparative interest. Rather, the affiliation of the other two poems— "Ode to the Sea," a composition that only survived in fragments and must have been started around 1904, and "Insomnia," tentatively dated 1906—is to be drawn more through the identity of sound than of theme.

The Bells
Edgar A. Poe

[. . .]
Hear the loud alarum bells—
Brazen bells!
[. . .]
Yet the ear, it fully knows,
By the twanging
And the clanging,
How the danger ebbs and flows:—
Yes, the ear distinctly tells,
In the jangling
And the wrangling,
How the danger sinks and swells,
By the sinking or the swelling in the anger of the bells—
Of the bells— / [. . .]
In the clamor and the clangor of the bells.
[. . .]
In the silence of the night
How we shiver with affright
At the melancholy meaning of the tone!
For every sound that floats
From the rust within their throats
Is a groan.
And the people—ah, the people
They that dwell up in the steeple
All alone,
And who, tolling, tolling, tolling,

In that muffled monotone,
Feel a glory in so rolling
On the human heart a stone—
They are neither man nor woman—
They are neither brute nor human,
They are Ghouls:—
And their king it is who tolls:— / [. . .]
And he dances and he yells;
Keeping time, time, time,
In a sort of Runic rhyme,
To the Paean of the bells—
Of the bells:—
Keeping time, time, time,
In a sort of Runic rhyme;
To the throbbing of the bells—
Of the bells, bells, bells:— / [. . .]

(*Poems*, 437–38)

Ode to the Sea (1904?)
Alexander Search

[. . .]
Hail, thou sea!
How thy fury taketh me,
Let it thunder, let it roar / [. . .]
More furious & more sounding rush
As if with force unstrained the frantic craze I'd crush

Soft is the sea!
How full in fulsome glee!
With its waters slowly tippling,
With its waters rippling, rippling. / [. . .]

Let it thunder, let it roar
O'er the panic stricken shore
Moving up in headlong rush
Hits at the rocks in rolling splash
The barks the waves with horror crush
Shatter and crash / [. . .]
Here were ships then; now here are wrecks
Men are swept in long-drawn torrent rash
While the thunder adds its might
With clatter and with crash!
Laughs & cackling in its glee
How thy fury taketh me!
Hail, thou sea!

(*Poemas Ingleses*, 173–74)

Insomnia (1906)
Alexander Search

[…]
And the clock, with its curst possession
    Of night with its monotone,
Is a madman mad with a word-obsession,
    Sorrowfully lone.

A thousand times a reeling
    Of reason around my world,
And around reason feeling
The very darkness wheeling
    In a blacker darkness whirled.

And the clock! Ah, its curst possession
    Of night with its monotone!
How it treasured well its word-obsession
    Dolorously lone!
[…]

(*Poemas Ingleses*, 90)

"Ode to the Sea" by Pessoa/Search offers an experiment in the accumulation of sound repetitions to induce gradual frenzy and excitement. The sea, in its various stages of calm, disquiet and anger, parallels strikingly the different chiming / tolling of Poe's "bells," as they fall from harmony into distress. The initial exclamation pointing to the changing object, followed by an imitative rendering of the quality of its sound, is remarkably attuned with Poe's poem, and the same pattern recurs in "Insomnia." In the latter, the focus of acoustic sensitivity shifts from the natural realm to the mechanical, man-made world, displaying a closer affinity with Poe's theme of humankind bound by the time-keeping devices it has manufactured, eventually undermining its conscious control of these. The first person recipient of monotone impressions seems to gradually identify with the personified clock, "a madman mad with a word obsession," whereas the repetitive use of the gerund— "reeling," "feeling," "wheeling" (cf. "tolling," "rolling," "throbbing" in "The Bells") underscores the omnipresent continuity of the unnerving sound whose distress is also meant to implicate the receiver/hearer of the poem.

In a manuscript draft headed "Poe," Pessoa offers a profound reading of the artist's "hiperacousia," or "extreme susceptibility to noises," in which he claims that "the hearing is the sense by which fear enters into the brain." Sound-hallucinations are said to precede "visions," and the state of fright in which the nervous man indulges by exposure to them is considered a "necessity," since "[t]he suspension of sound, i. e. absolute silence is, practically, for him the idea of death, or rather the tangible (so to speak) form of that idea." Pessoa's study, as we know it, ends by recalling how Poe did not forget to underscore "a rhythmic creation of beauty" in his definition of poetry. [11]

The existence of two translation drafts of "The Bells," both fragmentary, is also worthy of commentary. Quite probably they were produced more than one decade apart, thus testifying to Pessoa's continued interest in the poem, and both locate the emphasis of the initial stages of the translation process on getting rhymes and alliterations in place. The older fragment (Figure 1) isolates keywords in the third and fourth stanzas, such as "fogo" (fire) and "medo" (fear), and rehearses repetitions in keeping with short words and a single phonetic stress ("logo, logo, logo").

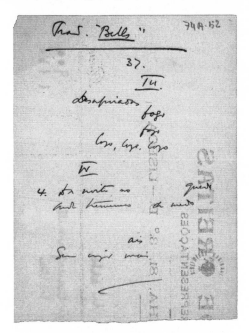

Figure 1

In a similar strain, the latter document (Figure 2) sets the rhyming dominant for each stanza—"in," "an," "en," "on (ai)"—and shows Pessoa's efforts and hesitations in mimicking the shrill "tintinnabulations" of the sleigh bells in the first stanza. [12]

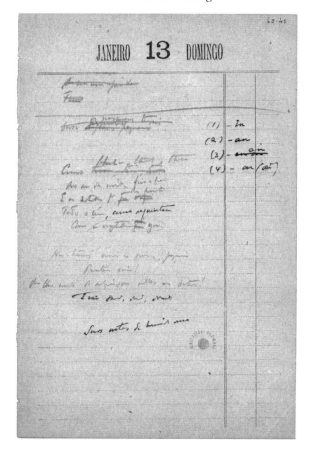

Figure 2

These drafts, therefore, confirm the importance that Pessoa attached to "verbal rhythm" in the translation of poetry, illustrated through his work on Poe, in a well-known note written in English:

> a poem is an intellectualized impression, or an idea made emotion, communicated to others by means of a rhythm. . . .The translation of a poem should therefore conform absolutely (1) to the idea or emotion which constitutes the poem, (2) to the verbal rhythm in which the idea or emotion is expressed; it should conform relatively to the inner or visual rhythm, keeping to the images themselves when it can, but keeping always to the type of image.
>
> It was on this criterion that I based my translations into Portuguese of Poe's "Annabel Lee" and "Ulalume."[13]

"Ode to the Sea" and "Insomnia," though each use a different set of images from "The Bells," seem to appeal to a very similar "emotion which constitutes the poem," in turn recalling the Poesque effect of the poem from whence they derive their rhythm. It is, perhaps, an emotion of the same kind, even if "Ode to the Sea" turns around the semantic cluster of the different aspects of the sea, and "Insomnia" deals with late night fancies, whereas Poe's "The Bells" presents an allegory of the universe's pull towards destruction: anguish, vertigo, dizziness. Significantly we are not in the realm of translation but of the poet's technical apprenticeship, and each of these rhythmic experiments yields, in what regards topoi, a contribution to two of the basic themes in Pessoa's mature work: 1) the conflict of mind and emotion, and its resolution through poetic craft; and 2) the troubled sea, whose representation in the national literary tradition of "The Discoveries" assumed giant proportions in the *Tragico-Maritime History* bound to loom over Pessoa's daydreams, even as a schoolboy in South Africa, and would later inform the modern epic of Pessoa's *Mensagem* as well as some of Álvaro de Campos's lengthy poems, namely "Maritime Ode," which I will explore further on.

It seems almost too easy and expedient to clothe these grand Pessoan themes in what some finely attuned English ears consider to be one of the most crass melodious mystifications in poetry. "How could . . . Baudelaire listen to Poe's music and remain unaware of its vulgarity?" asked a dismayed Aldous Huxley.[14] Should we consider, in Pessoa's case, the role of non-nativeness, albeit the ten years of his youth he spent immersed in the English language? Could Poe's resonant poetry have helped him to find a musical score in which to mold the expression of his verbal creativity into a second language? Did amplification result from the weaving of such prosodic qualities into the fabric of the Portuguese language, the transference from English of recognizable devices for sound effects? Note that one particular instance that horrified Huxley—Poe's shameless recourse to singsong "Do-Re-Mi" in the name of the poetic character "Dolermie"—is something to which Pessoa also resorted, in the original Portuguese of "Ode Maritima*"* by Álvaro de Campos (1915)—the Great Pirate is portrayed bellowing "la do re," in a melody that is corrupted by the mechanical rush of the sound "r": "A morte berrada do Grande Pirata a cantar /. . ./ Lá da ré a morrer, a berrar e a cantar."[15] It is worth recalling that the early Pessoa was deeply absorbed, just like Poe, in the effect of the monotone, a word that explicitly emerges in our example from "Insomnia" in association with time-keeping—"And the clock, with its curst possession / Of night with its monotone." Also, "Ode to the Sea" is, in the manner of "The Bells," composed of ending rhymes that are pervasively monotonic and onomatopoeic: "roar," "rush," "crush," "shore," "splash," "rash."

From the pages of criticism that Poe produced about poetry as "the rhythmical creation of beauty," the power of monotone is especially noteworthy. In the explanation in "The Rationale of Verse" its divine reach is concealed in the long-lost harmony of the spondee, "the rudiment of verse," and the metrical developments that ensued from "an attempt at its relief," surfaces the intuition that all stress gives way to distress. Accented syllables of equal duration, just as the bell's knell or the clock-sound, while at first numbing the senses with the cadence of oneness, are bound to be corrupted and to aggregate in disquieting clusters—or, in the words of *Eureka*, contain "*the Germ of their Inevitable Annihilation.*"[16] The parallel between Poe's conception of the universe and his theory of verse has been drawn by Martin Roth,[17] and it is quite impressive in "The Bells," where the principle of union leading to division / corruption and then an apparent chaos (though predetermined by its reversibility) is replicated in the routine where the monotone varies through alliteration, whose profusion in turn verges upon cacophony. The concentration of monosyllabic words highlights the variation of the monotone and its capacity of deviation—bells, swells, yells, tells, tolls, stone, steeple. It illuminates, furthermore, what Alexander Search dubs as "word-obsession," something he exemplifies with the puerile but effective collocation of "the madman mad." Word-obsession is not discourse-oriented, for it thwarts rationality and it is rather aimed at the haunting effect of association and disarticulation. Its practice must have suited the purpose of Fernando Pessoa's initial acts of disembodiment, as well as his need to accomplish something along the lines of what Richard Wilbur identified as Poe's attempt to short-circuit the intellect.[18]

AROUND REASON FEELING: EMOTION TURNED INTO RHYTHM BY THE MEANS OF THOUGHT

Among Pessoa's assortment of unpublished papers, there is a note written around 1913 that helps explain Pessoa's departure from symbolism and from the prevailing *saudosismo* in the Portuguese literary system, a neo-Romantic poetic trend advocating recollection through landscape contemplation and evoking the pan-psychic nature of the Portuguese soul. Pessoa found both tendencies to be lacking in complexity and bordering on vagueness, and ascribed to Poe the sobering cautionary remark against "obscurity of expression" when striving for the "expression of obscurity."[19] Pessoa's concern with complexity ties in with his idea of the poem as an intellectualized expression, and this affects his perception of the relationship between poetry and music: "Poetry is emotion expressed through rhythm by means of thought; music is that same expression, but more directly, without the mediation of the idea."[20] Recalling a Poesque formulation on the same subject, "Music, when combined with a pleasurable idea, is poetry; music without the idea is simply music,"[21] we may foreground Pessoa's insistence on thematizing poetry, rather than music, as well as his introduction of the word "thought" instead of "pleasurable idea." We should place Poe's formulation

in the context of his preface to his 1831 collection of poems, "Letter to B–,"
at a time when he was still assimilating Coleridge's optimistic Romanticism,
which he would later discard, not only by embracing rather ghastly and
clashing pleasures, but also by disputing the existence of a creative imagination and pursuing one that stemmed from combination, or intellectual con-
structiveness. Pessoa, however, as reader of Poe, was ambiguous about Poe's
poetry as a mature work, suggesting paradoxically that his "reasoning powers" marred his poetical propensity. In an unpublished note in English he
mused:

> Why did Poe write little poetry? Because the critical faculty was developed at
> the same time as the poetic propensity. He wrote verse with ease while at
> college, but then neither his true imagination nor his intellect were developed.
> These were developed at the same time. Hence the critical faculty, the analytic
> mind, being ever on the watch, allowed not inspiration to take its free
> course. [22]

Pessoa's emphasis on the "free course of inspiration" seems to take for
granted that, for all the pursuit of construction and complexity, poetry resides
somewhere else. Actually, Pessoa must have shared with Poe the notion that
poetry was intended for the excitement of beauty, and prose for the exercise
of reason. In an earlier note, more benevolent toward the poetic qualities of
his predecessor, Pessoa would praise in Poe the conjunction of the synthetic
power of poetry and the analytic faculty displayed in his mathematical reasoning. [23] Synthesis, in Pessoa, corresponds to "mental excitement," when the
mind creates powerful impressions, generating the sought-for overpowering
of sensations: "In me what feels is always / thinking" (*"O que em mim sente
'stá pensando"*). [24]

Pessoa's modernist hallmark—the forgery of emotion and commitment to
intellectual composition, was not dissociated from the belief in individual
genius and its correlation with madness. His early readings of Nordau and
Lombroso prompted him to explore the risk of madness through the excess of
reason, as well as of the power of delirium in transcending the realms of
physicality and rationality. [25] Experiments on the attainment of such states,
first attempted by Alexander Search, would be matured in Pessoa's accomplished neuropath heteronym, Álvaro de Campos, the naval engineer who
graduated in Glasgow and spoke the language of machines with a Scottish
accent. In "Insomnia," from the early Search, the monotone of the clock
marks the hypnagogy that, just as in Poe, leads to vertigo, and once the
machine of rhythmical poetry is set to motion, reason is wound up with
feeling through the effect of alliteration and of the consonant "r" (praised by
Poe as the "most producible" in "The Philosophy of Composition") and the
aid of the enveloping "l": "a *reeling* / Of *reason around* my wo*rld*, / And
a*round reason* fee*ling* / . . . / In a b*lacker* da*rk*ness whi*rled*."

In Álvaro de Campos, whose poetic breath pays a few explicit compliments to Whitman, we can't fail to hear also the echoes of Poe's resounding poetry, namely in the insistence on repetends, gradations and variations of single-stressed syllables to build the climax of "Maritime Ode," orchestrating sound and mechanical patterns of thought associations:

> Ecstasy stirs, increases, ascends in me
> And with a blind, riotous hum
> The flywheel's restless spinning intensifies.
> (*O extase em mim levanta-se, cresce, avança,*
> *E com um ruído cego de arruaçaacentua-se*
> *O giro vivo do volante.*)[26]

THE JESTER AND THE MECHANICS OF THE DOUBLE

Alexander Search is also allegedly the author of the following untitled poem, dated 1908:

> I asked an automaton
> What are you?
> But he being a machine
> Answered not
>
> I asked another one
> What are you It replied [*sic*]
> A being great full of power
> To whom naught is denied
>
> The mechanism did fall
> From the mind order it kept
> & said no more at all
> I found this funny and wept.[27]

Pessoa's interest in the workings of machines and their bearing on the affections of human beings, of whose perfectibility they became a controversial sign in modern times, might also have derived from readings of Edgar Allan Poe, namely "Maezel's Chess-Player," or "Von Kempelen and His Discovery." Pessoa's and Poe's treatment of the motif of the "Double / Other" deserves a more comprehensive analysis than I can undertake within the limits of this essay. It is my perception that Pessoa borrowed from Poe's insights on the craft of poetry as something obtained through synthesis and combination so as to tackle the theme of the divided self from an eminently modern point of view: that of the potentialities of duplication, and at a time that Walter Benjamin would famously label as "the age of mechanical reproduction."[28] Pessoa's "flywheel's restless spinning" ("*giro vivo do volante*") can be taken as a metaphor for writing as an automated (de)generative device in an age when the intervening stages between self-expression and the press were radically being swept away, precipitating interchangeability, role-play, and reversal between writer and reader. Thus, besides availing himself of the Romantic duality between observer and experiencer, on the verge of duplicity, Pessoa would embrace the mechanical complexity leading to the duplication of sender and receiver while eschewing the unity of identification. Arguably, such a concern is already to be found in Poe, namely in "William Wilson," where the protagonist's double is qualified both as "my rival" and "my namesake," and schizoid disorder ensues not only from loss of individuation but from the misguided denotation that might be ascribed to what the early Fernando Pessoa called "word-obsession," replicating rather than singling out a character: "I felt angry with him for bearing the name, and doubly disgusted with the name because a stranger bore it, who would be the cause of its twofold repetition."[29] Still, Pessoa's dissemination through alterity overcomes the tropos of simile, implying complete disembodiment, as he, unlike Poe, evades autobiographical surmises, and, rather than seeing the reader as "semblable" of himself (Baudelaire, "Hypocrite lecteur,—mon semblable,—mon frère"[30]), becomes the reader of successive selves—e.g. the untitled poem which starts "I don't know how many souls I have" (1930):

> Attentive to what I am and see
> I become them and stop being I.
> . . .
> That's why I read, as a stranger,
> My being as if it were pages.[31]
>
> (*Attento ao que sou e vejo,*
> *Torno-me elles e não eu*
> . . .
> *Por isso, alheio, vou lendo*
> *Como páginas, meu ser.*)

We have also seen that the above-quoted apprenticeship poem "Insomnia," by Alexander Search, associates the inexorable mechanics of the watch, intersecting midnight fancies (as in Poe's "Tell-Tale Heart") within another scission, most relevant to the alterity theme, that of reason and consciousness vs. feeling and dreaming, which Pessoa himself traced back to Poe. "Insomnia" bears the seeds of a central idea that would be crystallized in what is perhaps Pessoa's best known poem, "Autopsychography" (first published in 9132), where the mechanical imagery and the skill of fabrication promote an acute suffering that is as mind-induced as "factually" felt:

The poet is a faker
Who's so good at his act
He even fakes the pain
Of pain he feels in fact.
. . .
And so around its track
This thing called the heart winds,
A little clockwork train
To entertain our minds.

[*O poeta é um fingidor.*
Finge tão completamente
Que chega a fingir que é dor
A dor que deveras sente.
. . .
E assim nas calhas de roda
Gira, a entretar a razão,
Esse comboio de corda
Que se chama coração.][32]

The realization that pain and emotion can be produced by the intellect challenges the topos of authenticity in poetry, since it requires that the poet who
is master of his/her skill be also a "faker"—or, in Poe's apt phrase, a "literary
histrio," familiar with "the wheels and pinions—the tackle for scene-shift-
ing—the step-ladders and demon-traps—the cock's feathers, the red paint
and the black patches."[33]

The recognition of scission and artifice also represented a severe blow on
the equation of poetry with unity and sincerity—a debasement to which the
poet reacted either with despondency or bashful arrogance. Poe did both.
Pessoa opted for a sober variation of the latter and outdid the schism by
indulging in fragmentation, adding multiple combinations to the struggle
with a single projection or alter-ego. Pessoa's friend, Mário de Sá-Carneiro
(1880–1916), the poet of "Dispersion" (*Dispersão*, 1913), would, in a quite
different tone, employ his poetic energies to the cruel derision of the poet's
stance as a profoundly irreconcilable being: the "the double-masked," "the
liar," "the presumptuous jester."[34]

A passing reference should be made to the work of Sá-Carneiro, Pessoa's
comrade in the Portuguese revolution of Modernism, whose premature suicide at age twenty-six inhibited his career. A comparative study taking account of his texts, too, would bring an ampler insight into Poe's influence in
Portuguese modernism, as well as into an elaboration of what I described
above as the Romantic appeal to duplicity. Unlike Pessoa, Sá-Carneiro was
not very attuned to the Poesque rhythm, being rather more confessional and
colloquial—but he reflected the Poesque sense of artificial sumptuousness in
visual imagery and scenery. Working close to the stage—he studied acting

for some time—Sá-Carneiro revels in backdrops of gold and glitter, only to reveal their fake quality and the sick joke of grandeur in a world and age where the fall from unity is irrevocable and high-principled artists succumb to the "imp of the perverse." This impulse is explicitly invoked in Sá-Carneiro's seminal short story "Incest," where the protagonist, a playwright, "was prone to imagine, by a desire of perversity . . . that he was *of other opinion*," and goes on to recall the boyhood fantasy of throwing his pet—a *white* cat—out of the window.[35]

POE'S PERVERSENESS: "NOT A SIMPLE FACULTY OF THE MIND"

In Pessoa's reflections on genius, an unfinished note reads: "Poe's perverseness: not a simple faculty of the mind."[36] Textual evidence from Search's English poems suggests that the young Pessoa's susceptibility to perverseness materialized in an obscure presence, whose potential for destruction was ambiguously celebrated as a necessary impulse. In "Ode to the Sea," the raving element of troubled waves embodies that disturbing force, whereas in "Insomnia" it might be "the very darkness whirling / In a blacker darkness whirled." Considering both poems' indebtedness to "The Bells," we may venture to speculate that these forces of entropy and rage, but also of a might that is irresistibly vital, relate in function to the Poesque "ghouls" that arguably symbolize, in "The Bells," the "archfiend" quality that Poe ascribed to perverseness. Tellingly, Alexander Search will also feature the "Ghouls" in a poem aptly named "Horror" (c. 1907) that may be taken as yet another Poesque rewrite:

> In the darkness of my soul,
> Just as dark as the souls of men,
> By the blessing of their eternal curse,
> 　　Flashes like a bodiless ghoul,
> In its rare fullness above all ken,
> The sense of the sense of the universe[37]

The Ghoul here is a gateway to the above-mentioned glimpses beyond the limitations of men's earthly existence, which Poe referred to as "glories beyond the grave."[38] It also fulfils an exorcizing function in the exploration of limit states, such as self-destruction, suicide and nihilism, whose productiveness in Pessoa began with Search and afterward bloomed into modernist maturity through the heteronym Álvaro de Campos. Thus, we may trace back the Poesque foundations for such a self-induced trance, through mechanics and mnemonics where visions of blood and fire grow out of proclaimed ecstasies, to Campos's "Maritime Ode."

. . .
Douse with the cold depths the bones of my existence,
Scourge, cut and shrivel with winds, foams and suns
My cyclonic, Atlantic being,
. . .
Fire, fire, fire, inside me!
Blood! blood! blood! blood!
My brain is bursting!
The world as I know it explodes in red!
My veins snap with the sound of cables!
And from deep within booms the savage and insatiable
Song of the Great Pirate,
The bellowing death of the Great Pirate, whose singing
Sends a chill down the spine of his men.
Astern he dies, howling his song.
. . . .
Split keels, sunken ships, blood on the seas!
Decks awashed in blood, sectioned corpses!
Severed fingers left lying on gunwales!
Heads of children here and there!
People with gouged eyes shouting, screaming!
Hey-ey-ey-ey-ey-ey-ey-ey-ey-ey! [39]

Fire is a sign of the workings of the perverse in several Poesque texts, such as
"Hop-Frog," "The Imp of the Perverse" itself, or "the loud alarum" cries of
fire in "The Bells." Pessoa's surviving translated lines of this poem correspond to this momentum—"fogo, fogo, fogo"—a cry that may have echoed
in the Portuguese poet's mind until it found expression in Campos: "fire, fire,
fire, inside me! Blood, blood, blood, blood / My brain is bursting! . . ./ My
veins snap with the sound of cables." The overlapping of poetry veins and
sailing cables displays Pessoa's modernist technique of "interseccionism,"
but the metaphor itself is old and was used by Poe, namely in the correspondence between heart and lute-strings in "Israfel." In "The Bells," also, there
is the suggestion of mingling bells' and heart's ropes, furiously struck by the
Ghoul King: "and their King is he who tolls—/ And he dances and he yells; /
. . ./ Keeping time, time, time, / In a sort of Runic rhyme: / To the throbbing
of the Bells." In "The Maritime Ode," "the Great Pirate" with his "savage
and insatiable song" and his "bellowing death . . . whose singing / sends a
chill down the spine of his men" is, I suggest, another avatar of "the imp," or
of "the sense of the sense of the universe." An embodiment of vertigo amid
the whirling sea of the wrecks of ancient voyages, "split kills and sunken
ships," he furthermore recalls the great Poesque creation of the looming
shrouded figure that, in *Arthur Gordon Pym*, a novel Pessoa had read, [40]
awaits the hero on the verge of the great chasm.

With such a suggestion of wonder, conflating reason and madness, while numbing the senses of physical reality through the rhythmic induction of rush and arousal, I close this attempt at identifying certain Poesque traits whose creative appropriation, traced back to Pessoa's writing apprenticeship, may have facilitated the processes and techniques which marked early Portuguese modernism.

NOTES

1. T. S. Eliot, "From Poe to Valéry," Library of Congress Lecture, November 29, 1948; repr. in *The Recognition of Edgar Allan Poe*, ed. Eric W. Carlson (Ann Arbor: The University of Michigan Press, 1966), 205–220; Bloom (ed.), *Edgar Allan Poe* (New York: Chelsea House, 1985), 4.

2. Bloom, *The Western Canon: The Books and Schools of the Ages* (New York: Harcourt, 1994), 485.

3. Fernando Pessoa, *Escritos Sobre Génio e Loucura,* ed. Jerónimo Pizarro (Lisbon: Imprensa Nacional–Casa da Moeda, 2006), I: 417.

4. Ibid., 619. For Pessoa's assessment of the impact of his English education, see *Correspondência Inédita*, ed. Manuela Parreira da Silva (Lisbon: Livros Horizonte, 1996), 92.

5. George Monteiro, "The Bat and the Raven," *Edgar Allan Poe Review* 11:1 (Spring 2010): 105–120; Monteiro, "The Wing of Madness: Poe," *Fernando Pessoa and Nineteenth-Century Anglo-American Literature* (Kentucky: University Press of Kentucky, 2000), 111–128; Monteiro, "Fernando Pessoa," in *Poe Abroad. Influence, Reputation, Affinities*, ed. Lois D. Vines (Iowa City: University of Iowa Press, 1999), 210–214; Monteiro, "Poe/Pessoa," *Comparative Literature* 40: 2 (Spring 1988): 134–149; Margarida Vale de Gato, "Poetics and Ideology in Fernando Pessoa's Translations of Edgar Allan Poe," *Edgar Allan Poe Review* 11: 1 (Spring 2010): 121–131; Vale de Gato, "Poe's 'Nevermore,' Lisbon's Ravens, and the Portuguese Ideology of Saudade," *Trans/American, Trans/Oceanic, Trans/Lation: Issues in International American Studies*, ed. S. Araújo, J. F. Duarte and M. P. Pinto (Cambridge: Cambridge Scholars Publishing, 2010), 219–232. Luis Juan Solís Carrillo: "Edgar Allan Poe y su presencia en Fernando Pessoa," *Espéculo: Revista de Estudios Literarios* 42 (July–Oct. 2009), web; Duarte, "America in Exile: Pessoa Translator of Poe," in *Americas' Worlds and the World's Americas/Les mondes des Amériques et les Amériques du monde*, ed. Amaryll Chanady, George Handley and Patrick Imbert (Ottawa: University of Ottawa/Legas, 2006), 391–400; Maria Eduarda Keating, "Das Fronteiras do 'Estranho': Edgar Allan Poe por Baudelaire, Mallarmé e Pessoa," in *A Tradução nas Encruzilhadas da Cultura/Translation as/at the Crossroads of Culture/La Traduction aux carrefours de la culture*, ed. J. F. Duarte (Lisbon: Colibri, 2001), 119–30; Badiaa Bourenanne Baker, "Fernando Pessoa and Edgar Allan Poe / Fernando Pessoa and Walt Whitman," *Separata dos Arquivos do Centro Cultural Português* (XV, Paris: Fundação Calouste Gulbenkian, 1980), 247–321; Maria Leonor Machado de Sousa, "Fernando Pessoa e a Literatura de Ficção," in *Actas do I Congresso Internacional de Estudos Pessoanos* (Brasília Editora: Porto, 1978), 527–545; António Ralha, "A Tradução Portuguesa do Poema 'Ulalume' por Fernando Pessoa," *Biblos* 51 (1979): 153–172; Manuel Tanger Correa, "Mallarmé e Fernando Pessoa perante o 'Corvo' de Edgar Allan Poe," *Ocidente* 65 (1963): 4–20.

6. Luísa Freire, *Fernando Pessoa: Entre Vozes, Entre Línguas* (Lisbon: Assírio e Alvim, 2004).

7. Ibid., 30–38.

8. Fernando Pessoa, *Escritos Autobiográficos, Automáticos e de Reflexão Pessoal*, ed. Richard Zenith (Lisbon: Assírio e Alvim, 2003), 22.

9. Pessoa, "Impressões do Crepúsculo," *Renascença* 1 (Feb. 1914); translated as "Twilight Impressions" by Richard Zenith, *A Little Larger Than the Entire Universe: Selected Poems* (London: Penguin Classics, 2002), 279.

10. Besides Monteiro's already quoted essay in "Poe / Pessoa," see Maria Aliete Galhoz, "Em Torno ao Poema de Fernando Pessoa 'Ó Sino da Minha Aldeia'—nota preliminar e breve achega ao seu estudo," in *Estudos Portugueses. Homenagem a Luciana Stegagno Picchio* (Lisbon: Difel, 1991), 743–757; and Fátima Freitas Morna, "Ecos de Vários Sinos," in *Estudos de Tradução em Portugal: Novos Contributos para a História da Literatura Portuguesa,* ed. Maria Teresa Seruya (Lisbon: Universidade Católica Editora, 2001), 109–122.

11. Fernando Pessoa, Portuguese National Library, E 3 / 14 D—45 and 46 (manuscript written in English); reimpr. in *Principais Poemas de Edgar Poe,* edited and translated by Margarida Vale de Gato and Fernando Pessoa (Lisboa: Guimarães [Col. Fernando Pessoa Editor / Olisipo], 2011), 191–192.

12. Fernando Pessoa Papers, Portuguese National Library, E 3 / 74 A—52 and 65–45. The first draft is written on the back of an invoice of a company in the name of Mário N. Freitas, Pessoa's cousin for whom he had worked on and off since 1908, and matches, in its annotations, another Poe translation draft from c. 1913; the second draft uses the page of a diary for January 13, 1924.

13. Pessoa, *Páginas de Estética e de Teoria e Critica Literárias,* ed. Georg Rudolf Lind and Jacinto Prado Coelho (Lisbon: Ática, 1973), 74–75.

14. Huxley, "Vulgarity in Literature," 1930; repr. in *The Recognition of Edgar Allan Poe,* ed. E. W. Carlson, 165.

15. Pessoa / Álvaro de Campos, *Poemas de Álvaro de Campos* (Lisbon: EdiçõesVercial), 92.

16. Poe, *Eureka,* ed. Stuart Levine and Susan F. Levine (Urbana: University of Illinois Press, 2004), 57.

17. Martin Roth, "Poe's Divine Spondee," *Poe Studies,* XII: 1 (June 1979): 14–18.

18. Wilbur, intr. *Poe: Complete Poems* (New York: Dell Publishing Co., 1959), 35.

19. Pessoa, *Escritos sobre Génio* (Lisbon: Nacional-Casa de Moeda, 2006), I: 381. Pessoa took Poe's idea from his review of Elizabeth Browning's *A Drama of Exile* (Jan. 1845): the relevant passage is underlined in the edition *The Choice Works of Edgar Allan Poe* (London: Chatto and Windus, 1902) of the personal library of Fernando Pessoa preserved in his Museum-House in Lisbon.

20. Pessoa, *Páginas de Estética,* 73 (my translation).

21. Poe, *Critical Theory: The Major Documents,* ed. Stuart Levine and Susan F. Levine (Urbana: University of Illinois Press, 2009), 11.

22. Fernando Pessoa Papers, Portuguese National Library, E3 / 146–51.

23. See Pessoa's note in French, "L'activité de synthèse est liée à l'excitation mentale, comme celle d'analyse l'est à la depression . . . Un cas de coëxistence des deux activités, Edgar Poe (remember also his success at mathematics)," *Escritos sobre Génio,* I: 53.

24. Pessoa, *Poesia do Eu,* 2nd ed, edited by Richard Zenith (Lisbon: Assírio e Alvim, 2006), 171; transl. Richard Zenith, *A Little Larger,* 284.

25. Pessoa had the project of writing a monograph on the subject of genius, madness, and degenerescence. Jeronimo Pizarro's compilation of the existing material in *Escritos sobre Génio* includes notes and marginalia on Lombroso and Nordau, particularly in 1907–1908.

26. Pessoa / Campos, *Poemas de Álvaro de Campos,* 87; transl. Richard Zenith, *A Little Larger,* 172.

27. Pessoa / Search, *Poemas Ingleses* II, vol. 5 of *Edição Crítica de Fernando Pessoa,* edited by João Dionísio (Lisbon: INCM, 1997), 43.

28. Walter Benjamin, "The Work of Art in the Age of Mechanical Reproduction" (1936); repr. *Illuminations, Essays and Reflections,* ed. Hannah Arendt, trans. H. Zohn (New York: Schocken, 1969), 217–252.

29. Poe, *Tales & Sketches,* vol. 1 of *The Collected Works of Edgar Allan Poe,* ed. T. O. Mabbott (Cambridge, MA: Belknap Press of Harvard University, 1978), 433, 445 and 435 respectively.

30. Baudelaire, *Les Fleurs du Mal,* 1861; repr. *Oeuvres Complètes,* ed. Claude Pichois (Paris: Gallimard, 1975), 6.

31. Pessoa, *Poemas de Fernando Pessoa, 1921–1930*, tomo III, vol. I of *Edição Crítica de Fernando Pessoa*, edited by Ivo de Castro (Lisbon: INCM, 2001), 197. Transl. Richard Zenith, *Forever Someone Else: Selected Poems*, ed. and trans. Richard Zenith (Lisbon: Assírio e Alvim, 2008), 241.

32. Pessoa, *Poesia do Eu*, 241; transl. *A Little Larger*, 314.

33. Poe, *Critical Theory*, 61.

34. Mário de Sá-Carneiro, "Aquele Outro" (1916): "O dúbio mascarado—o mentiroso /. . . . / Em vez de Pajem, bobo presunçoso," in *Poemas Completos*, ed. Fernando Cabral Martins (Lisbon: Assírio e Alvim, 2005), 131 (my translation).

35. Sá-Carneiro, "O Incesto," *Princípio: Novelas Originais* (1912; repr. Editora Orfeu: Porto, 1985), 157 (my translation, my italics).

36. Pessoa, *Escritos sobre génio*, I: 97.

37. Pessoa / Search, *Poemas Ingleses* II, 146.

38. Poe, *Critical Theory*, 184.

39. Pessoa / Campos, *Poemas de Álvaro de Campos*, 90–93; transl. Richard Zenith, *A Little Larger*, 172–179. All further references to "Maritime Ode" will go unmentioned.

40. *Arthur Gordon Pym* features in Pessoa's reading list of 1907 (10th May); see *Escritos sobre Génio*, II: 623.

Chapter Nine

Poe in Place

Charles Cantalupo

The four poems of "Poe in Place" focus on Edgar Allan Poe's three extant residences in the United States—in Baltimore, Philadelphia and the Bronx (or Fordham, to name it as in Poe's time)—and on one imagined location: the winter palace of the twentieth-century Ethiopian emperor, Haile Selassie, in Massawa, a city in Eritrea on the coast of the Red Sea. Heavily damaged by war, the extravagance of the palace still survives and strikes me as the kind of setting Poe might have used in a short story. After my first visit, as I looked at the pictures I had taken, I saw perched on one of its shattered marble cornices what I had not noticed when I was actually there: a raven. It confirmed the Poe-like presence I had felt, later reinforced in my reading about Haile Selassie, which made him seem, too, like a character out of Poe. Yet his poem, "The Haunted Palace," offered a form as well as content upon which to base a poem that the appearance of the raven seemed to demand that I call "Poe in Massawa."

I justify creating an imagined place for Poe because I come to him primarily through his fiction and poetry, the work of his literary imagination. Subsequently, in the next three poems of "Poe in Place," I see the actual places where he lived more through his biography, his fame and even his notoriety, although I would emphasize that the physical locations where Poe lived concern me more than how he lived there: the former, admittedly, far less intractable than the latter. Furthermore, my perspective on the three buildings still standing where Poe actually lived also involves the people who now live around them: who may know of him without knowing much about him or his work or who may not know or care about him at all. They represent one extreme, and a strict biographical analysis of Poe's life when he actually went in and out of the doorways on Spring Garden, Amity and the Grand Concourse or thereabouts offer another extreme, with the four poems of "Poe in Place" ranging in between. Nevertheless, as "Poe in Massawa" relates to "The Haunted Palace," so does "Poe in Philadelphia" to "The Coliseum," "Poe in Fordham" to "The City in the Sea," and "Poe in Baltimore" to "Eldorado": poems by Poe ostensibly titled as places. Therefore, the forms of these "place poems" become another determining factor in the composition of "Poe in Place."

Veering among biographical, historical and literary understandings of Poe and observations about the three houses now remaining where he lived, not all of the allusions in "Poe in Place" may be clear. Generally, the poems juxtapose what the places look like now and what they might have looked like in Poe's time—an inescapably subjective endeavor. At times the poems echo phrases from Poe's writing, including his letters, particularly if it has been identified as originating from the time when Poe lived in a particular house. More obscurely, perhaps, in "Poe in Philadelphia," "Qohaito" refers to an elaborate, ancient city for the most part still unexcavated in the highlands of Eritrea. I characterize Poe's writing the same letter, word for word, over and over, describing his plans for "The Penn Magazine," to potential benefactors—which never appeared—as obsessive compulsive disorder or OCD. The first stanza of "Poe in Baltimore" includes purported lines from a headstone for his grave that was planned in the 1860s. The poem also includes the fanciful story that a freight train derailed on a nearby track and smashed the stone.

Poe in Massawa

> *In state his glory well befitting,*
> *The ruler of the realm was seen.*
> —Edgar Allan Poe, "The Haunted Palace"

Square with seven arches on each side
Of marble and blue enamel,
The emperor's palace says he died
Horribly but lived well.
The grand entrance stairs blasted in two,
The gaping dome, bullet holed, crumbling
Walls and missing floors the light pours through
Recall a King of Kings

Who rarely slept, fed conspirators
To his leopards and lions at dawn,
Acted peacefully amidst total war,
Scattered flamingoes across his lawns,
Lived without the written word,
Barely spoke and punished silence.
He only remembered
What he thought made sense

And strengthened him as head of state.
Anything else meant disease.
He also thought it wisdom to wait,
Seeing everyone on their knees
Had a knife behind their back.
But now the railings' shattered filigree,
A foundation full of cracks
And viscera of masonry

Dangling in oriental doors
Speak of a greater power here.
It says, ignore.
Climbing on a balcony, I peer
Through the shutters at a rich table
And chairs lined up, but nobody comes.
The elevator without car and cables
And the belfry stripped deaf and dumb

Faze no one, and a shirtless man
Walks by barefoot in a sarong.
A delivery van
And a boat in dry dock don't seem to belong
Next to the palace, but they portend
No more spirit
To haunt him and the fishing dhows that bend
Among the container ships that sit

In the harbor doing business,
Or haunting you and me
As we join a chorus
Of camels silhouetted against the sea,
Particles clinging to a grinding stone . . .
And a raven's *nevermore*
In a corner of the emperor's bones
Upon the Red Sea shore.

Poe in Philadelphia

Potsherds from Qohaito, a chartreuse chip
Of Corinth, Roman mosaic bits and
Merely seeing the original manuscripts
Of "Daffodils" or "Kubla Kahn" lead me
To Seventh and Spring Garden Streets to pick
A lip of molding off the basement floor:
Great relic, I think, as I crack my head
On a low beam and read at the same time,
Do not use steps, where he wrote as *a man*

Who looks steadily up two months before
He left as a failure—his most famous
Tales for sixteen cents a day and blotting
The need for poetry into lost drafts
Or the OCD of single columns,
Clear type, hand press, woodcuts and pure paper:
French stitched immortality with readers.

No Worcester Street, fruit, flower and vegetable
Gardens, fresh meat markets, women scrubbing
Stoops and white-washing stalls on the cluttered
Outskirts of America's publishing
Capital—I see a spotless cottage
With insipid mulch amidst abandoned
Lots and, inside from his tiny study
Window, the requisite housing project,
My vulnerable Volvo on the street,

And not much else except what I make up:
The extra wide floorboards, blood and writing
On each layer of wallpaper, each stair's
Riser up to the bedrooms kicked and kicked
And kicked, but no other show of anger
Or frustration amidst the gangs, riots,
Hate, fires, filth, addicts, strikes, poor, sick, and the dead.

What echoes in this neat, three story brick:
Incongruously clear views to downtown,
And twenty haunted palaces amidst
Store front churches, greasy garages, fast food,

Vacant manufacturers, mass transit
And a huge university up Broad?
Something more than glory that Poe lived here?

I am deep in the Aegean, boating
From monastery to monastery,
Pilgrim among pilgrims trading stories:
I touched the bone of John the Baptist's hand.
I ran my fingers on the holy Virgin's belt.
They mean these people really lived and died.
A chip of molding? A piece of the true cross.

Poe in Fordham

Death sets up a throne in Fordham
And takes a queen—Virginia Clem.
Entering to lilac music
Perfuming the fresh air, she's sick.
Who cares she dies nine months later?
The throne remains, love or hate her,
Doesn't it? Slope east. Face west. See
The rivers so clean, woods, fruit trees,
Dahlia gardens and mockingbirds,
Orioles, owls, and canaries
Caged or free, all feeding my words?

Jasmine and honeysuckle wreathe
And crown the air—only breathe!
If this is only what I've read,
No throne remains except the dead
Or drunk: denial ground into
Dust of poverty. . . . No breakthroughs?
No art? Beauty? Romance? Poem?
No place finally to call home?
What if everything created
Could be good and never wasted?
If not at first, remade that way
After the end of the last day?

Dying of tuberculosis,
No Virginia Clem to kiss,
Throwing up a bucket of blood. . . .
Such a loss transformed and made good?
She rolls and spirals inward where,
Revolting against my despair,

I find the perfect plot: the end
Becomes a dream from her girl friend:
A city where she's never been,
Virginia circled by children,
And the answer to "where am I."
It's Richmond again, who knows why,
Only without separation:
The beginning and end as one
Heart—throbbing, swelling, subsiding
Between the divine and nothing.
Virginia's dream, her friend's, or mine,
Who cares? I worship at a shrine

That can't survive but somehow does,
Moved from where it really was:
Its language, stones, hanging bookshelf,
Shingles, planks, rocking chair and self
Lost amidst a million faces
And songs from different places
Never together before here
And now . . . but without any fear
No matter how the traffic roars.
A Spanish spiritualist store
Nearby offers *Velas, Séance*
Criptographia with reverance.

Poe in Baltimore

Spare these remains.
A runaway train
Smashes a marble headstone.
On one side, these words—
And on the other, more absurd,
He is finally happy here.

What remains? Where?
In the wheelchair
And shattered lamp
On the broken porch with no ramp
For the abandoned
To watch a boy with a gun

At 11:00 a.m.
Chasing his neighbor's son?
In the burnt out frames,
Collapsed foundations
And missing doors
Of row house after row house

With no heat
Rented to the poor?
Gangs block off the corners—
Nowhere trees or stores,
Plastic bags and tape
Instead of car windows.

Happy? Spared? Where?
More like *in despair*, *dead*.
America doesn't care
About this slum.
Who is to blame?
Sunshine or *shadow*?

At least *the lovely name*
Of *the lowly street*
And *the little house*
Built in 1830,
As Edgar Allan Poe
Described it,

Where he lived
From 1832 or 33 to 35,
Remains: *Amity.*
America doesn't care,
And touching the powdery bricks
I'm singing *in . . . Eldorado.*

Chapter Ten

Ligeia—Not Me!: Three Women Writers Respond to Poe

Daniel Hoffman

The best Poe biography is Kenneth Silverman's *Edgar A. Poe*. His subtitle quotes a line of Poe's: "Mournful and Never-Ending Remembrance." This sad sentiment alludes to what Silverman rightly considers the shaping events of Poe's life—the deaths, from tuberculosis, of his mother when he was not yet three years old, his stepmother when he was in his teens, and his wife Virginia when he was in his thirties. These were losses from which he did not, could not, recover. They shaped his attitude to women.

The result of this "mournful and never-ending remembrance" was the idealization of women. In his story, as I've summarized it in my study of Poe's life and work,

> "the learning of Ligeia was immense." She epitomizes all knowledge, all wisdom, all learning. She is also the epitome of ideality, or spirit, a quality imparted to Husband by the haunting expression of her eyes. No merely human eyes, however lovely, ever held such mysteries, such clues to the unifying spirit which invisibly presides over the wayward chaos of our mortal world. [1]

After she dies, he marries another woman, and in this truly scary story, he comes to hate his second wife, Rowena, because she is not Ligeia. But as Rowena sickens and dies, she becomes Ligeia—a frightening fable of the impossibility of finding a substitute for his first, idealized love.

I give all these details to suggest the problems that might face a woman interested in Poe's work and wishing to write about him. Interestingly, the first critic to propose the influence on Poe's imagination of these losses was his first female critic, Princess Marie Bonaparte, a student of Sigmund Freud's. In the past few years, three distinguished women authors have been moved to deal with Poe. They are the English fiction writer Angela Carter, the greatly talented, prolific novelist and short story writer Joyce Carol Oates, and the award-winning poet Mary Oliver. Each approaches Poe at a different point in his life and the life of his works: Carter is fascinated by Poe's birth and infancy, Oates by his last days and death, and Oliver by the lasting effect of his writings, we might say, his afterlife.

Angela Carter is not as well known in the United States as she should be. She was born in England, and before her death at fifty-two in 1992, she had been nearly as prolific a fiction writer as Joyce Carol Oates. Carter published nine novels, eight volumes of short stories, two books of poems; wrote four radio plays, two film scripts, an opera, six children's books; edited four collections of fairy tales; and wrote four collections of nonfiction, mainly on feminist themes. Very few works of this whole library were published in the United States. A critic wrote of Angela Carter that she offered "strange events and bizarre characters . . . possessed a gift for controlled grotesquery, stylistic flourish, and thematic elegance . . . an original voice meshed to original subject matter."[2] The tale she is best known for in the United States is her grimly detailed, nightmarishly realistic story "The Fall River Axe Murders"—we all know the skip-rope rhyme—

> Lizzie Borden took an axe
> And gave her mother forty whacks.
> When she saw what she had done
> She gave her father forty-one.

—but no one till Carter had made Borden's crimes both so repellent and so believable.

Carter spent three years in Japan, where she met French surrealist writers who influenced her. Of them, in an essay, "The Alchemy of the Word," published in *Expletives Deleted,* she wrote, "[she] thought the surrealists were wonderful, [but] had to give them up in the end. They were, with a few patronized exceptions, all men and they told me that I was the source of all mystery, beauty, and otherness, because I was a woman—and I knew that was not true."[3] She found herself cast by the surrealists into the feminine role that I've described as obsessive in the tales of Poe. Not for her—she'd not play Ligeia to anyone else's imagination; she rejected being "the source of all mystery, beauty and otherness" because she was a woman. And because she was a woman, she wrote, "I wanted my fair share of the imagination, too. . . . Just an equal share in the right to vision."[4]

In view of her nondidactic feminism, let's see how she deals with Poe and his mother. One book of her short fiction, *Saints and Strangers* (published in Great Britain as *Black Venus),* has the tale I'll describe. Its title is "The Cabinet of Edgar Allan Poe." Angela Carter had lived in America for a couple of years while she taught at Texas and at Brown universities, so her description of American life is not entirely imaginary, as when on her opening page she says,

> Imagine Poe in the Republic! when he possesses none of its virtues. . . . Where is the black star of melancholy? Elsewhere; not here. Here it is always morning; stern, democratic light scrubs apparitions off the streets down which his dangerous feet must go . . . up here, up north, in the levelling latitudes, a man must make his own penumbra if he wants concealment because the massive, heroic light of the Republic admits of no ambiguities. Either you are a saint; or a stranger. He is a stranger.[5]

And a paragraph later, "Poe staggers under the weight of the Declaration of Independence. People think he is drunk. He *is* drunk. The prince in exile lurches through the new-found land."

Angela Carter thus dramatizes Poe's incompatibility with the egalitarian, expanding, forward-thrusting culture around him, the characteristics of America that Tocqueville described during Poe's lifetime. This she merges with his drinking, to make Poe completely odd man out. If you think Poe "overacts," "[t]here is a past history of histrionics in his family. His mother was, as they say, born in a trunk, grease-paint in her bloodstream," and Carter describes how Eliza Poe, already attached to a traveling repertoire company at age nine, "skipped on to a stage . . . to sing an old-world ballad clad in the pretty rags of a ballet gypsy. Her dancer's grace, piping treble, dark curls, rosy cheeks—cute kid! And eyes with something innocent, something appealing in them that struck directly to the heart." She became a star, "a shooting star; she flickered briefly in the void." Being slightly built, she continued after puberty to play juvenile roles, like Little Pickle in a comic sketch, but "also tried her hand at Juliet and Cordelia and, if necessary, could personate the merriest soubrette; even when racked by the nauseas of her pregnancies."

This ingenue was in her second marriage, her first husband dead of fever at twenty; she was now married to David Poe, son of a Revolutionary War general, whose Baltimore family opposed his giving up the law for the stage. They were right; he was an incompetent actor, pilloried in the press while Eliza was the darling of reviewers. They traveled, two children—Eddie and his older brother, William Henry, with them, until David Poe deserted them—Carter says, "before his sons' bewildered eyes. . . . He unbecame. . . . The air shuddered with the beginning of absence."

Angela Carter deeply imagines what little Eddie, not yet three years old, saw backstage while his mother performed. "Consider the theatrical illusion with special reference to this impressionable child, who was exposed to it at an age when there is no reason for anything to be real." Here is "a Gothic castle all complete with owls and ivy. . . . Nothing is what it seems." A child kicks a throne; it's only *papier mâché*; he "could sit in it and be a king or lie in it and be in pain."

The little boy saw "another mystery and made less sense of it . . . allowed to stay in the wings and watch; the round-eyed baby saw that Ophelia could . . . die twice nightly. All her burials were premature." Not only that, but he could see her in a blonde wig, then as a brunette—everything was illusory; all was illusion. When his mother died, "although Mr Allan told Edgar how all of his mother that was mortal had been buried in her coffin, Edgar knew the somebody elses she so frequently became lived in her dressing-table mirror." So Ligeia repossesses the body of Rowena as she lay dying. Death itself is not real, yet it is inexorable, and mourning is never-ending.

* * *

Joyce Carol Oates, reviewing a later book by Angela Carter, wrote that "it inhabits its own manic universe."[6] This is true of much of Oates's own writing. I'm not an Oates expert, have read only a couple of her more than twenty volumes of stories or thirty-nine novels—she seems to give us a new book every few weeks, hard to keep up. I'm sure, though, that Poe has been an influence on her work, for she has written two volumes of tales of the grotesque, and, in 2007, *The Museum of Dr. Moses: Tales of Mystery and Suspense,* these tales in addition to the nine mystery novels she published under pseudonyms. She is surely indebted to Poe, who pioneered these genres and who described some of his own fiction as "Tales of the Grotesque." But in the books I've mentioned, Poe's relation to Oates's work is indirect. But Poe himself is the subject of the opening tale in her recent book, *Wild Nights!: Stories About the Last Days of Poe, Dickinson, Twain, James, and Hemingway.* It is titled "Poe Posthumous; or, The Light House."

She has based her tale on the fragment "The Light House"—only a little over two printed pages. I quote T. O. Mabbott, from his edition of Poe's complete works, "This is the last of Poe's tales of terror, and was never finished . . . he was prevented from completing it by his sudden death."[7] Although the brief text provides no evidence, Mabbott says, "That Poe's lighthouse was doomed to fall cannot be doubted, but whether the dog, . . . was to save only the diary, or his master, must be left to the reader's imagination."[8] Poe's fragment breaks off with his narrator, who has been left alone to tend a lighthouse far from land (the location resembles that in "A Descent into the Maelstrom"); he will keep a diary, but we have his entries only for January 1 and 3, 1796.

Joyce Carol Oates sets her tale to begin on October 7, 1849, the date of Poe's death. Her unnamed narrator has just been left on "the fabled Light-House at Viña de Mar," his "Soul filled with hope!"[9] He has been sent there by Dr. Shaw, to whom he has promised to keep a diary of his experience, for "there is no predicting what may happen to a man so entirely alone as I am. . . . My soul, long depressed . . . has miraculously revived in this bracing *spring air*" (3). Accompanied by his "good-hearted" dog, Mercury, he climbs to "the pinnacle of the tower" (3) and gazes on "Sky, sea, earth: ah, vibrant with life!" (4).

As the days pass, he is "eager to begin what posterity will perhaps call *The Diary of the Fabled Light House at Viña de Mar,* a document to set beside such celebrated investigations into the human psyche as the *Meditations* of Rene Descartes" (6) as well as the works of Rousseau and Richter. He is reading Plotinus, the most idealistic of philosophers, and is translating Jeremias Gotthelf. (I thought Oates had made up this author of whom I'd never heard, but find, in the eleventh edition of *Encyclopedia Brittanica*, that he was a Swiss writer, contemporary with Poe, best known for his novella about a monster spider that makes a pact with the devil and spreads the plague over Europe.)

Poe rejoices at having freed himself from "cards, & drink, & riotous company. (By my agreement with Dr. Shaw, my debts of some $3,500 were erased as by the flourish of a magician's wand.)" (7). By his third night, forebodings begin to oppress him. Still, he and Mercury feel "more 'at home' in this strange place" (8), exploring the rocks on which the lighthouse tower is built. Within a month, the island is assaulted by gales, dispersing the clouds of stinging insects that have afflicted him. He still thinks of his late wife: "As V. dreaded the bestial, which permeates so much of human intercourse, within even the marital bed, I have a like aversion" (13). He has, strangely, been hearing the voice of Dr. Shaw and seeing his face in the clouds above.

> *My boy* he has called me—tho'in my forty-first year I am scarcely a boy— *what a role you are destined to play, in advancing the cause of scientific knowledge.* My deep gratitude to this gentleman, who rescued me from a life of dissolution & self-harm, to engage me in this experiment into the effect of "extreme isolation" upon an "average male specimen of *Homo sapiens.*" The irony being lost on Dr. Shaw, seemingly, that tho' I am quite a normal male specimen . . . I am hardly average. (13)

Gales wash onto the rocky isle "sea-filth, (some of it yet wriggling with the most repulsive life)"(14). Gradually, Mercury feeds on carcasses of horrible sea creatures and refuses to obey commands, becoming more savage. On December 19, Narrator makes a disturbing discovery. Leafing through a stack of papers of the Philadelphia Society of Naturalists that had been put ashore with him, he comes on an article by "one Dr. Bertram Shaw, Ph.D., M.D., for 1846" (19). This recounts the effects of extreme isolation on "a rat; a guinea pig; a monkey; a dog; a cat; a 'young horse in good health'" (19). Imprisoned in pens, given food and water but no intercourse with any person or creature, by degrees the animals lost appetite, energy, and strength, lapsing at last into stupor, in which they died. "[T]he creatures, trapped in isolation, were thus trapped in their own beings, & 'smothered' of boredom; their vital spirits, a kind of living electricity, ceased by degrees to flow" (20).

Poe is confident that, not being merely "an average specimen," he will not be a subject in such an experiment, but, of course, this is exactly what is happening. Dr. Shaw is a mad scientist who has bought, by paying off his gambling debts, a human subject for his sci-fi experiment. The rest of Oates's tale records Poe's nightmarish descent into slovenliness (why shave, wash himself or his bedclothes, with no one to observe?), records his disgust at the horrible sea creatures his dog brings, bloody and gory to the lighthouse and eats. The dog becomes disobedient, Poe in a rage hits him in the head, the dog dies, and Poe is left with no companion. Repulsive sea-creatures come ashore, carnivorous, boar-sized animals.

Poe has lost track of time, declines to climb the stairs to light the beacon although a fleet of ships is visible. His journal is disjointed; he's losing control of himself. He now dines with relish on the eggs and flesh of some of the sea creatures. A species he named *Cyclophagus*, with "its single eye . . . which emerges out of its forehead, twice the size . . . & with the liquid expressiveness of a human eye" (30); it is "covered with a velvety hide, wonderfully soft to stroke. . . .To think of *Cyclophagus* is to feel, ah!—the most powerful and perverse yearning" (30). Poe is becoming bestial, has "learned to go on all fours" (31). By now Poe has imagined the rest of the world, and all its people are destroyed; he is the only survivor. "[H]aving fled breathless & whimpering to me, a virginal *Cyclophagus* female pursued by an aroused . . . male . . . emerging as Venus from the sea. To be rescued in my arms from a most licentious & repulsive brute" (33).

His scribbles, no longer dated, record "How terrified my darling was" (40). He has named her HELA, for Helen of Troy. When, it must be a year has passed, "invaders came ashore . . . in a small rowboat," to pick him up and return him to shore, "he hides with Hela in 'our snug burrow'" (40), and the rescuers depart without him. "[I]n this chalky bedchamber Hela has given birth to eight small hairless & mewing babies . . . sucking fiercely at her velvety teats . . . each of the young is unmistakably imprinted with its father's patrician brow My nose that has been called 'noble' in its Roman cast . . . Ah, a doting father holding them aloft!" (34–35). This he calls "our Kingdom by the Sea . . . her soulful eye so intense, in devotion to her hunter-husband . . . we shall be the progenitors of a bold & shining new race of immortals Hela my darling forevermore" (34–35).

This ugly story is Oates's response to Poe's idealism, dramatizing his descent from reading Plotinus to becoming a brutish beast, his devotion to his wife V. and his abhorrence of sex parodied and mocked by his mating with a repulsive monster. I would hazard that Oates is satirizing Poe's obsessive idealism, for the tale, which begins with an air of realism in its depiction of Poe, is by its conclusion a caricature. In an article on another satirical writer, Flannery O'Connor, Oates writes,

> Is the art of caricature a lesser or secondary art, set beside what we might call the art of complexity or subtlety? Is "cartoon" art invariably inferior to "realist" art? The caricaturist has the advantage of being cruel, crude, reductive, and often very funny; as the "realist" struggles to establish the *trompe l'oeil* of verisimilitude . . . the caricaturist wields a hammer, or an ax, or sprays the target with machine-gun fire, transmuting what might be rage—the *savage indignation* of Jonathan Swift, for instance—into devastating humor.[10]

Satire is the weapon of rectitude, a way of meting out punishment. Satire regrets nothing, and revels in unfairness in its depiction of what Flannery O'Connor called "large and startling figures." Her treatment of Poe doesn't partake of humor; its savagery doubtless expresses Oates's deep rejection of what she sees as Poe's vapid idealization and of the physical realities of life that are faithfully transcribed by the realist writer. Her grotesque plot has the feel of a great antagonism by its author to the real Poe. Her description of his transformation is convincingly written but has the effect of undermining the reader's sense of who Edgar Poe really was and diminishing the bequest of his actual writings.

* * *

In her book of essays, *Winter Hours* (1999), in "The Bright Eyes of Eleanora: Poe's Dream of Recapturing the Impossible," the poet Mary Oliver has a very different version of Poe's immortality. Unlike Carter or Oates, Oliver has not made Poe a figure in her own work; her poems do not draw upon his *noir* or grotesque images nor do they participate in the popular genres he pioneered—mystery, science fiction, tales of exploration. This poet has no agenda descended from Poe; she is a disinterested reader and interpreter of his work. She takes Poe at his own measure and finds his work serious, courageous, and of universal relevance and appeal.

Her title, "The Bright Eyes of Eleanora," is fulfilled in her demonstration of the essential unity, the oneness, of Poe's work, by examining his recurrent description of the eyes of his characters. This emphasis was first noted by Marie Bonaparte, examining the daguerrotype of Eliza Poe in the locket that was among the few material things she bequeathed to Edgar. She had large, dark, haunting eyes. His concentration on the eyes of Ligeia, Eleanora, Berenice, the old man murdered in "The Tell-Tale Heart," the eye-like windows of the House of Usher—all these allusions are, in Oates's tale, subsumed in the hideous and bizarre single large eye protruding from the forehead of the repulsive creature on whom Poe begets offspring, his immortality.

Oliver, instead, writes that while in Poe "we hear about plague, and torture, and revenge . . . the real subject of [his] work . . . is the anguish of knowing nothing for sure about the construct of the universe, or about the existence of a moral order within it—anything that would clarify its seemingly total and imperial indifference toward individual destiny.[11] Hence the subtitle of her essay: "Poe's Dream of Recapturing the Impossible." Poe, she writes, "was without confidence in a future that might be different from the past. He was, forever, reliving an inescapable, original woe. . . . His enterprise is to dissolve a particular fact or circumstance that represents the natural order of things—specifically death's irreversibility" (38, 43–44).

To do this requires Poe to dissociate himself from the world as we know it and to create an alternative to that reality. This is why, comparing his tales of terror to those by Henry James and Kafka, she finds Poe's tales are "frightening" but not in the way those of the other two authors are, for Kafka's and James's "are, horribly and unmistakably, descriptions of life a we know it, or *could* easily know it. While Poe's stories . . . never fail to thrill as *stories.* But literature, the best of it, does not aim to be literature. It wants and strives . . . to be a true part of the composite human record—that is, not words, but a reality" (46–47).

Yet, at the same time, she regards Poe's "inability to incorporate loss and move on" to be not only a response to his own experience but "also an invention, an endlessly repeatable dark adventure created by his exceedingly fertile mind. For Poe . . . doesn't write only about his own argument with the universe, but about everyone's argument" (47).

> In the mystery and energy of living, we all view time's shadow upon the beloved as wretchedly as any of Poe's narrators . . . we never forget it: the beloved shall grow old, or ill, and be taken away finally . . . no matter how ferociously we fight, how tenderly we love, how bitterly we argue, how persuasively we berate the universe . . . this is what shall happen. (47)

This, the "mournful and never-ending remembrance," is Poe's real story. As it is ours. "And this is why we honor him, why we are fascinated far past the simple narratives. He writes about our own inescapable destiny" (47–48).

Thus Mary Oliver avows that, despite all the Gothic machinery of his stories, all his efforts to escape what is commonly accepted as reality, Poe nevertheless grips us because his unreal characters have unlocked in us real emotions, his wraiths relive the grief of our inevitable losses of those we love. This poet helps us to recognize and acknowledge the seriousness of Poe's aims and the success of his strange, haunting tales. Poe will continue to fascinate contemporary authors, and we may be sure that more of them will make him a character in plots of their own devising, with their ends rather than his in view. Some of these may distort or diminish our sense of Poe, but there will be those that enhance his heritage and lead us to unsuspected appreciations of his achievements.

NOTES

1. Daniel Hoffman, *Poe Poe Poe Poe Poe Poe Poe* (Garden City: Doubleday, 1972; repr. Baton Rouge: LSU Press, 1998), 244. Further references cited parenthetically.

2. Jeff VanderMeer, "Angela Carter," *The Modern Word: The Scriptorium.* http://www.themodernword.com/scriptorium/carter.html. Accessed on December 30, 2010 .

3. Ibid.

4. Ibid.

5. Angela Carter, "The Cabinet of Edgar Allan Poe," in *Black Venus. Scribd.* http://www.scribd.com/doc/46674785/30521383–Angela-Carter-Black-Venus. Accessed on December 30, 2010. Further quotes from this story are from this edition.

6. Joyce Carol Oates, "The Parables of Flannery O'Connor," *New York Review of Books*, April 9, 2009, 16.

7. Edgar Allan Poe, *Collected Works of Edgar Allan Poe, Volume III*, ed. Thomas Ollive Mabbott (Cambridge: Belknap Press, 1978), 1388.

8. Mabbott, 1388–89.

9. Joyce Carol Oates, *Wild Nights* (New York: HarperCollins, 2008), 3. Further references will be noted parenthetically.

10. Joyce Carol Oates, "Large and Startling Figures: The Fiction of Flannery O'Connor," in *Rough Country: Essays and Reviews* (New York: Ecco Press, 2010), 109.

11. Mary Oliver, *Winter Hours* (Boston: Houghton Mifflin, 1999), 37. Further references will be noted parenthetically.

Chapter Eleven

Gothic Windows in Poe's Narrative Space

Shoko Itoh

In her "Afterword: Reflections on the Grotesque" in *Haunted: Tales of the Grotesque*, Joyce Carol Oates discusses Poe's influence on the Gothic genre as being "so universal as to be incalculable"; she goes on to ask, "Who has not been influenced by Poe?"[1] Oates, herself, provides evidence for the lengthened shadow Poe continues to cast over contemporary writers. One of the short stories she includes in *Haunted*, for instance, is "The White Cat," a postmodern homage to "The Black Cat," and, more recently, in "Poe Posthumous; Or the Light-House,"[2] the first chapter of *Wild Nights* (2008), Oates imagines Poe living on after October 7, 1849, to an unnumbered day in March 1850. While, even in the imagination of Joyce Carol Oates, Poe finally succumbs, his influence survives into the twenty-first century. Much of his impact on postmodern writers is his treatment of settings. Poe's Gothic houses, room-tomb-womb can be considered great archetypal sources for the "haunted house" genre.

Chief among Poe's haunted settings is the house of Roderick and Madeline Usher. In *The Gothic Vision*, Dani Cavallaro pays attention to the "rhetoric of haunting" in "The Fall of the House of Usher" as a formula for "haunted house" literature.[3] Dennis R. Perry and Carl H. Sederholm also present us with the "Usher formula" as a framework of the "philosophy of horror."[4] Until now, however, even in extensive studies on Poe's fictional houses and the "haunted house" formula—which typically employs melancholy houses, twins, sentient stones, premature burial, dark tarns, incestuous brothers and sisters, among other Gothic motifs—the significance of the many windows one finds in Poe's works has not been examined in detail, while the closed or sealed rooms have been variously discussed.

This chapter considers the role and significance of the windows in the houses and rooms of Poe's narrative space. These windows have a particularly Gothic quality because of their uncanny and theatrical character in the mansion or in the chamber of mystery symbolically associated with nightmarish loss of an Eden-like past. Windows in Poe's works are often juxtaposed with a hybrid element of artistically repeated coincidental sounds combined with the natural indefinite power of darkness. In order to grasp the essence of Poe's Gothic window, the analysis will first compare Poe's special mode of windows with that of Faulkner and then discuss Poe's use of windows in "The Fall of the House of Usher" and other tales. Poe's Gothic window functions as a dangerous threshold between the inside and the outside and reveals the external world as the inner depth of the psyche. Moreover, once a window is opened, the borderless situation invites chaos into the room and reminds us of the mirror-like world wherein the inner self is projected onto the outer world. At the same time, we notice that in Poe's descriptions of Gothic windows, strange sounds are heard from afar or at the lattice of the windows. These sounds gradually begin to reverberate within the room and are a sign of the cosmic intrusion of magical powers into the enclosed space. Sounds represent time just as the clock does in the black room in "The Masque of the Red Death." It is very interesting that the opening of windows and shutters triggers the mystery of the cosmic ending of the room and that sounds could control and calculate the process to the ending. Gothic windows in Poe awaken another dimension of space-time like "windows" do on a computer.

WINDOWS TO THE GOTHIC DOMAIN IN *ABSALOM, ABSALOM!*

In my essay, "Poe, Faulkner, and Gothic America,"[5] I discussed the relation between Usher and Sutpen, Poe and Faulkner, and Usher's house and Sutpen's Hundred from various perspectives and examined how each pair shares many elements of the "haunted house" story. I based my study on Leslie Fielder's socio-historical study *Love and Death in the American Novel* and David Leverenz's "Poe and Gentry Virginia,"[6] as well as the racialized structure in Poe addressed by Teresa Goddu in *Gothic America: Narrative, History, and Nature.*[7]

"Poe, Faulkner, and Gothic America" reveals how both texts begin with a similar entrance into narrative spaces through "a singular summons" conveyed by a black boy to Quentin and probably by a "black" valet of "stealthy steps" in Usher's case. The study then goes on to show how both works end with the fall of the houses and the decline of the Southern mansion. It also points out the remarkable similarity in the descriptions of the apocalyptic events that occur at the end of both works, particularly the supernatural and ominous zigzag line running from the roof and visible against the dark night with a bloody moon and three hot stars. The line "from the roof of the building, in a zigzag direction, to the base" in "The Fall of the House of Usher"[8] is echoed by the modernist ending of *Absalom Absalom!* when a "jagged" and "ragged segment of the sky" suggesting a lightning flash leads to the cosmic destruction of Sutpen's Hundred.[9]

Based on these similarities, we must realize that, in the last chapter of *Absalom, Absalom!*, the windows of Harvard College are referred to strangely and often as the target of Quentin's gaze as he finishes the story of the Sutpen Dynasty. The target of Quentin's eyes is a window, whose rectangular frame becomes identical with the square shape of a letter from another world. For him, the window is also the passageway into the Gothic narrative domain that is an essential part of the South. While staring at the window, Quentin feels "Nevermore of peace, Nevermore of peace, Nevermore" (298–299), like the speaker in Poe's "The Raven." As in Poe's works, windows in *Absalom, Absalom!* serve as entryways into an other-worldly Gothic domain quite different plane of the just prior narrative mode.

> Then the darkness seemed to breathe, to flow back; the window that Shreve had opened became visible against the faintly unearthly glow of the outer snow as, forced by the weight of the darkness. . . . He lay watching the rectangle of windows, feeling warming blood driving through veins, his arms and legs. Quentin did not answer, staring at the window; then he could not tell if it was the actual window or the window's pale rectangle upon his eyelids, though after a moment it began to emerge. It began to take shape in the same curious, light, gravity-defying attitude the-once-folded sheet of the wisteria Mississippi summer, the cigar smell, the random lowing of the fireflies (301).

The window here functions as a passageway from the real world into the Gothic domain, from which a "faint heavenly snow light" (288) comes to shine against the last hot segment of red fire seen in the burning house in the final section of the narrative. "Gothic narrative domain" refers to the magical field created by the connection between fire and snow, and the transgression or warp of time and space half a century back from Quentin's Harvard room in 1910. Quentin's gaze through the Gothic window into the complete fall of the Sutpen Dynasty and the South achieves the same effect of eternal despair as Poe does in "The Raven" with the word "Nevermore."

Another kind of window in *Absalom, Absalom!* reveals a hidden crack and opens up the text to Gothic terrain. *Absalom, Absalom!* has often drawn attention as the story of two doors, but we need to be attentive to the relationship between doors and windows in this work. After being rejected at the front door of a plantation house, the boy Sutpen comes to an understanding about life with his discovery of societal and political codes. Charles Bon is killed at the gate of Sutpen's Hundred and is thereby denied entrance to it eternally. The front gate and door are both social and class barriers, locking out all but those who are qualified to enter. The back door, where Sutpen was ordered to go by a "Negro ape-faced slave," is open to everyone unqualified to use the front door. Doreen Fowler regards the front door as Freud's "Superego" or Lacan's "Law of the Father," since many figures in *Absalom, Absalom!* are excluded from it.[10] A door finally makes a prison of impenitence for Henry, Bon, and Rosa. Goodhue Coldfield nails his attic door shut from the inside, thereby sealing the passage between himself and his community and family, and ultimately starves to death.

While access via doors is tightly and socially regulated in *Absalom, Absalom!*, windows become secret and private means of ingress and egress. In many scenes characters must enter through windows because the door is shut. For example, Rosa's aunt flees out of a window to run away with a man, and after locking himself in the attic Goodhue Coldfield is supplied food from a window. In the last scene, when Quentin and Rosa come to the ghost house and the door cannot be opened, they try to open the window with a hatchet like the one wielded by the nameless narrator in "The Black Cat."

Faulkner's heroes and heroines, blocked and confined by the Law of the Father, repeatedly perform illegal escapes and intrusions through windows. Windows embody the unsocial and sentimental secret codes that make it possible to flee from the closed space of the South. In *Children of the Dark House*, Noel Polk describes the meaning of windows in Faulkner's other novels: "Often at crucial moments in their lives characters in Faulkner stand at windows looking out, immobilized in that frame, an icon of impotence and frustration. Some escape through those windows into sexual experience (Caddy, Miss Quentin, Joe Christmas, Lena Grove), others feel a certain comfort and security being on the inside and not having to face the life outside."[11] Beyond these similarities between the two houses, we must realize that the grounds on which the House of Usher and Sutpen's Hundred are built are wetlands beyond "the causeway." As is repeatedly mentioned in the story, Usher's house stands on the marshland rising up from a tarn, which ultimately swallows all the fragments of the House of Usher. The darkness in Poe's work is connected to his interest in the atmospheric power of the tarn, where the miasma of the stagnant water settles over and determines everything. Swamps in Poe and Faulkner's works are a chaotic psychic plane under the plot. For instance, in "Ulalume" spirits of the dead roam beyond the human power of solace in the region of the tarn. In *Absalom, Absalom!*, Sutpen robbed the Chickasaw Indians of the bottomland where he and his slaves worked hard in the mud for two years to cultivate a "garden out of virgin swamp" (30). Faulkner's swamps are filled with the regular and shrill rhythms of unnamed evil birds and woodpeckers, which Southern black people call prophets. Though invisible in "The Bear" and *Sanctuary*, the birds "now and then sang back in the swamp, as though it were worked by a clock; twice more invisible automobiles passed along the highroad and died away. Again the bird sang."[12] The ominous birds in Faulkner's swamps sing with a mechanical and ruthless precision reminiscent both of automobiles and the calls of "nevermore" issued by Poe's Raven.

DRAMATIC GOTHIC WINDOWS IN "THE FALL OF THE HOUSE OF USHER"

The basic meaning of the window in Poe's work can be understood through an examination of Poe's poem "The Sleeper." Typically, windows in "The Sleeper" are very dangerous, especially at night, and permit "wanton airs" to enter the chamber through the lattice and "flit . . . in and out."

> Oh, lady bright! can it be right—
> This window open to the night?
> The wanton airs, from the tree-top,
> Laughingly through the lattice drop—
> The bodiless airs, a wizard rout,
> Flit through thy chamber in and out,
> And wave the curtain canopy
> So fitfully—so fearfully—
> Above the closed and fringéd lid
> 'Neath which thy slumbering soul lies hid,
> That o'er the floor and down the wall,
> Like ghosts, the shadows rise and fall. (I, 187)

The windows here may invite a supernatural evil power in the room and cause a momentary breakthrough to a different spatial dimension. Windows in "The Fall of the House of Usher" also serve a dramatic function similar to that of a sealed room. A magical power enters Roderick Usher's room after he "hurried to one of the casements, and threw it freely to the storm," (II, 412) to welcome the destructive gale from outside controlled by atmosphere welled up the tarn. Windows in "Usher" serve as a way for supernatural powers from the outside world to enter the haunted house. This is a typical example of Poe's Gothic window, through which we may observe the spectacle of the evolution of the story. Without these windows, the narrative would be frozen or walled in by a dead end.

Usher's Gothic windows appear to funnel destruction into the haunted house, precipitating its total collapse and raising the body of Madeline, heretofore buried in an underground mortuary. The correspondence between the gale outside and the strange sounds in the house creates a cumulative series of coincidences driving toward the catastrophic final scene that parallel the narrated words of a story within a story, the "Mad Trist" (a mad meeting of fiction and reality). It is important that Poe's Gothic art replaces or infuses virtual sounds in a narrative story with "real" sounds in the house, because it gradually makes the imaginary tangible. The sounds in the following four paragraphs develop from an auditory hallucination ("echoes") into the "counterpart" of a sound, then into a "ringing sound" in the fiction, and finally into a clear recognition of the "reverberation" of a shrill sound:

> At the termination of this sentence I started, and for a moment, paused; for it appeared to me (although I at once concluded that my excited fancy had deceived me)—it appeared to me that, from some very remote portion of the mansion, there came, indistinctly, to my ears, what might have been, in its exact similarity of character, *the echo* (but a stifled and dull one certainly) of the very cracking and ripping sound which Sir Launcelot had so particularly described. . . . Here again I paused abruptly, and now with a feeling of wild amazement—for there could be no doubt whatever that, in this instance, I did actually hear (although from what direction it proceeded I found it impossible to say) a low and apparently distant, but harsh, protracted, and most unusual screaming or grating sound—*the exact counterpart* of what my fancy had already conjured up for the dragon's unnatural shriek as described by the romancer. . . . "And now, the champion, having escaped from the terrible fury of the dragon, bethinking himself of the brazen shield, and of the breaking up of the enchantment which was upon it, removed the carcass from out of the way before him, and approached valorously over the silver pavement of the castle to where the shield was upon the wall; which in sooth tarried not for his full coming, but fell down at his feet upon the silver floor, with *a mighty great and terrible ringing sound.*" No sooner had these syllables passed my lips, than—as if a shield of brass had indeed, at the moment, fallen heavily upon a floor of silver—I became aware of a distinct, hollow, metallic, and clangorous, yet apparently *muffled reverberation.* (II,414–15; emphasis added)

Thus, the window in "Usher" is not only a boundary between two worlds but also provides the determinative moment that produces the step-by-step in-crease of sound in reverberation of a theatrical effect. Windows become invitations for Gothic power to enter into the narrative and break through the different dimensions of space and time in the text. The most impressive "door" sequence in the work provides this "entrance-like" effect during the last scene, where Madeline stands outside: "'*Madman! I tell you that she now stands without the door!*' As if in the superhuman energy of his utterance there had been found the potency of a spell—the huge antique panels to which the speaker pointed, threw slowly back, upon the instant, their ponder-ous and ebony jaws. It was the work of the rushing gust—but then without those doors *did* stand the lofty and enshrouded figure of the lady Made-line of Usher" (II, 416). Although every opening and shutting of a door in this story is an important step toward the final catastrophe, this particular "panel," which is opened by both a spell and the power of the wind coming from a Gothic window, brings the house itself into the jaws of the underworld. Thus, the windows in "The Fall of the House of Usher" work in concert toward a finale marked by the morphing of fictional sound into real sound.

THE PLUTONIAN WINDOW IN "THE RAVEN" AND "THE BLACK CAT"

The raven also enters into the room through the "lattice" window after it has been rejected at the door: "Surely," said I, "surely that is something at my window lattice; / Let me see, then, what thereat is, and this mystery explore" (I, 366). In the case of "The Raven," it is very important that the raven comes into the room through the window, not through the door. This is especially so given that the speaker in the poem initially misunderstands the tone of the knock at the door, the conventional and social means by which a visitor enters or exits a room. As in *Absalom, Absalom!*, the window in "The Raven" is contrasted with the door. A window can be used not only as an emergency, unlawful, or secret exit, but also as a kind of passageway for ghostly and magical powers.

We have a typical example of a Gothic window in *Wuthering Heights*. The lattice window in Catherine's bedroom at Wuthering Heights plays an important role. Lockwood sees the ghost of Catherine at the lattice window after a gust brushed the branch of a fir tree against the meeting: "the branch of a fir . . . touched my lattice, as the blast wailed by, and rattled its dry cones against the panes."[13] Thus, the lattice window has been connected to sounds of stormy wilderness, and suggests something for a passageway for the ghost as well.

Sound plays a key role in the raven's entry into the room. "'Tis some visitor," I muttered, "tapping at my chamber door / Only this, and nothing more." After the "fantastic terrors never felt before" evoked by "the silken sad uncertain rustling of each purple curtain" and the lapse of 6 stanzas worth of hesitation (after his step-by-step determination), the poet says, "I flung the shutter," and the raven enters the room very dramatically. Here, the contrast between stillness and sound "with many a flirt and flutter" precipitates a radical change similar to the one seen in "Usher," and the raven becomes the master, taking control of the chamber. Both in "Usher" and "The Raven," invasion through a Gothic window brings about a sudden change and initiates the total collapse of the house or chamber. The raven, whether through spell or for solace, comes from another Plutonian world and leads the room's occupant into a desperation without salvation.

It is quite significant that the raven is called upon to "Tell . . . what thy lordly name is on the Night's Plutonian shore" (I, 366). There is a scene from the "The Black Cat" in which Pluto, a cat named for the king of the underworld that had been earlier hung from a tree, was thrown into the narrator's bedroom from the outside. "Upon the alarm of fire, this garden had been immediately filled by the crowd—by some one of whom the animal must have been cut from the tree and thrown, *through an open window*, into my chamber. This had probably been done with the view of arousing me from sleep (III, 853; emphasis added). This window is another passage through which the strange and powerful return to the ordinary everyday world of a room. The room becomes an uncanny space; it changes into a magical dimension after the inflow of the power caused by the carcass of the cat. Sometimes the traces of power leave "impressions" on the walls of the everyday space: "I approached and saw, as if graven in bas relief upon the white surface, the figure of a gigantic cat. The impression was given with an accuracy truly marvelous. There was a rope about the animal's neck." One paragraph later, the "impression" is mentioned again: "Although I thus readily accounted to my reason, if not altogether to my conscience, for the startling fact just detailed, it did not the less fail to make a deep impression upon my fancy" (III, 853). A trace of magical power invades the imagination and becomes fused with the morally motivated accusation against the misbehavior of the narrator. This image of a rope is an uncanny antitype, prefiguring the narrator's fate on the gallows.

According to studies about the racial undercurrent in "The Black Cat" by Goddu, Itoh, and Leland S. Person in "Poe's Philosophy of Amalgamation,"[14] this story is a work that exposes a murder latent in the dangerous inter-dependence and struggle between a pet, an obedient and mute wife, and her husband, master. The story concludes in a victory for the domestic animal, who succeeded in sending his owner/master to the gallows. The beginning of the story filled with many pets intensifies the contrast between Gothic or Baroque feelings and those of the homely, commonplace, ordinary world. It may heighten the effects of the inseparable situation of the Gothic and the Baroque with the homely life from the beginning paragraph.

This intermingling of "homely, common, ordinary" with "wild, mad, baroque" is in accordance with the ambiguity of Gothic discourse which challenges uncertainty and the motif of the return of the repressed. The cat's presence at the last scene represents not only the transgression of an evil spirit, but also the fusion of everyday gesture and magical power. The opening of the wall through the narrator's "tapping" of the cane signs the opening of the window to the sealed domain within the tomb as in "The Raven." Before the cat appears as a black body against the white wall of the tomb, the cat gives the gradual amplification of the sounds: from "silence" to "a voice" to "a cry" to "a scream" to "a howl" and finally to "a wailing shriek":

No sooner had the reverberation of my blows sunk into silence, than I was answered by a voice from within the tomb!—by a cry, at first muffled and broken, like the sobbing of a child, and then quickly swelling into one long, loud, and continuous scream, utterly anomalous and inhuman—a howl—a wailing shriek, half of horror and half of triumph, such as might have arisen only out of hell, conjointly from the throats of the dammed in their agony and of the demons that exult in the damnation. (III, 858–59)

This sequence is a typically Poesque art of sound connected with the opening of Gothic windows. The last scene in which the cat opens its red mouth while on top of the wife's head becomes an unforgettable tableau that exposes the failure of reason and consciousness through the vengeance of the cat and the wife. Thus, "The Black Cat" is a subversive narrative about the repressed that fails to remain repressed. Pluto's vacant eye socket may serve as another example of the Gothic window. Gothic windows provide a kind of opening, fissure, or chasm where the ordinary world is invaded by the Baroque or a region of horror. Gothic windows introduce strange, unbelievable, ominous, and unforeseen horrors that lead to the vengeful chasm of the bloody mouth. It is suggested that the black cat has been feeding on the corpse of the walled-up wife: the gentle pet has been transformed not only into a gruesome icon of revenge but also into a forbidden image of "cannibalism" as pets are often so humanized as to become part of the family.

UNLOCKED WINDOWS OF "THE MURDERS IN THE RUE MORGUE"

The windows in "The Murders in the Rue Morgue" and "Hop Frog" present a different aspect of Poe's Gothic window art. In "The Murders in the Rue Morgue," the word "window(s)" is used at least twenty-six times. Windows are at the core of this mystery. The importance of this word can be explained first by Dupin's view that "most of the people have an open window inside" (II, 533). Clearly, then, Dupin's vision (or imagination) barges into people's "sealed rooms" through windows. As the sentence "it seized first the corpse of the daughter, and thrust it up the chimney, as it was found; then that of the old lady, which it immediately hurled through the window headlong" (II, 567) indicates, the assassin hauled bodies in and out of windows; a sailor peeped into a window and saw the atrocities, and a victim was hurled headlong through the window. All of the key elements of the story and plot are constructed using the apparently locked window and the paradoxical "open shutters." This window plays an important role in overturning the old world order defined by the dual dichotomy of within/without boundaries by windows. The reflected image of the headless bodies of the L'Espanayes is presented to the readers by a newspaper article. The illustration of the dead bodies in the *Gazette* is, in Poe's words, a "reflected image of the reality" and is expressed in daguerreotype style with the text displayed as a polished daguerreotype panel.

Poe praised the daguerreotype in *The Alexander Weekly* in January 1840 as the most accurate tool for presenting reality. I quote from Clarence S. Brigham's *Edgar Allan Poe's Contributions to Alexander's Weekly Messenger*: "All language must fall short of conveying any just idea of the truth, and this will not appear so wonderful when we reflect that the source of vision itself has been, in this instance, the designer. Perhaps, if we imagine the distinctness with which an object is reflected in a positively perfect mirror, we come as near the reality as by any other means."[15] Poe's admiration for the accuracy of photography prompted him to alter his method of landscape construction radically.

The basic function of a window is to act as a boundary between two worlds, the inside and the outside, with the private world inside the window and the public world outside. In Poe's story, however, windows turn the inside into the outside and vice versa. The within/without dichotomy is completely lost in the landscape of the Rue Morgue. The window that should have been closed was actually pushed open by a secret spring mechanism. Outside the room, a wild orangutan that was kept as a pet by a French sailor was running around the city of Paris. The doubly chaotic outside world, which contains both wild animals and everyday human activity, suddenly fuses and jumps like a lightning bolt on a lightning rod into the private room of mother and daughter, creating a horrific scene involving a swinging razor. Moreover, the shutters are not shut, but are instead left "swinging." The discovery of the "truth" shown by Dupin's magnifying lens is, in other words, the discovery of the identity of recreated image in a photograph and complete reality as Poe remarked regarding the daguerreotype.

Ronald Thomas, in his work on the Victorian visual imagination, explains that the photograph reveals the female bodies that have been hidden within the room; it ruthlessly focuses on the dead bodies and turns them into a "text to read" that can be controlled by specialist readers.[16] As the photograph created a new way to view the world, the window becomes a tool that externalizes the inside and becomes the medium of dangerous powers, both the inflow from the street and the outflow of female bodies to be read in the newspapers.

THE FINAL WINDOWS IN "HOP-FROG OR EIGHT CHAINED OURANG-OUTANGS"

Finally, we have another different kind of window or skylight in "Hop Frog." The function of the window in this text is to serve as an exit by which one may escape from a sealed room. Although Poe based "Hop Frog" on Shakespearean comedy (as he did with "The Masque of the Red Death"), he added elements (such as the "tar and feathers," "chained ourang-outangs," and "revenge by fire") drawn from the practice of American slavery, while also exploring the irony of torture by showing the animalization of humans and slave auctions. This story is thoroughly theatrical in its setting. Hop-Frog, as a director, has the key to the door of the masquerade ball room. Similar to "Usher," grating sounds at the window are heard twice in the middle of the story and in the catastrophic final scene. Although Hop-Frog explains that the sounds are an "odd noise outside the window," the sound is a clear sign of his hidden plot:

> There was a dead silence for about half a minute, during which the falling of a leaf, or of a feather, might have been heard. It was interrupted by a low, but harsh and protracted *grating sound* which seemed to come at once from every corner of the room. . . . It was broken by just such a low, harsh, *grating sound,* as had before attracted the attention of the king and his councillors when the former threw the wine in the face of Trippetta. But, on the present occasion, there could be no question as to whence *the sound* issued. It came from the fang-like teeth of the dwarf, who ground them and gnashed them as he foamed at the mouth, and glared, with an expression of maniacal rage, into the upturned countenances of the king and his seven companions. (III, 1349, 1353; emphasis added)

Like the black room in "The Masque of the Red Death," the grand saloon is a cosmic space that will eventually become shattered. A reversal of stage space and of the relationship between the king and the fool is completed by the fool's revenge for having been persecuted and humiliated as a prisoner of war. The captive and crippled dwarf and his girlfriend hang eight chained men—the king and his ministers disguised as ourang-outangs—on the chandelier's ceiling hook. The window in this room is a sky-light. This roof window makes "Hop-Frog" quite different from other works. In a mechanical maneuver, the "revenge by fire" motif is completed through the use of the elevation via "counter-balance" (III, 1353). The window opened in the midst of their confinement enables the impossible escape to their homeland.

Hop-Frog completes his plot of fiery revenge and flight from the confined space at the same time. Prospero destroys himself in the aesthetic closed castle, with the colored stained glass windows, that was his universe, and the space turns into darkness. With the "immense strength in his crooked arms" and the "strength in his legs," Hop-Frog manages to escape from that universe by climbing the chain up to the sky-light. That very "immense strength in his crooked arms" and the "strength in his legs" is similar to the hybrid Dirk Peters in *The Narrative of Arthur Gordon Pym* and represents another Gothic technique by which Poe has created a Gothic window opening onto an alien space where one can never be pursued, because it is a kind of hyperspace, "out of time and out of space."

NOTES

1. Joyce Carol Oates, *Haunted: Tales of the Grotesque* (New York: Plume Book, 1994), 305.

2. Joyce Carol Oates, "Poe Posthumous; Or the Light-House," in *Wild Nights* (New York: Harper Perennial, 2008).

3. Dani Cavallaro, *The Gothic Vision: Three Centuries of Horror, Terror and Fear* (New York: Continuum Intl Pub Group, 2002).

4. Dennis R. Perry and Carl H. Sederholm, *Poe: "The House of Usher," and the American Gothic* (New York: Palgrave Macmillan, 2009), 5.

5. Shoko Itoh, "Poe, Faulkner, and Gothic America," *The Faulkner Journal of Japan* 3 (2001): 17–31.

6. David Leverenz, "Poe and Gentry Virginia," in *American Face of Edgar Allan Poe*, ed. Shawn Rosenheim and Stephen Rachman (Baltimore: Johns Hopkins University Press, 1995), 210–36.

7. Teresa A. Goddu, *Gothic America: Narrative, History, and Nature* (New York: Columbia University Press, 1997).

8. Edgar A. Poe, *The Collected Works of Edgar Allan Poe, Vol. II*, ed. Thomas O. Mabbott (Cambridge, MA: Belknap Press of Harvard University Press, 1984), 417. All references to Poe's work are from the Mabbott edition: from volume I: *Poems* (1969); volumes II and III: *Tales and Sketches* (1978), hereafter referenced parenthetically by volume and page number in the text.

9. William Faulkner, *Absalom Absalom! The Corrected Text* (New York: Vintage International, 1986), 293. All further references are from this edition and noted parenthetically.

10. Doreen Fowler and Ann J. Abadie, eds., *Faulkner and Race* (Jackson: University Press of Mississippi, 1987), 95.

11. Noel Polk, *Children of the Dark House: Text and Context in Faulkner* (Jackson: University Press of Mississippi, 1990), 31.

12. William Faulkner, *Sanctuary: The Corrected Text* (New York: Vintage International, 1993), 5.

13. Emily Bronte, *Wuthering Heights* (New York: AMS Press, 1973), 24.

14. Leland S. Person, "Poe's Philosophy of Amalgamation," in *Romancing the Shadow: Poe and Race*, ed. J. Gerald Kennedy and Liliane Weissburg (New York: Oxford University Press, 2001), 205–24.

15. Clarence S. Brigham, *Edgar Allan Poe's Contributions to Alexander's Weekly Messenger* (Worcester: American Antiquarian Society, 1943), 20–22.

16. Ronald R. Thomas, "Making Darkness Visible," *Victorian Literature and the Victorian Visual Imagination*, ed. Carol T. Christ and John O. Jordan (Berkeley: University of California Press, 1995), 152–53.

Chapter Twelve

Poe's Progeny: Varieties of Detection in Key American Literary Texts, 1841–1861

John Gruesser

I shall seek this man, as I have sought truth in books;
as I have sought gold in alchemy.

—Nathaniel Hawthorne, *The Scarlet Letter*

"What are you knotting there, my man?"
"The knot," was the brief reply, without looking up.
"So it seems; but what is it for?"
"For some one else to undo," . . .

—Herman Melville, *Benito Cereno*

I knew his cunning nature too well not to perceive that this
was a trap laid for me; and so all my friends understood it.
I resolved to match my cunning with his cunning.

—Harriet Jacobs, *Incidents in the Life of a Slave Girl*

Two-thirds of a century have passed since Edmund Wilson published a trio of essays attacking detective fiction in the *New Yorker*,[1] yet skepticism, if not hostility, still often greets the genre, and it remains largely marginalized in American literary scholarship. Although critics readily credit Poe with inventing modern detection and grudgingly acknowledge that subsequent figures, including Mark Twain and William Faulkner, dabbled in it, they tend to devote little attention to the form—and the strategies for reading it—outside of the rapidly increasing number of critical essays and books devoted exclusively to detective and mystery writing. Yet from its inception detective fiction has been a remarkably "fluid" form, as Raymond Chandler termed it, that has evolved as modern society and modern literature has evolved. Thus, if we as scholars of American literature take the genre seriously, then we can see detection—and more importantly the different varieties of detection—in key mid-nineteenth-century American texts by authors not normally associated with the form.[2] Foremost among these are *The Scarlet Letter*, *Benito Cereno*, and *Incidents in the Life of a Slave Girl* by Poe's contemporaries Nathaniel Hawthorne, Herman Melville, and Harriet Jacobs respectively.

Hawthorne, who told Poe in a 17 June 1846 letter that he "could never fail to recognize the force and originality" of his tales,[3] uses the word "detect" frequently in his first novel, particularly after Roger Chillingworth commits himself to solving the mystery of Pearl's paternity. Therefore, it is appropriate to regard this character as a kind of detective, as critics such as Richard Kopley and George Dekker have done, although a very different one from Poe's Dupin.[4] When poor sales forced Melville to turn from novels to short fiction, contemporary observers, including Evert Duyckinck and Thomas Powell, noted similarities to Poe's prose,[5] and recent critics have made similar connections.[6] Because of Amasa Delano's inability to recognize and draw proper conclusions from the clues before his eyes, his role as an incompetent detective—a kind of anti-Dupin—in Melville's novella may not at first be readily apparent; however, there can be little doubt that the retrospective narrative structure and the heterogeneous content of the story link it to detection. There is no evidence that Jacobs ever met Poe, and her long-time employer Nathaniel Parker Willis by no means encouraged Jacobs to write her narrative. However, she had access to the books and periodicals owned by Willis, who was not only a friend and defender of Poe but also played a key role in bringing him considerable fame when the *New York Evening Mirror*, which Willis edited, published "The Raven" in its 29 January 1845 issue.[7] Jacobs's narrative cannot properly be called a detective story; however, there are links between Dupin's rivalry with the criminal mastermind D_____ in "The Purloined Letter" and that in the "Competition in Cunning" between Linda Brent and her master Dr. Flint in *Incidents in the Life of a Slave Girl*. The connections to and the divergences from Poe's detective stories in the texts by Hawthorne, Melville, and Jacobs serve to highlight not only the influence of detection from the 1840s through the early 1860s but also the particular concerns and the achievements of each writer, namely Poe's penchant for challenging and deceiving readers; Hawthorne's fascination with the intersections between morality and psychology; Melville's biting critique of Northern white Americans' willful obtuseness in matters of race, especially slavery; and Jacobs's efforts to create a hybrid text that reworks the conventions of the African American slave narrative and multiple Anglo American fictional genres.

Tales of detection have been around almost as long as literature itself, with stories from the Bible, *Oedipus the King*, "The Three Princes of Serendip," *Hamlet*, Voltaire's *Zadig*, and William Godwin's *Caleb Williams* standing out as some of the most notable examples. Critics generally agree, however, that Poe founded modern detection in the 1840s. This was an era known for its hoaxes, including P. T. Barnum's notorious Feejee Mermaid, concocted by sewing a monkey's upper body to the lower half of a fish.[8] Poe debunked but also perpetrated such frauds, which, despite being rigged in the house's favor, appealed to audiences because they offered diversions from the daily grind and an opportunity to match wits with the hoaxer. In three tales featuring C. Auguste Dupin, Poe conceives of detection as competition between himself and his readers, whom he challenges to arrive at the solution to the mystery while stacking the deck in his favor by using stratagems designed to throw them off the trail. He also stages a series of contests between characters and makes reference to games of skill and games of chance to underscore the competitive nature of detection and explain the analytical ability that enables the protagonist to come out on top.[9] Moreover, after creating the first story, "The Murders in the Rue Morgue" in 1841, he in effect competes with himself in its two sequels. Poe based "The Mystery of Marie Rogêt" (1842–1843), an extended exercise in armchair (i.e., purely textual) detection, on a real case, and in "The Purloined Letter" (1844), he produced his most concise and, in the opinion of many, his most successful story of detection, which concerns the location of a pilfered document and pits his brilliant sleuth against a worthy opponent, the criminal mastermind D_____. By striving to rework and outdo what he has already done, Poe weaves authorial competition into the fabric of detection, inspiring a diverse range of writers to vie with him—and each other—to bring innovations to the form.

In *The Scarlet Letter* the use of terminology typically associated with the detective form is not limited to the words "detect" and "detection"; rather, "mystery," "solution," "clew," "investigation," "investigator," "case," and "crime" appear one or more times between chapter 4 when Roger Chillingworth sets out to discover the identity of the man who impregnated Hester and the conclusion of chapter 10 when he has his answer. Echoing the statement from Sir Thomas Browne to the effect that even the most "puzzling questions" are not insoluble, which Poe uses as the epigraph to "The Murders in the Rue Morgue," the healer, herbalist, and erstwhile alchemist Chillingworth tells Hester, "there are few things—whether in the outward world, or to a certain depth, in the invisible sphere of thought—few things hidden from the man who devotes himself earnestly and unreservedly to the solution of a mystery."[10] Clearly the man formerly known as Roger Prynne regards himself as someone capable of solving the most arcane enigmas.[11]

Whereas Poe conceives of detection as an intellectual duel between one or more sets of opponents, Hawthorne takes morality as his subject in his novel, thereby anticipating the defining aspect of G. K. Chesterton's detective stories. Unlike conventional crime solvers, Father Brown does not necessarily seek to expose the wrongdoer and subject him to a public trial and community-mandated punishment. The same is true for Chillingworth. However, in contrast to Chesterton's man of God, who strives to save the souls of those whose crimes he has detected, Hawthorne's "man of science" allows his search for Pearl's father to devolve into an obsessive personal vendetta. Chillingworth may believe he acts "with the sense and impartial integrity of a judge, desirous only of truth" (129), yet, as Hawthorne's narrator notes, "as he proceeded, a terrible fascination, a kind of fierce, though calm, necessity seized the old man within its gripe, and never set him free again, until he had done all its bidding" (129). J. Gerald Kennedy's characterization of the narrator of Poe's "The Man of the Crowd" as a "deluded detective" aptly describes Chillingworth. According to Kennedy, "the psychological tension between the narrator's detached, analytical view of human experience and his mounting fascination with" the object of his inquiry functions as "the real conflict" in Poe's 1840 tale. [12] As evidenced by the regimen of private torture Chillingworth imposes on Arthur Dimmesdale, however, Hawthorne portrays the physician as a much more sinister figure than the narrator of "The Man of the Crowd." Brook Thomas notes that even though "various states began applying the so-called unwritten law by which a husband who killed his wife's lover in the act of adultery was acquitted" in the 1840s, *The Scarlet Letter* "generates little sympathy for Hester's husband." [13] In the eyes of Hawthorne's narrator, who explicitly compares him to Satan at the end of chapter 10, Chillingworth is guilty of a greater moral crime than that committed by Hester and Dimmesdale in conceiving Pearl or by the Minister in failing to own up to what he has done.

If Poe's interest in detection in the Dupin tales is primarily intellectual and aesthetic and Hawthorne's use of it in his most famous novel is largely moral and psychological, Melville incorporates key elements of the genre into *Benito Cereno* to serve a political purpose. The novella's initial publication in *Putnam's Monthly*, as Andrew Delbanco reminds us, "was in a partisan magazine committed to the anti-slavery cause." [14] In its far-from-straightforward structure, incorporation of documentary evidence, and depiction of a person confronting a puzzling mystery, the novella draws upon the nascent detective form. Yet in contrast to the brilliant Dupin, the detective figure, Captain Amasa Delano of Massachusetts, utterly fails to read the ample clues before his eyes correctly because of his naiveté and race prejudice. Although, as Cereno notes in the coda to the story, Delano's innocence and obtuseness have saved him from death at the hands of the black mutineers, Melville's narrative predicts that terrible bloodshed lies ahead for Northern whites precisely because of their willful ignorance about race and slavery.

Kevin J. Hayes accurately remarks, "Structurally 'Benito Cereno' recalls Poe's detective stories."[15] Near the end of the short novel, Melville calls attention to the story's idiosyncratic organizational scheme when the narrator states, "Hitherto the nature of this narrative, besides rendering the intricacies in the beginning unavoidable, has more or less required that many things, instead of being set down in the order of occurrence, should be retrospectively, or irregularly given."[16] The novella, in other words, resembles tales of detection, which are written backward in order to produce a specific effect, as Poe indicates in a 9 August 1846 letter to Phillip Pendleton Cooke:

> These tales of ratiocination owe most of their popularity to being something in a new key. I do not mean to say they are not ingenious—but people think them more ingenious than they are—on account of their method and *air* of method. In the "Murders in the Rue Morgue," for instance, where is the ingenuity in unravelling a web which you yourself (the author) have woven for the express purpose of unravelling?[17]

Moreover, similar to the first Dupin tale, in which newspaper accounts of the killings are quoted at length, and especially "The Mystery of Marie Rogét," in which the detective solves the case using only textual evidence, much of which appears in the story verbatim or in summarized form, Melville devotes almost one-fifth of the narrative to testimony given in court in connection with the events that occurred on the *San Dominick*. However, Melville uses this information to provide the solution to the mystery instead of presenting such raw data as clues, as Poe does.

From the start, Melville stresses Delano's limitations as an analyst. A "blunt thinking American" (57) of "a singularly undistrustful good nature" (47) who is "incapable of sounding . . .wickedness" (112) and who later acknowledges that "acuteness might have cost me my life" (115), the Yankee captain misses the clues indicating that a slave mutiny has taken place, including the decay and disorder of the ship, Cereno's odd behavior, the lack of white officers aboard the vessel, and the inappropriate attire of the surviving Spaniards. As Delbanco aptly observes, "In Amasa Delano, Melville created a character whom we recognize as an ancestor of those callow Americans who walk through the novels of Henry James mistaking malice for charm, botching uncomprehended situations with the unintended consequences of their good intentions."[18] In "The Murders in the Rue Morgue," as in the aforementioned letter to Cooke, Poe compares the solving of a mystery to the disentangling of a snarled thread, imagery which Melville incorporates into the plot of *Benito Cereno* when a Spanish sailor tosses a complicated knot he has been weaving at Delano, urging him to "Undo it, cut it quick" (76).[19]

However, the dull American captain, "knot in hand and knot in head" (76), as Melville's narrator refers to him, is unequal to the task of solving the riddle before his eyes.

Melville makes clear that Delano's incomprehension derives not simply from his inability to perceive evil but from his prejudice against blacks. Delano, who is quick to offer assistance to a slaver in distress (but not to aid a group of enslaved blacks fighting for their freedom), and who regards scenes of black subservience as "pleasing" but the sight of two blacks pushing a white as a "spectacle of disorder" (70), fails to interpret correctly what is happening on the ship because he regards whites as intellectually superior to blacks and slavery as an acceptable practice. Although on several occasions he perceives that the whites and blacks on board the vessel are performing a kind of masquerade, he can only imagine that the person orchestrating it for some kind of an evil purpose is the Spaniard Cereno. Confident that the whites are "the shrewder race" and the blacks are "stupid" (75), Delano never once suspects that a slave mutiny has taken place and that Babo is in charge. As Laurie Robertson-Lorant points out,

> Melville builds suspense by limiting his third-person narrative to Delano's point of view until the point where Delano himself realizes with a shock that the Africans have taken over the ship and slaughtered most of the whites, and that Babo has woven an elaborate web of deception from the American's own prejudices. By the end of the story, Melville has drawn readers who adopt Delano's view of the *San Dominick* into the same entangling web.[20]

As the court documents incorporated into the text reveal, Babo relies upon Delano's and his men's prejudice to make convincing the performance he is stage directing. To cite just one example, Babo has a hatchet tied to a white clerk's hand to make him look like a "renegade seaman" (113) as the crew of Delano's vessel the *Bachelor's Delight* prepares to board the slave ship.

In the novella's coda, we are told that Cereno remains haunted by "The negro" (116) until his early death, having had to alter his notions about the intellectual capabilities of blacks because of Babo, "whose brain, not body, had schemed and led the revolt" (116). However, there is no indication at the end of the story that Delano has been similarly transformed.[21] Ultimately, then, the short novel suggests that Delano and by extension Northern whites who share his beliefs about race and slavery remain unenlightened and may, consequently, in an eerie anticipation of the Civil War, be destined for a harrowing experience of their own. In the words of Eric J. Sundquist, *Benito Cereno* stands as that "most troubled and explosive tale of America's antebellum destiny."[22]

Harriet Jacobs's *Incidents in the Life of a Slave Girl* concerns competition, morality, and the politics of slavery in the antebellum United States. Similar to the battle of wits between Dupin and the Minister D_____ in "The

Purloined Letter," the moral and intellectual struggle between Linda Brent and her master Dr. Flint dominates the slave narrative. In terms of their status in society and access to power, the middle-aged, affluent, white, male slave-holder and physician Flint and the young, black, female slave Linda could not differ more. Nevertheless, the latter at times presents the competition between them as a fair fight because of her high moral purpose and willpower: "My master had power and law on his side; I had determined will. There is might in each."[23] As critics such as Jean Fagan Yellin, Henry Louis Gates, and Valerie Smith have pointed out,[24] in writing *Incidents* Jacobs draws upon the African American male slave narrative and the white, female sentimental novel to create a hybrid text that critiques and revises both traditions. Confronted with the black-white and slave-free oppositions dominating antebellum America, Jacobs emphasizes gender, asserting the common womanhood of Northern white free women and southern black slave women and exhorting the former to take a personal and political stand against the moral abomination of slavery. What I am suggesting here is that Jacobs turns to another Anglo American genre, namely detective fiction, in portraying Linda's battle with Flint. Just as G_____'s prejudices cause him to underestimate and thus be outwitted by D_____ in "The Purloined Letter," and racism causes whites generally, and Delano in particular, to underestimate Babo in *Benito Cereno*, Flint consistently underestimates Linda's cunning and is frequently outmaneuvered by her.

At key moments, Linda gambles with her own life—something which, it is worth noting, she does not legally own—to get the better of Flint. As the tenth chapter, "A Perilous Passage in the Slave Girl's Life," details, Linda enters into a sexual relationship with another white man that ultimately results in two children to escape her master's long-held obsession with making her his concubine. Then, in a scheme to prevent her children from being broken in on Flint's plantation that eventually proves successful, Linda runs away. Unable to reach the North, she uses a stratagem that to some extent recalls the one used by D_____ in outwitting the police prefect G_____ (and by Poe himself in misleading readers) in "The Purloined Letter" by secreting herself in a place that Flint passes by every day and thus somewhere he would never think to look for her. In Poe's story, Dupin explains that to hide something effectively, it must be positioned so obtrusively as to escape notice, exemplifying his point by referring to a game of location in which the experienced player chooses a word composed of large letters that stretch across the page of a map because people will miss it, instead choosing the most inconspicuous word:

> There is a game of puzzles, . . . which is played upon a map. One party playing requires another to find a given word—the name of town, river, state, or empire—any word, in short, upon the motley and perplexed surface of the

> chart. A novice in the game generally seeks to embarrass his opponents by
> giving them the most minutely lettered names; but the adept selects such
> words as stretch, in large characters, from one end of the chart to the other.
> These, like the over-largely lettered signs and placards of the street, escape
> observation by dint of being excessively obvious; and here the physical over-
> sight is precisely analogous with the moral inapprehension by which the intel-
> lect suffers to pass unnoticed those considerations which are too obtrusively
> and too palpably self-evident. [25]

The letter is right in front of G_____ and his men all the time, but they miss it
because they expect it to be hidden. Although Linda does not conceal herself
in plain sight as the Minister does the pilfered letter, she does hide in a
cramped space in her grandmother's house a mere two hundred yards from
Flint's home rather than some out-of-the-way location. According to Daneen
Wardrop, who sees more than one link between "The Purloined Letter" and
Incidents, the "loophole in the garret owes its success, in remaining impossible to expose, precisely to the fact that it is so obvious."[26]

Linda manages to transform this uninsulated and vermin-infested crawl-
space from a place of seeming limitation, danger, and weakness into a site of
possibility, safety, and empowerment. Her "loophole of retreat," as she calls
it—a phrase she derived from William Cowper, perhaps via Lydia Maria
Child, but makes completely and uniquely her own[27]—enables her to become, like Ralph Ellison's invisible man in fiction and the little-known Mary
Elizabeth Bowser in real life, a spy in enemy territory. The Union operative
Bowser, an educated, free black person with a photographic memory, worked
in the home of Jefferson Davis during much of the Civil War, disguising
herself as a dimwitted but diligent bondwoman. She availed herself of household materials to transmit information to her spymasters, hiding military
plans in empty eggshells, conveying messages in a food tray with a false
bottom, and even using the clothes she hung up to dry to send coded messages.[28] From her loophole, Linda assembles and draws upon an intelligence
network comprised of family members and other blacks in the community to
monitor and thus be able to counter Flint's actions.

In the twenty-fifth chapter, entitled "Competition in Cunning," Linda
describes how, from her loophole, she succeeds in tricking Flint into believing she has reached the North by writing him letters about her fictional life in
the free states, which she addresses and arranges to have sent to him from the
North. To make them credible, she inserts realistic details, such as New York
City street names, which she has culled—perhaps we could say purloined—
from a copy of a pro-slavery Northern newspaper: "Early the next morning I
seated myself near the little aperture to examine the newspaper. It was a
piece of the New York Herald; and, for once, the paper that systematically
abuses the colored people was made to render them service" (164). Although
by no means a full-fledged story of detection but rather a narrative that

chronicles a black woman's desperate struggle to avoid or at least limit the moral degradations of slavery, *Incidents in the Life of a Slave Girl* nevertheless incorporates the competition that characterizes such stories, and in particular the rivalry between the canny detective and the master criminal in Poe's "The Purloined Letter," in order to portray vividly the battle of wits and wills between Linda and Dr. Flint.

Amenable to a range of purposes, detective fiction over the years has appealed to a wide variety of writers. Critics such as Catherine Ross Nickerson, Kathleen Gregory Klein, Stephen Soitos, and Frankie Y. Bailey[29] have asserted that by the turn to the twentieth century, women and African American writers embraced detection as a means to address issues of gender and race. What I have tried to suggest in this essay is that the process of taking the malleable genre Poe created and using it to serve a specific moral, political, and/or artistic program begins much earlier with Poe's contemporaries in the 1850s and early 1860s in such famous texts as *The Scarlet Letter*, *Benito Cereno*, and *Incidents in the Life of a Slave Girl*. By no means do I wish to overstate the role that detection plays in these writings by Hawthorne, Melville, and Jacobs but rather propose that, along with British and French novelists, the German romantics, and American transcendentalists and reformers, we include Poe among the writers who influenced these texts.

NOTES

1. "Why Do People Read Detective Stories" (14 October 1944), "Who Cares Who Killed Roger Ackroyd" (20 January 1945), and "'Mr. Holmes, They Were the Footprints of a Gigantic Hound'" (17 February 1945); reprinted in *Edmund Wilson: Literary Essays and Reviews of the 1930s & 1940s*, ed. Lewis M. Dabney (New York: Library of America, 2007), 657–61, 677–83, and 684–90.

2. Drawing on the work of several critics, in this essay I will be using the following definition of detection: a fiction that features 1) a person or persons confronted with a puzzling mystery or disordered state of affairs, 2) the presentation of clues related to the mystery or disordered state of affairs, 3) some sort of solution to or resolution of the mystery or disordered state of affairs, and 4) some sort of an explanation of the solution to or resolution of the mystery or disordered state of affairs.

3. Nathaniel Hawthorne, *The Letters, 1843–1853, The Centenary Edition of the Works of Nathaniel Hawthorne, Vol. XVI*, ed. William Charvat et al. (Columbus: Ohio State University Press, 1985), 168.

4. Richard Kopley, *Edgar Allan Poe and the Dupin Mysteries* (New York: Palgrave, 2008), 88; George Dekker, *The American Historical Romance* (New York: Cambridge University Press, 1987), 324.

5. Hershel Parker, *Herman Melville: A Biography Volume 2, 1851–1891* (Baltimore: Johns Hopkins University Press, 2002) 188, 283, and 285.

6. See, for example, Parker, 176; Andrew Delbanco, *Melville: His World and Work* (New York: Vintage, 2006), 213, 242; and Daniel A. Wells, "'Bartleby the Scrivener,' Poe, and the Duykinck Circle," *Emerson Society Quarterly*, vol. 21 (1975): 35–39.

7. Jean Fagan Yellin, *Harriet Jacobs: A Life* (New York: Basic, 2004), 70ff; Kenneth Silverman, *Edgar A. Poe: Mournful and Ever-ending Remembrance* (New York: HarperCollins, 1991), 237–39.

8. For promotional material relating to the Feejee Mermaid, as well as contemporary reactions to this and similar spectacles, see James W. Cook, ed., *The Colossal P. T. Barnum Reader: Nothing Else Like It in the Universe* (Urbana: University of Illinois Press, 2005), esp. 185–90. On Barnum's hoaxing, see Neil Harris, *Humbug: The Art of P. T. Barnum* (Boston: Little, 1973).

9. For a reading of Poe's work, including his detection, in relation to competition, game playing, and revenge, see Kopley 21–24, and Scott Peeples *Edgar Allan Poe Revisited* (New York: Twayne, 1998), 106–32. For a reading of the Dupin tales and detective fiction generally in connection with competition and game playing, see John Gruesser, "Never Bet the Detective (or His Creator) Your Head: Character Rivalry, Authorial Sleight of Hand, and Generic Fluidity in Detective Fiction," *Edgar Allan Poe Review*, vol. 9, no. 1 (Spring 2008): 5–23.

10. Nathaniel Hawthorne, *The Scarlet Letter*, *The Centenary Edition of the Works of Nathaniel Hawthorne, Vol. I*, ed. William Charvat, et al. (Columbus: Ohio State University Press, 1962), 75. Subsequent references to the novel will be provided parenthetically in the text.

11. The objection could be raised that Chillingworth has no mystery to unravel because the reader knows (or strongly suspects) that Dimmesdale is Pearl's father. However, the fact that the audience knows that Oedipus himself is the pollution that plagues Thebes does not make him any less of a detective figure. Similarly, even though viewers learn the identity of the killer at the start of each episode of the old *Columbo* television series, this does not make the eponymous police investigator any less of a sleuth.

12. J. Gerald Kennedy, "The Limits of Reason: Poe's Deluded Detectives," *American Literature* vol. 47, no. 2 (May 1975): 186.

13. Brook Thomas, "Citizen Hester: *The Scarlet Letter* as Civic Myth," in Nathaniel Hawthorne, *The Scarlet Letter*, 2nd ed., ed. Ross C. Murfin (Boston: Bedford/St. Martin's Press, 2006), 443.

14. Delbanco, 230.

15. Kevin J. Hayes, *The Cambridge Introduction to Herman Melville* (New York: Cambridge University Press, 2007), 80.

16. Herman Melville, *Benito Cereno*, in *The Piazza Tales and Other Prose Pieces 1839–1860*, ed. Harrison Hayford, Alma A. MacDougall, G. Thomas Tanselle, et al. (Evanston, IL: Northwestern University Press, 1987), 114. Subsequent references to the novella will be provided parenthetically in the text.

17. Edgar Allan Poe, "Letter to Cooke," in *The Collected Letters of Edgar Allan Poe, 3rd ed., Vol. I*, ed. John Ward Ostrom, Burton R. Pollin, and Jeffrey A. Savoye (New York: Gordian Press, 2008), 595.

18. Delbanco, 242.

19. Although he stops short of calling Delano a detective, Dekker comments on the American captain's obtuseness in this episode, 202–3.

20. Laurie Robertson-Lorant, *Melville: A Biography* (Amherst: University of Massachusetts Press, 1998), 349.

21. It may indeed be the case that Delano is simply too obtuse to learn anything from his experience—something which the court documents quoted in the text obscure on the one hand and reveal on the other—thereby leaving the issue of slavery ominously unresolved.

22. Eric J. Sundquist, "'Benito Cereno' and New World Slavery," in *Herman Melville: A Collection of Critical Essays*, ed. Myra Jehlen (Englewood Cliffs, NJ: Prentice Hall, 1994), 186.

23. Harriet A. Jacobs, *Incidents in the Life of a Slave Girl*, ed. Jean Fagan Yellin, enlarged ed. (Cambridge, MA: Harvard University Press, 2009), 110. Subsequent references to the narrative will be provided parenthetically in the text.

24. Jean Fagan Yellin, "Introduction," in Harriet A. Jacobs, *Incidents in the Life of a Slave Girl* (Cambridge, MA: Harvard University Press, 2009), xli; Henry Louis Gates, Jr., "Introduction," in *The Classic Slave Narratives* (New York: Signet, 2002), 12; Valerie Smith, "Introduction," in Harriet Jacobs, *Incidents in the Life of a Slave Girl* (New York: Oxford University Press, 1988), xxxi–xxxiii.

25. Edgar Allan Poe, "The Purloined Letter," in *The Collected Works of Edgar Allan Poe, Vol 3,* ed. Thomas Olive Mabbott (Cambridge, MA: Harvard University Press, 1978), 989–90.

26. Daneen Wardrop, "'I Stuck the Gimlet in and Waited for Evening': Writing and *Incidents in the Life of a Slave Girl*," *Texas Studies in Literature and Language,* vol. 49, no. 3 (Fall 2007): 226.

27. According to Jean Fagan Yellin, Cowper's phrase was used in 1838 in a column called "The Curtain" published in *Freedom's Journal*; Jacobs, 373.

28. For more on Bowser, see John Cullen Gruesser, "Introduction," in *Loopholes and Retreats: African American Writers and the Nineteenth Century*, ed. John Cullen Gruesser and Hanna Wallinger (Vienna: Lit Verlag, 2009), 9–10.

29. Catherine Ross Nickerson, *The Web of Iniquity: Early Detective Fiction by American Women* (Durham: Duke University Press, 1998); Kathleen Gregory Klein, *The Woman Detective: Gender and Genre*, 2nd ed. (Urbana: University of Illinois Press, 1995); Stephen Soitos, *The Blues Detective: A Study of African American Detective Fiction* (Amherst: University of Massachusetts Press, 1996); Frankie Y. Bailey, *African American Mystery Writers: A Historical and Thematic Study* (Jefferson: McFarland, 2008).

Index

About the Contributors

Barbara Cantalupo is editor of *The Edgar Allan Poe Review* and associate professor of English at The Pennsylvania State University. Her edited books include a re-issue of Emma Wolf's novel *Other Things Being Equal* (Wayne State University Press), *Emma Wolf's Short Stories in "The Smart Set"* (AMS Press), and, with Richard Kopley, *Prospects for the Study of American Literature* (AMS Press). Her most recent book, *Edgar Allan Poe and the Visual Art*s, is currently under review by an academic press. She has published numerous articles on nineteenth-century American authors and a series of interviews with Poe scholars including Ray Bradbury, Daniel Hoffman, Burton Pollin, and Richard Wilbur, among others.

Charles Cantalupo is distinguished professor of English, comparative literature, and African studies at Penn State. His memoir, *Joining Africa: From Anthills to Asmara*, was recently published by Michigan State Univeristy Press. His poetry translations include *We Have Our Voice*, *We Invented the Wheel* (poems by Reesom Haile), and, with Ghirmai Negash, *Who Needs a Story?: Contemporary Eritrean Poetry in Tigrinya, Tigre and Arabic*. A monograph, *War and Peace in Contemporary Eritrean Poetry,* is based on the poetry in *Who Needs a Story?* His other books include two collections of poetry—*Anima/l Woman and Other Spirits* and *Light the Lights*, as well as two edited collections on Ngugi wa Thiong'o, and a monograph, *A Literary Leviathan: Thomas Hobbes's Masterpiece of Language*.

William O. Gardner is associate professor of Japanese at Swarthmore College. He is the author of *Advertising Tower: Japanese Modernism and Modernity in the 1920s* (Harvard University Asia Center, 2006) and numerous articles on Japanese modernism, including "Japanese Modernism and 'Cine-

159

Text': Fragments and Flows at Empire's Edge in Kitagawa Fuyuhiko and Yokomitsu Riichi," in *The Oxford Handbook of Global Modernisms* (Oxford University Press, 2012).

John Gruesser is professor of English at Kean University, author of four books, including *The Empire Abroad and the Empire at Home: African American Literature and the Era of Overseas Expansion* (University of Georgia Press, 2012), as well as editor of four others, most recently the anthology, *A Century of Detection: Twenty Great Mystery Stories, 1841–1940* (McFarland, 2010). He has written several articles on Poe and currently serves as president of the Poe Studies Association.

Daniel Hoffman, former poet laureate, is the author of *Poe Poe Poe Poe Poe Poe Poe*. Among his other critical studies are *Form and Fable in American Fiction* and *Faulkner's Country Matters*. His fourteenth book of poems, *Next to Last Words*, will appear from Louisiana State University Press in April 2013, on his ninetieth birthday. He is the Felix E. Schelling Professor of English Emeritus, University of Pennsylvania.

Shoko Itoh is professor emeritus of Hiroshima University, vice president of the Edgar Allan Poe Society of Japan, and president of the Ecocriticism Society of Japan. Her publications include *A Road to Arnheim: The World of Edgar Allan Poe* (1987) and *Sauntering into Inner Wilderness: Thoreau and American Nature Writing* (1998), among twenty-five other coauthored books on Thoreau, Poe, and ecocriticism. She also translated into Japanese Poe's "Al Aaraaf," Thoreau's *Wild Fruits*, and Buell's *Future of Environmental Imagination*. Her recent book is *Listen to the Alternative Voice: A Selection of the Present Day English Environmental Literature, 103* from Otowa-Tsurumi Publisher, Tokyo.

Seth Jacobowitz is assistant professor in the Humanities Department at San Francisco State University. He is primarily a specialist in modern Japanese literature and visual culture. His most recent book is *The Edogawa Rampo Reader* (Fukuoka: Kurodahan Press, 2008).

Isabel Oliveira Martins is assistant professor in the Faculdade de Ciências Sociais e Humanas, Universidade Nova de Lisboa. Her main research and teaching interests are connected to four areas: Anglo-Portuguese studies (mainly British and American travelers in Portugal), Portuguese-American studies, North American literature, and literary translation. She is a member of CETAPS (Centre for English, Translation and Anglo-Portuguese Studies) and of ULICES (University of Lisbon Centre for English Studies) as well as of other international associations of literature, languages, translation, and American studies, namely ESSE, EAAS, ACLA, and PSA.

Mark Silver is a senior program officer on the staff of the Research Division at the National Endowment for the Humanities in Washington, D.C. He is the author of *Purloined Letters: Cultural Borrowing and Japanese Crime Literature, 1868–1937* (Honolulu: University of Hawaii Press, 2008); a chapter on photographs of atom-bombed Nagasaki that appeared in *Imagining the War in Japan: Representing and Responding to Trauma in Postwar Literature and Film* (Leiden: Brill, 2010); and articles and reviews in the *Harvard Journal of Asiatic Studies,* the *Journal of Asian Studies,* the *Journal of Popular Culture,* and *Japan Forum.*

Diane M. Smith is professor of English at SUNY Farmingdale. Her research on the international influence of nineteenth-century French naturalism, championed by Émile Zola, has appeared in *Comparative Literature Studies, Excavatio* and *Works and Days.* She also coauthored a series of interdisciplinary studies tracing links between literary naturalism, photography, and silent film. These studies, published in *Zola et le texte naturaliste en Europe et aux Amériques* and the international journals *Griffithiana* and *Dedalus,* explore the early biograph films of D. W. Griffith and other American filmmakers and the graphic arts, photography, and silent film of Weimar, Germany, in relation to Zola's naturalism. More recently, Smith's comparative research into Asian literatures led to her interest in the reception of Poe's works in China.

Alexandra Urakova is a senior researcher at the Gorky Institute of World Literature and associate professor of English at the Russian State University for the Humanities, Moscow, Russia. She is the author of *The Poetics of Body in the Short Stories of Edgar Allan Poe* (in Russian), and has published on Poe both in Russian and in English.

Margarida Vale de Gato is guest auxiliary professor in the areas of translation and literature at the Faculty of Letters of the University of Lisbon and at the Faculty of Social and Human Sciences in the New University of Lisbon. As a literary translator, she has produced versions of several French and English canonical texts into Portuguese. She also published a number of essays on North American literature, translation, and reception studies, including *Edgar Allan Poe em Portugal* (2009) and the edition of Fernando Pessoa's *Principais Poemas de Edgar Poe* (2011). She is the author of the poetry collection *Mulher ao Mar [Woman Overboard]* (2010).

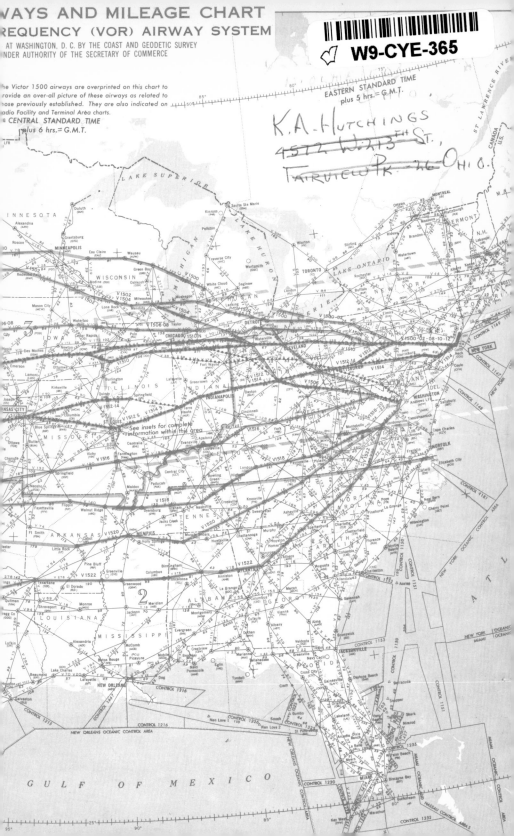

Flying the Omnirange

Flying the Omnirange

A pilot's guide to the omnidirectional radio range, distance
measuring equipment, and the Victor airways

by

CHARLES A. ZWENG
author of "Radio & Instrument Flying,"
"Airline Transport Pilot Rating," etc.

and

JOHN DOHM
former flight navigator with TWA, Pan American
Grace Airways, and American Airlines

fifth edition

published jointly by

PAN AMERICAN NAVIGATION SERVICE
North Hollywood, California

and

WEEMS SYSTEM OF NAVIGATION
Annapolis, Maryland

FLYING THE OMNIRANGE

5th revised edition June 1959
Reprinted November 1960

Library of Congress Catalog Card Number: 59-11139

Preface

Like its predecessors, this newly revised fifth edition of "Flying the Omnirange" is designed as a pilot's guide to the use of the VHF omnidirectional radio range. By this we mean that it is written from the pilot's point of view, and that its chief purpose is to explain how the omnirange is used, in the air, for navigation.

The omnirange has been operating now in the U.S. for about 15 years, and it is the basis of our complete nation-wide short-range navigation program. Nevertheless, there are evidently thousands of student, private and commercial pilots who have not yet been introduced to the relative pleasure and safety which the omnirange has brought to cross-country flying. This book is offered to those pilots.

"Flying the Omnirange" is not a technical book in the sense that it is concerned with the electronic principles of the equipment. It is written in the familiar terms of pilot language, and it attempts to explain how to fly a VOR course, how to take and plot VOR bearings, how to fly the VOR Victor airways — all with a view toward the fact that the average pilot's aircraft is equipped only with the basic omni instruments.

Through the medium of a typical cross-country flight from San Francisco to Burbank, Calif., you can follow the step-by-step procedures of omnirange operation in actual practice, and in the next chapter learn how omni has helped to take much of the tedium and guesswork out of approaches under conditions of low ceiling and restricted visibility.

Next is a survey of the principal omnirange receivers on the current market, followed by suggestions for maintaining and checking the accuracy of your receivers both on the ground and in flight. There are also chapters on distance measuring equipment (which adds a touch of luxury to your radio navigation equipment if you're wealthy enough to afford it) and the course-line computer. Finally, there is a brief discussion of the omnirange-TACAN controversy which raged a few years ago, and the new VORTAC system compromise which resulted from that controversy.

Near the back of the book you will find a number of questions and answers on VOR and DME operation, a sort of self-test on modern radio navigation. Beyond that you will find a glossary of words and terms commonly used in very high frequency radio.

We hope that this edition of "Flying the Omnirange" will stimulate those of its pilot-readers who are unfamiliar with omnirange flying to take a demonstration flight and experience for themselves the ease and safety of it all.

For the contribution of valuable material to the book we should like to thank the following individuals and organizations: the Federal Aviation Agency and Mr. Ben Stern, its Director of Aviation Information when it was still called the Civil Aeronautics Administration; the LearCal Division of Lear, Inc.; the Collins Radio Company, through its offices in both Cedar Rapids, Iowa, and Burbank, Calif.; the Aircraft Radio Corp., Boonton, New Jersey; National Aeronautical Corporation, Fort Washington, Penn.; the Radio Division of Bendix Aviation Corp., Baltimore, Md.; Mitchell Industries, Inc., Mineral Wells, Texas; Sperry Gyroscope Co., Great Neck, N. Y.; Dayton Aviation Radio & Equipment Corp., Troy, Ohio; and Wilcox Electric Co., Inc., Kansas City, Mo.

John Dohm
Charles A. Zweng

Contents

1

The VHF system

Any pilot who ever tried to make an instrument letdown on one of the old four-course low-frequency radio ranges during bad weather probably still recalls the experience with something less than pleasure.

In the first place, it was likely that when the radio range was most vitally needed—when the weather was bad—the reception was poorest. The static in the earphones sounded like a grease fire in an all-night diner, and the headaches that resulted from trying to separate the range signals from the interference were standard equipment. In many cases there weren't even any signals to be heard through the static.

It was obvious that the ranges—which had served a useful purpose in the days when air traffic was less of a problem—were operating in a frequency band (200 to 400 kilocycles) that was too vulnerable to atmospheric noise.

Moreover, the ranges were subject under certain conditions to annoying and dangerous eccentricities such as bent beams, night effect, and multiple courses. Bent beams caused pilots who started out to follow the leg of a four-course range to end up over the station on a heading as much as 45°away from the initial heading, even in nearly calm air. Multiple courses and night effect resulted not only in misleading indications but actually hazardous approaches as well.

But the greatest disadvantage of the old ranges was the plan that created four quadrants—two "A" quadrants and two "N" quadrants lying on opposite sides of the range station. This plan meant that a pilot who was lost, or whose position relative to the station was uncertain, with only the quadrant signals to guide him, had to proceed through one of the several methods of standard range orientation in order to make sure in which of the two similarly identified quadrants he was located. Orientation was a complicated and

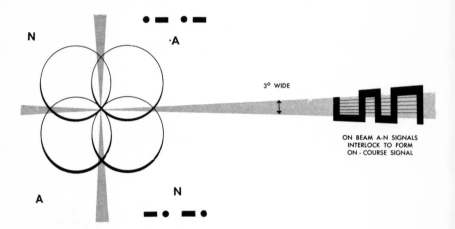

Old four-course low-frequency radio range pattern. A pilot receiving an A signal could be located in either one of two A quadrants.

time-consuming business: instrument approaches and letdowns had to be spaced out so far apart that it took only a minimum of traffic to saturate any airport's facilities.

The private or sportsman pilot, too, was aware of the inadequacy of the four-course ranges, even though he may have used them only for occasional checkpoints during a cross-country flight. Unless he was flying directly toward a range station and his course lay along one of the four legs, he had to have a direction-finder in order to derive any directional value from the range. Light planes aren't ordinarily equipped with automatic pilots, which meant that he used one hand for controlling the aircraft . . . and needed two more to take radio bearings and plot the fix on the chart. As a result, most light-plane pilots shied away from using the ranges.

As the amount of air traffic continued to build up, it became increasingly clear that the four-course ranges—and the airways of which they were the signposts—could not possibly meet the needs of present-day aviation let alone those of the future.

Since the days before War II, specialists from both military and civil aviation had been working on a new system of radio navigation and air traffic control. By 1950 they had agreed on the nature and extent of such a system, and from that time on the problem was a matter only of money, time, and electronics. The system is now installed and functioning along the airways of the U.S.

The foundation of the system is very high frequency radio (VHF) operating in the spectrum between 108 and 144 megacycles (mc). Aeronautical VHF embraces the Instrument Landing System (ILS), air-to-ground and ground-to-ground communications, and the omnidirectional radio ranges that replaced the old four-course ranges. The omnirange alone has completely changed the whole pattern of radio navigation.

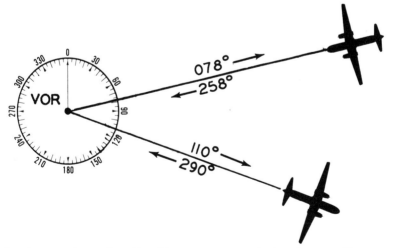

Omnirange gives the pilot his exact magnetic bearing at all times, to or from the station.

BACKGROUND FOR PROGRESS

At one time the then Civil Aeronautics Administration, Air Force, and Navy were all working independently on new radio navigation and traffic control programs. There was some justification for this since the needs of each are by no means identical.

Eventually, however, it became clear that aviation could not afford the luxury (and confusion) of three, or even two, different kinds of airway systems operating side-by-side. A group called the Radio Technical Commission for Aeronautics (RTCA), representing all aviation interests in the nation, was then set up to study the problem of air navigation. Finally the divergent viewpoints were reconciled and the RTCA came up with a detailed and forward-looking program, one that would fill the needs of the airlines, private fliers, the military, and the non-scheduled carriers. The plan was divided into two parts—a transition program to be completed in five years and an ultimate program which would require another ten years.

This plan is now considered the "Bible" for all future work in air navigation and traffic control.

Until recently there were nearly 400 of the old low-frequency ranges located along 72,000 miles of civil airways in the U.S. About 88 of these have been retained and are still operating, primarily for the Air Force and Navy. Another 60 or so LF ranges have been retained as weather broadcasting stations, in remote areas. The A and N signals are no longer transmitted from these 60 stations, and consequently there are no course legs, although the continuously transmitted signal can be used for homing. Eventually even these LF ranges will be decommissioned.

The period of changeover from LF ranges to omniranges and from LF to complete VHF communication was the transition period in the RTCA program. This period also saw the installation of the first distance measuring equipment (DME), which works in conjunction with the omnirange to provide the pilot with not only course and bearing information but distance information as well. This means an almost instantaneous and continuous fixing of position.

The ultimate objective of the RTCA program is a system of navigation and communication wholly based on VHF and even ultra high frequency (UHF) radio, with as much directly visual and automatic control as possible.

Here is the long-range program as visualized by the **FAA** and planned for completion in the 1960's:

Before a pilot takes off on a flight a landing time will be reserved for him at his airport of destination. While he is enroute a dial will tell him continually, in minutes and seconds, whether he is ahead of or behind his precise schedule, and he will slow his plane down or speed it up accordingly. On a screen in the cockpit the pilot will see a pictorial presentation of everything around him. This picture, probably televised from the ground, will show his own aircraft in relation to others in his vicinity, indicate obstructions or other hazards, and even show the location of storms and turbulent air.

At the same time, radar will be continuously watching him from

Airway and airport surveillance radar play an important part in the traffic control program. (FAA photo)

the ground. By means of a block system, something like that used on railroads, the pilot will be assured that he is in safe air space at all times.

His aircraft will carry equipment which continuously transmits to the ground the readings of the cockpit instruments. Electronic brains on the ground will check these readings automatically against information derived from radar and other sources. If, for example, the altitude shown by ground radar differs from the altimeter reading in the cockpit, the pilot will be instantly and automatically notified.

If the pilot wishes to change his altitude or his flight plan he will be able to communicate with the ground stations by pushing an appropriate button. Approval or disapproval will be flashed back to his cockpit in a fraction of a second, since the calculations will be made by automatic machines on the ground.

This system may sound a bit fantastic in some respects, especially since it is due for realization within the next 6 or 7 years. Nevertheless, nearly all of the mechanisms and instruments upon which it is predicated already are in development and some of them are in actual use. The program will almost completely solve the weather problems which plague aviation today, and it will permit aircraft to fly their schedules with clocklike precision and absolute reliability.

The new system is designed with military as well as civil requirements in mind. The system could give instant warning of an enemy attack, if such calamity should come to pass, and permit interceptors to be vectored for counter attack. It would permit quick and heavy concentration of airpower anywhere it is needed within the country, and then assist in maintaining a continuous flow of supplies and manpower to the area.

These, then, are the possibilities for air navigation and control in the immediate future. The point to be emphasized, however, is that the transition period has been completed and the omniranges and distance measuring equipment—which form the spine of the new system—are functioning. The pilot who doesn't realize that the old ways of radio navigation and control are changing will be left as far behind aviation progress as the triplane.

ADVANTAGES OF THE VHF SYSTEM

A few of the many advantages inherent in the omnirange-DME system of navigation should be listed:

(1) The pilot flies by eye instead of ear. Instead of listening hour after hour to the monotonous dit-dah or dah-dit of the range signal, he holds his course by watching the indications of a vertical needle on his instrument panel.

(2) The omnirange operates in the very high frequency part of the radio spectrum. In this band, as pointed out earlier, there is a minimum amount of static to interfere with the signals.

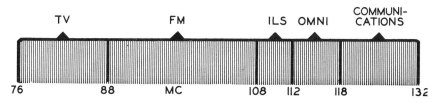

Omnirange operates in the VHF band between 112 and 118 megacycles.

(3) The omnirange produces a theoretically infinite number of courses which radiate from the station like the spokes from the hub of a wheel.

(4) With the omnirange there is no possibility of quadrant confusion. The pilot can read on a simple indicator his direction in degrees from the station at all times. A simple "to-from" indicator tells him whether the bearing shown on the dial is to the station or from it.

(5) The DME indicator—simplicity personified—tells the pilot continuously how far his aircraft is from the VOR-DME station.

(6) Unless terrain clearance is a problem, no plotting of fixes or bearings is necessary: the pilot merely holds the course indicated by the omnirange and calculates his estimated time of arrival according to the indication of the DME dial.

On the basis of these advantages alone, the omnirange provides easier, safer and more reliable air navigation. The airborne omnirange receiver, the equipment which the pilot actually carries in his plane and uses for navigation, is extremely simple to operate. Anyone who can fly by magnetic compass can learn basically all he needs to know about the use of the receiving equipment in a short time. The best way to become acquainted with omnirange is to (1) study the fundamental principles of transmission and reception, and (2) ask one of the local omnirange equipment dealers for a demonstration. Anyone who first takes the trouble to learn something about the theoretical operation of omnirange is obviously bound to get the most value from this new facility.

The least expensive omnirange receiver currently available sells for around $400.00. However, continued research on cheaper materials, combined with mass production, no doubt eventually will bring costs down to a figure more attractive to private plane owners.

Instrumentation in this Beech Bonanza includes Lear omnirange receivers and VHF communications equipment. (Lear, Inc., photo)

The course-line computer brings even more flexibility to the omni-range-DME combination. The computer, a lightweight airborne electronic "brain," makes it unnecessary to fly directly to or from an omnirange. Using the computer, DME, and omnirange, a pilot can fly a straight course between any two selected points on the map.

In order to set the computer the pilot adjusts its dials for a proposed course angle, bearing of destination from station, and distance of destination from station. Then the computer, absorbing additional data from nearby omniranges and DME transmitters, continuously solves the specific navigation problem involved; that is, it furnishes the pilot with a course and distance to his destination. All the pilot must do is keep the vertical needle on the dial centered, as he does in flying to or from an omnirange.

These three units working together—omnirange, DME and computer—make off-airway navigation as easy and accurate as on-airway flying. For congested airways the units make possible multiple airways, parallel to each other and a few miles apart, in whatever number current traffic demands.

The air navigation and traffic control program also calls for complete VHF communication between air and ground. All FAA airway and airport facilities are equipped with transmitters and receivers operating in this nearly static-free radio band, and an increasing amount of private-plane traffic is being controlled over the new and higher frequencies. All airline and military air-ground communications is by means of VHF.

Any pilot, private or otherwise, who has received landing instructions or a weather report over VHF facilities, wonders how he ever managed to survive with only low-frequency communication. On VHF the tower operator's voice comes through loudly and clearly, free of interference. There is little chance of misinterpreting instructions on VHF.

Inasmuch as omnirange also operates in the VHF band, nearly all radio equipment manufacturers package VHF voice receivers and transmitters along with the omnirange receivers, even though both units are also available independently. This means that more and more lightplane pilots are discovering the wonders of VHF air-to-ground communication.

Also included in the program are greatly expanded facilities for ILS (instrument landing system); precision beam radar (in which an operator watching a radar screen on the ground "talks" the pilot down to the runway over ordinary voice radio); surveillance radar (used to guide aircraft to a point where precision beam radar can pick them up for ground controlled landings), and new electronic devices to replace the laborious hand-posting system now used in airway traffic control offices to keep track of enroute planes.

If you are one of the approximately 60,000 light-aircraft owners in the United States, it is possible that you are one of the majority who restrict your flying to your local area. If such is the case, it isn't likely that you will become the owner of expensive dual omnirange receivers, distance measuring equipment, or a course-line computer. On the other hand, it is quite possible that very soon you will install one of the smaller and less elaborate VOR receivers designed to fit the needs of the lightplane owner. If and when you do, it won't be long before you'll be off on a cross-country flight. And you may be agreeably surprised that cross-country navigation can be so simple . . . when you fly by omnirange.

2

How omnirange works

VHF RADIO WAVES

In order to understand the operating principles of the omnirange
it is first necessary to know something of the characteristics of
VHF radio waves.

Standard radio broadcasting stations operate in a frequency band
of approximately 550 to 1,600 kilocycles, slightly higher than low-
frequency aeronautical radio (200 to 400 kilocycles). In the range
above 1,600 kilocycles are the shortwave bands used for international broadcasts, police calls, and some forms of aeronautical
communication. Above this latter range in the frequency ladder,
measurements are made more conveniently in megacycles, which are
kilocycles multiplied by 1,000.

The frequencies just above the standard broadcast band, like
those below it, are plagued by overcrowding and static traceable to
weather, night effect, and so on. The frequency range from five to
30 megacycles, occupied chiefly by international broadcasts, amateur radio communication, and extremely long-range transmission, is
often unreliable for short-range communication.

The next step up the frequency ladder, in the wide band between
30 and 300 megacycles, is the new realm of VHF aeronautical radio.

As anyone knows who has listened at home to frequency modulation radio (FM), which operates between 88 and 108 megacycles, this VHF area is almost completely free of static and interference. FAA aircraft communication facilities start just above the FM broadcast band.

VHF waves have characteristic properties. Low-frequency waves are transmitted over long distances because they are reflected back and forth between the earth and the ionosphere. VHF waves, on the other hand, ordinarly do not "bounce." They continue straight out

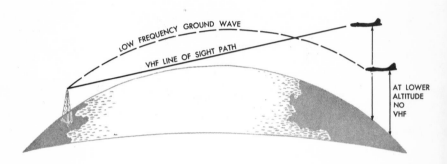

into space. They can be received, therefore, only slightly below a line-of-sight course from the transmitter. Obviously there are disadvantages inherent in line-of-sight transmission, one of which is the limitation on range. At higher altitudes, however, VHF signals can be received 200 miles away. Furthermore, because of their line-of-sight signal pattern, VHF stations below the horizon and located several hundred miles apart cannot interfere with each other, even when transmitting at or near the same frequency.

Because the majority of aircraft operate between 2,000 and 10,000 feet above the terrain, the line-of-sight characteristic makes VHF ideal for aeronautical purposes. Even at 1,000 feet an aircraft is in VHF range of every station within a radius of 50 miles.

In addition, airborne VHF transmitters are smaller and lighter than the corresponding low-frequency equipment, and for normal purposes of communication less power is required with VHF.

VHF communication facilities are available at all major airports in the U.S., but low-frequency facilities are also in operation.

Here is the approximate range for VHF transmission over flat terrain:

Aircraft Altitude	Range
1,000 feet	55 miles
1,500 feet	65 miles
2,000 feet	75 miles
2,500 feet	85 miles
5,000 feet	110 miles
10,000 feet	150 miles
15,000 feet	185 miles
20,000 feet	210 miles
30,000 feet	255 miles
40,000 feet	290 miles
50,000 feet	320 miles

OMNIRANGE TRANSMITTER OPERATION

The word "omnirange" is a combination of the Latin "omnis" (meaning "all") and the familiar word "range." The VHF omnirange is abbreviated VOR.

Transmitting VHF radio waves in all directions of the compass, the omnirange produces a theoretically infinite number of courses which radiate out like spokes from the hub of a wheel. These courses are called radials. Directional information is thus generated at the station and transmitted to the aircraft continuously. Airborne omnirange equipment intercepts this signal and converts it into a visual directional indication for use by the pilot.

The principle of the omnirange is based on the comparison of the phase difference between two radiated audio-frequency signals, the difference in phase varying with change in azimuth.

One of these signals is non-directional. It has a constant phase throughout its 360° of azimuth and is called the "reference" phase. This signal is radiated from the center antenna of a five element group. In order to separate the two signals for comparison in the receiver, a 10-kilocycle FM subcarrier is used to carry the reference signal.

The second signal rotates at a speed of 1,800 rpm, varies in phase with azimuth, and is called the "variable" phase. It is produced by a group of four stationary antennas connected in pairs to a motor-driven goniometer, or inductor. As the goniometer revolves,

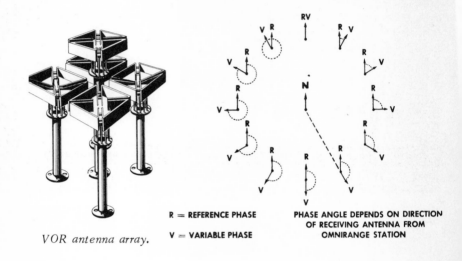

VOR antenna array.

R = REFERENCE PHASE

V = VARIABLE PHASE

PHASE ANGLE DEPENDS ON DIRECTION OF RECEIVING ANTENNA FROM OMNIRANGE STATION

RF voltage fed to each pair of antennas varies sinusoidally at the rate of 30 cycles per second to produce the rotating field.

The rotating signal is initially set so that at magnetic north the reference and variable signals are exactly in phase. In all other directions the positive maximum of the variable signal occurs at some time later than the maximum of the reference signal. The fraction of the cycle which elapses between the occurrence of the two maxima, at any point in azimuth, identifies the azimuth angle of that point.

One of the best ways to visualize the method of determining bearings from an omnirange transmitter is to use the analogy of an airport light beacon. If the identification flasher cam is so adjusted that the green airport identification light flashes each time the light beam sweeps past magnetic north, and if the beacon rotates clockwise at the rate of six revolutions per minute (i.e., one revolution

Omnirange and DME transmitter housing. VOR antenna is enclosed within plastic dome. Vertical pipe-like structure above is DME antenna. (FAA photo)

each 10 seconds, or 36° per second), we can determine our direction from the beacon.

We would, in this case, start a stop-watch at the instant we see the beginning of the green flash, and then stop the watch when the rotating beam sweeps past us. If we multiply by 36 the number of seconds shown on the stop-watch we obtain our magnetic bearing from the beacon.

For example, if precisely five seconds elapse from the time of the beginning of the green flash until the rotating beam flashes past us, then our bearing from the beacon is 180°(5 X 36 = 180).

It is evident that the same time would elapse and the same bearing be obtained should the observer move directly toward or away from the beacon without changing direction with respect to the beacon, regardless of distance. If the observer should move around counterclockwise toward the beacon, less time should elapse between the green flash and the beacon flash. If the observer moved around clockwise, the interval would be greater. In effect, the reference and variable voltages of the omnirange provide the same information electronically that the flasher and beacon supply visually in the above example.

RECEIVER OPERATION

The airborne receiving system used with the omnirange is composed of a special V-type dipole antenna and three basic circuit groups: (1) frequency control, (2) conventional superheterodyne receiver, and (3) navigation circuits.

The function of the navigation circuits is to measure the phase angle between the reference voltage and the variable voltage. As described previously, each point or degree of azimuth radially from the VOR transmitter has a definite, fixed phase difference between the reference and the variable signals. Therefore, if the receiving equipment can translate and provide in readily usable readings on the instrument panel the phase difference existing at the receiving position, a bearing from the transmitter is obtained. Similarly, if the equipment can be adjusted to any desired bearing (or phase difference), and indicate when the aircraft has reached that bearing, it is possible to preset courses and then fly to and continue along them. This is exactly what the VOR receiver is designed to do, and a great deal of navigational information is available to the pilot who takes advantage of all its possibilities.

Thus the navigation circuits are connected to a manually-operated course selector, a left-right or deviation indicator (the familiar localizer pointer of the ILS indicator), and a special device known as a to-from or sense indicator. (There are some differences in VOR indicators but for the most part the designs are somewhat similar. All of the principal receivers are discussed in detail in Chapter 5.)

TUNING THE RECEIVER

Some VOR receivers are equipped with two-stage frequency selectors that automatically tune in the transmitters at the point of best reception. On this kind of selector there are two tuning dials, a smaller one for the fractions of a megacycle and a larger one for the units of whole megacycles. Since all omnirange, ILS, and most VHF communications channels operate in the range between 108 and 136 mc, there is no need to change the selector from the 100 mc position. Thus, a pilot tuning to a VOR station with a frequency of, say, 117.6 mc, turns the larger selector dial until 17 appears in the window directly below the 1 that represents 100 mc. He then turns the smaller dial until .6 appears in the window below 117. The receiver is now tuned to the point of maximum signal reception from the VOR transmitter.

Positive or automatic frequency selector, left, and conventional rotatable tuning unit, right. (Collins Radio Co. and Lear, Inc.)

Other airborne receivers are equipped with frequency selectors that are tuned in the conventional manner: a rotating dial is turned until the proper frequency is aligned beneath an index. With these selectors it is necessary to tune the dial manually until the point of maximum reception is reached. This point can be determined aurally by listening through the headphones or loudspeaker to the station's identification signals.

In any case, after the station is tuned in it should be identified positively since VHF facilities in the 108-136 mc band are separated by very small frequency-margins. Each station transmits its three-letter coded identification continually. Most stations are identified by letters that suggest the names of the cities near which they are located. San Francisco, for example, is identified as SFO, Dallas as DAL, Albany, New York, as ALB, and so on.

THE SUPERHETERODYNE RECEIVER

All radio waves striking an aircraft's receiving antenna induce electrical impulses into the antenna. It is the function of the receiver to select the impulses from the station whose frequency has been tuned on the frequency selector, and then to convert these impulses into useful navigation information.

THE NAVIGATION COMPONENTS

The navigation circuits of most VOR receivers are connected to three basic components that provide omnirange course or bearing information: (1) the course selector, (2) the left-right indicator (also called course indicator), and (3) the to-from indicator.

The course selector may be either one of two types. One is a 360° azimuth dial with a manually rotatable pointer, and the other is a three-digit mechanical counter on which any value from 0° to 360° may be set. In either case, it is used to establish the magnetic bearing or course of an aircraft to or from a VOR station.

The to-from indicator may be either a small needle that points to the words "to" or "from" printed on the dial or it may be a simple indication of either word as it appears in a small window in the dial.

The left-right indicator is a vertical needle pivoted at the top of a dial—the same needle used to indicate left or right deviation from the ILS localizer during an approach and letdown on the Instrument

Standard course-deviation or left-right indicator, which is also used in ILS flying, and (right) A.R.C. instrumentation combining all three functions of left-right indicator, course selector, and to-from meter. (Aircraft Radio Corp.)

Landing System. In omnirange flying, the left-right indicator tells the pilot when he is left or right of a selected course to or from the VOR station. When the needle is centered, the magnetic course the aircraft is making good is the value set on the course selector.

These are the three basic navigation components of the airborne omnirange receiving system—the course selector, to-from indicator, and left-right indicator. Some receivers combine the indications of all three on one dial, and still others combine two of the indications on a single dial. Two other omnirange receivers—those made by Collins and Bendix (See Chapter 5)—include a fourth instrument, the radio magnetic indicator (RMI), which combines the presentation of a gyrosyn compass and radio compass.

The RMI includes a circular compass card that rotates as the aircraft turns, so that the compass heading (or magnetic heading if all deviation is removed from the compass) is always indicated under the reference point at the top of the instrument. The double-barred needle always points toward the VOR station to which the receiver is tuned. When the aircraft is headed directly toward the station, the pointer of the double-barred needle and the magnetic heading of the aircraft are both directly under the reference point at the top of the dial. When the aircraft is turned 90° to the right, the compass card rotates 90° in a counterclockwise direction. At the same time, the double-barred needle also rotates 90° inasmuch as it always points toward the station. However, it rotates with the compass card and therefore its position relative to the compass card does not change except as the aircraft's position relative to the station changes. Thus, the indication of the double-barred needle is always the magnetic bearing of the aircraft to the station.

The single-barred needle is identical in operation, and is provided for simultaneous bearings on a second station. It may be connected to the omnirange receiver as a dual installation or to a radio compass receiver for bearings on low-frequency navigation aids.

DETERMINING A BEARING

To determine the bearing of an aircraft from an omnirange station:

(1) Tune in the station, and identify it aurally by means of its three-letter code transmission. When the station is too far from the aircraft or is otherwise receiving a weak signal, the to-from needle points to a red warning sector rather than "to" or "from."

(2) If the station's signal is being received properly, rotate the course selector until the left-right indicator is centered.

(3) The magnetic bearing of the aircraft to or from the station is then indicated on the course selector, regardless of the aircraft's heading.

Suppose, for example, that a pilot flying in a general west-to-east direction is passing somewhere to the south of a VOR station, and decides to take a bearing on it. He tunes in the station and receives a strong signal. The left-right indicator is at the extreme side of the dial. The pilot slowly rotates the course selector, and the needle begins to move toward the center. When it is finally centered vertically, the pilot notes that the course selector is set at 152° and the to-from needle points to "from." This means that at that moment the aircraft bears 152° from the VOR station.

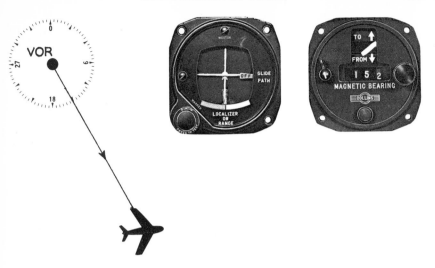

The heading of the aircraft does not in any way enter into the determination of this bearing. The bearing is as rigidly fixed in space as a highway is on the earth's surface: regardless of the aircraft's heading, the aircraft bears 152° magnetic from the station.

FLYING A VOR COURSE

Flying a course directly toward or away from a VOR station is even simpler than taking bearings, since no plotting or chart work is involved. Suppose a pilot wants to fly directly toward a station. He tunes in the station and rotates the course selector until the left-right needle is centered. If the to-from indicator points to "to," the value on the course selector is the magnetic course to fly to the station. If it points to "from," the pilot can either fly a course reciprocal to the one indicated on the course selector or else rotate the course selector approximately half way around the dial until the left-right needle is centered again and the to-from indicator points to "to."

If the pilot wants to fly a course away from a station, the procedure is reversed. That is, the course selector is rotated until the left-right needle is centered and the to-from indicator points to "from."

In either case, whether he wants to fly a course toward or away from a station, he takes up a magnetic heading approximately the same as the value set on the course selector when the left-right needle is centered. As long as he keeps the needle centered he is making good a course that will bring him directly over the station, assuming of course that the to-from needle indicates "to."

In effect, the omnirange automatically compensates for drift. A crosswind can cause the aircraft to drift from a selected VOR course, but not if the pilot keeps the left-right indicator centered. In the process he may have to alter the compass heading to left or right, but the point is that he will automatically find the heading necessary to hold the course as long as he keeps the left-right indicator centered.

In cases where the plane does drift off course, the left-right indicator can be re-centered and a new course flown to the station. When an aircraft drifts off course while flying away from a station, however, the aircraft should be returned to the original course by altering the heading, as usual, in the direction toward which the left-right needle points.

In most cases the pilot will preselect a course that he wants to make good to a VOR station. Suppose, for example, he wants to fly from A to B, as in the illustration. This course leads directly across an omnirange station. The true course from A to B (090°) he measures with a plotter on the chart, and then applies the average variation (5° westerly) to determine the magnetic course (095°). He

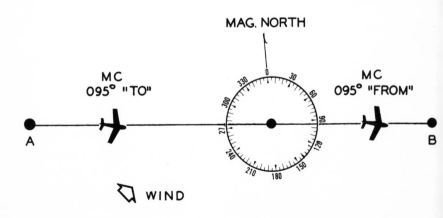

turns his aircraft to a magnetic heading of 095°, and rotates the course selector also to 095°. The left-right indicator is centered and the to-from needle points to "to."

Eventually, the left-right indicator begins to move to the right of center, although the pilot is still holding a magnetic heading of 095°. This means that the aircraft is drifting to the left of course. The indicator, as usual, points the way back to course. The pilot increases the magnetic heading to 105°, and slowly the left-right needle returns to center. Further on along the course, however, the needle moves slightly to the left of center. The pilot has corrected heading too much to the right, and the aircraft has now drifted a small distance to the right of course.

This time the pilot corrects the magnetic heading back to 100°—a correction of only 5°. The left-right indicator now reaches center and holds there. The pilot has found the heading that, under prevailing wind conditions, holds the aircraft on the 095° magnetic course to the VOR station. The wind component is from the right, and the amount of drift correction is 5° right, but the pilot is not concerned with this fact. All he's interested in is keeping the left-right indicator centered. The omnirange takes care of the rest.

As the pilot approaches the station the left-right needle begins to oscillate slightly. Finally, as the aircraft crosses the station, the to-from indicator changes abruptly from "to" to "from." The course selector and the magnetic heading remain the same—095°—as the aircraft proceeds away from the station. The left-right needle indication is also the same. If the aircraft drifts off to the right, the needle still points to the left and the pilot corrects the heading to the left.

In other words, regardless of whether the aircraft is heading toward or away from the station, the left-right needle points to the omnirange course set on the course selector. If there is any convenient rule about omnirange flying, it is this:

Always fly into the needle. When the needle points to the left, the aircraft must be turned to the left in order to return to course. When it points to the right, a correction to the right is required.

Like most rules, this one involves a minor exception. It was seen in the foregoing example how the to-from indicator changed from "to" to "from" as the aircraft passed over the VOR station but the pilot continued on the same heading and the left-right needle maintained the same sense indication. However, if the pilot after passing over the station had made a 180° procedure turn without changing the course selector, the to-from indicator would still indicate "from" but the left-right needle would now point away from the 095° course rather than toward it. The simplest procedure in this case would be for the pilot to rotate the course selector to the reciprocal bearing of 275° while making the procedure turn. The to-from indicator would then indicate "to" and the 275° course would be flown by making corrections toward the left-right needle as usual.

This exception to the "fly into the needle" rule occurs ordinarily only during VOR instrument approaches, and for the most part will not confuse the pilot if he remembers that the magnetic compass and the course selector should be in general agreement when flying an omnirange course—that is, the rule does not hold when there is a difference of approximately 180° between the readings on the compass and the course selector.

To summarize the procedure for flying a VOR course:

(1)   Rotate the course selector to the value of the magnetic course desired.

(2)   Turn the aircraft to approximately the same magnetic heading.

(3)   Adjust the aircraft heading as necessary until the left-right needle is centered and the to-from indicator points to "to" when flying toward a station, or "from" when flying away from it.

(4)   When the needle deviates from center, turn the aircraft into the needle, that is, to the left when the needle points to the left, and to the right when it points to the right.

(5)   When the aircraft passes over the station, the to-from indicator changes from "to" to "from."

(6)   If the same course is to be flown away from the station, maintain that course by keeping the left-right indicator centered in the same way, with the same setting on the course selector and an indication of "from" on the to-from indicator.

OFF—COURSE VOR FLYING

In aircraft equipped with a single VOR receiver but not equipped with distance measuring equipment or a course-line computer, the simplest method of flying the omniranges is to fly a course from station to station. However, it is also possible to fly VOR between any two points not equipped with omnirange facilities but which are within signal-reception range of a VOR transmitter.

For example, a pilot plans to fly from St. Clair to Laurelgrove. Laurelgrove has no omnirange facility, but is located 25 miles south of Woodbridge, which does have. On his chart the pilot draws a course line from St. Clair to a point intersecting the bearing line from the Woodbridge VOR to Laurelgrove. This course is set definitely to one side or the other of the destination in order to prevent any uncertainty about which way to turn once the Woodbridge VOR bearing is intercepted. In the example the course is set to the right of Laurelgrove simply because it represents the shorter distance between St. Clair and Laurelgrove.

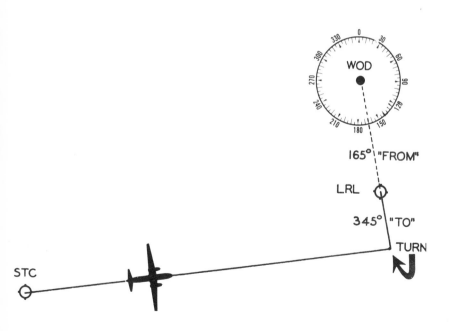

The pilot sets 165° on his course selector, the value of the bearing from Woodbridge to Laurelgrove, and then maintains by dead reckoning a heading calculated to make good the course between St. Clair and the turning point to Laurelgrove. When he starts out from St. Clair the left-right needle is at the extreme left position on the dial. As he approaches the 165° radial from Woodbridge, however, the needle moves toward center.

When the needle is finally centered and the to-from indicator points to ''from,'' the pilot knows he has reached the bearing line extending from the Woodbridge VOR through and beyond Laurelgrove. He resets the course selector to 345°, the reciprocal of the 165° bearing, and the to-from indicator changes to "to." The pilot turns the aircraft to a magnetic heading of 345° and keeps the left-right needle centered until he arrives over Laurelgrove, his destination.

If Laurelgrove should be within range of a second VOR station the pilot could obtain a definite fix over his destination, even if he were on instruments, by taking a cross-bearing on the second station.

PLOTTING VOR BEARINGS AND FIXES

Flying an omnirange course or taking a single bearing on an omnirange course does not fix an aircraft's position—it provides only a single line of position somewhere along which the aircraft is located. A definite VOR fix is obtainable only (1) when the aircraft is directly over the station, (2) when a VOR bearing is crossed with another bearing from a second station, or (3) when the aircraft crosses an airway marker beacon while on an omnirange course. In fast aircraft this limitation of the single VOR bearing is not important, since VOR stations are spaced along the airways about every 100 miles, providing a fix nearly every 20 or 30 minutes. Fixes for off-airway flying in slower aircraft, however, require the plotting of two or more bearings on a chart.

All aeronautical charts used in civil flying in the U.S. show the location, frequency, and identification of VOR stations. In addition, a 360° compass rose is printed around each station. These compass roses are oriented to magnetic north, which means that they are offset from true north by the amount of magnetic variation at the omnirange site. The compass rose around each station thus represents the exact magnetic bearing of each radial from the station.

To plot a VOR bearing on a chart:

(1) Tune in the station, rotate the course selector until the left-right needle is centered, and note whether the bearing is "to" the station or "from" it.

(2) If the bearing is from the station, place the straight-edge of a plotter along the VOR site and through the value on the compass rose corresponding to the value on the course selector. Draw a light pencil mark along the straight-edge in the approximate vicinity of the aircraft's estimated position. This is a single line of position.

(3) If the bearing is to the station, either (a) add or subtract 180° from the value on the course selector, or else (b) rotate the course selector about 180° until the left-right needle is again centered and the to-from indicator reads "from." Plot the bearing on the chart exactly as above.

To plot a position fix, select a second VOR station and plot the bearing from it in the same way as outlined in (2) and (3) above.

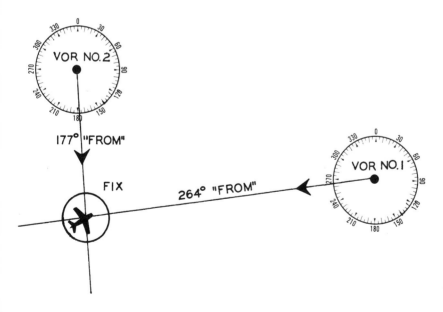

The point where the two bearings intersect is the aircraft's position.

The most accurate fixes result when the bearings are about 90° apart. The first of two bearings should always be made on the station most closely in line with the fore-and-aft axis of the aircraft—off the nose or the tail. If this practice is followed, it is unnecessary to advance the first bearing along the course to the time of the second bearing. Ordinarily, however, even when both stations are to the side and abeam of the aircraft, the first of the two bearings need not be advanced if only two or three minutes elapse between bearings. The loss of accuracy is usually small, especially when small-scale charts are used.

A second method of saving time when determining a VOR fix, although rather crude by precision flying standards, is to plot the bearings by what might be called the "line-of-sight" method. The compass roses around the VOR stations on the Sectional and World Aeronautical charts are 35 miles in diameter and printed in dark blue, which means they are prominently displayed. It is quite possible (and even practical if you're flying without a co- or auto-pilot) to draw the bearing out from the station through the proper radial by freehand, with nothing more to guide your line than the eye's "logic." With a little practice the results can be surprisingly accurate.

For practical purposes, no plotting at all is necessary in airways flying. In the first place, the aircraft is flying between VOR stations, on a course from one station or to the other. This represents one continuous line of position. The stations are seldom more than 100 miles apart, and the nationwide average may be close to 70 miles. Thus, groundspeed checks from station-to-station are fairly frequent. Moreover, the VOR airways are literally dotted with marker beacons. Every time the pilot crosses one of these beacons he has another fix—one line of position from the omnirange radial he is following, one from the beacon located in the center of the airway.

This is literally pencil-less, plotter-less navigation.

THE VOR AIRWAY SYSTEM

The VOR "Victor" system of civil airways in the United States is composed of both "main" and "alternate" airways, each 10 statute miles wide. The main airways normally follow a straight line between successive omnirange stations. The alternate airways are laid out to the sides of the main airways, usually departing from the main airways at an angle of at least 15° and returning at the next station also at an angle of at least 15°.

The alternate airways are designed mainly for the purpose of creating lateral separation between aircraft operating on instrument flight plans required by traffic conditions. Lateral separation of this kind, however, is not used within 15 miles of a VOR station. Altitude or time separation is used instead.

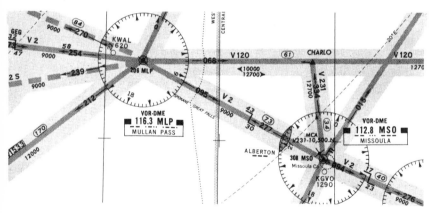

Section of VOR Victor airway as shown on Radio Facility Chart.

The VOR airways are numbered the way U.S. highways are: those that run generally north and south have odd numbers, and those that run east and west have even numbers. Any airways segment common to two or more routes bears the numbers of all airways that coincide for that segment. For example, between St. Louis and

Farmington, Mo., the airways labeled Victor 9 (Chicago to New Orleans) and Victor 69 (St. Louis to Walnut Ridge) share the same airway in common, and aeronautical charts show both numbers.

Alternate airways are identified by location relative to the main airways with which they are connected. Victor 9 West, for example, identifies an alternate airway associated with, and lying to the west of, Victor 9. Since there are a number of west alternate airways along Victor 9, a traffic clearance specifying Victor 9 West also includes the names of the omniranges comprising the particular alternate airway.

A pilot who plans an airway flight using VOR facilities simply specifies in his flight plan the identification of the appropriate Victor airway or airways. For example, a flight from Chicago to New Orleans at 8,000 feet is designated as: "Departing Chicago-Midway, cruising 8,000 feet, via Victor 9 to Moisant International."

It is also possible, of course, to conduct a flight by means of both omnirange and low-frequency navigation aids, that is, by both Victor airways and the LF/MF airways identified as either Green, Amber, Red, or Blue. Flight plans and traffic clearances, in such cases, must stipulate which segments are to be flown on Victor airways, and which on the LF/MF airways.

The Victor airways are marked not only by omnirange stations but by compulsory reporting points and numerous marker beacons, which operate on 75 megacycles and transmit an elliptical pattern about three miles wide and 12 miles long.

A WORD ABOUT MAPS AND CHARTS

Whether you call them maps or charts, they're indispensable for omnirange flying—or any other kind of flying, for that matter. The kind of chart you select should depend on the kind of flight you are making, the size and speed of your aircraft, and of course your personal preferences.

Here is a brief summary of the charts used for flying in the U.S.:

Sectionals: for short flights in smaller planes; omnirange compass roses and VOR airways overprinted in blue; also provide much topographical detail.

World Aeronautical Charts: for medium-range flights; good detail for pilotage combined with omnirange flying; VOR compass roses and VOR airways printed in blue.

Jet Navigation and Route Charts: very little topographical detail for pilotage and designed mainly for high-altitude high-speed flying, particularly by omnirange; VOR airways and VOR compass roses overprinted; not recommended for lightplane flying except as planning charts.

Radio Facility Charts: strictly for airways flying, but with the most complete VOR and VHF information available on any chart series; can be used either alone for instrument flying or in conjunction with Sectionals or WAC's for pilotage and omnirange flying combined.

3

SFO *to* BUR *by* omnirange

Probably the best way to stress the simplicity of cross-country flying by means of omnirange is to follow the course of a flight based on actual facilities and experience. Our demonstration flight here is from San Francisco International Airport down the airways to Lockheed Air Terminal in Burbank, Calif., via Fresno and Bakersfield. The airport-to-airport distance is 307 nautical miles; our aircraft is a medium-range executive transport.

PRE-FLIGHT AND TAKEOFF

On the ramp in front of the transient aircraft hangar we check the fuel tanks to make sure they have been filled, and then run the engines up, check the VHF radio—both transmitters and receivers—for proper operation, and in general complete the pre-flight inspection of our aircraft. We've been to the Weather Bureau for the latest enroute and terminal forecasts, and after consulting the winds-aloft charts we've decided on 8,000 feet as the best cruising altitude for our southbound flight. The forecast is for contact weather all the way, but with enroute and terminal visibility restricted by haze.

We are flying under Visual Flight Rules and no flight plan is required, but we know it's sound practice to file one anyway, and we have done just that.

Cruising altitude: 8,000 feet.

True airspeed at 8,000 feet: 162 knots.

Forecast winds at 8,000 feet:
    SFO-FNO: 245°/18 knots.
    FNO-BUR: 200°/12 knots.

Average magnetic courses:
    SFO-FNO: 95°
    FNO-BUR: 141°

Distances:
    SFO-FNO: 138 nautical miles.
    FNO-BUR: 169 nautical miles.

On the basis of this information, and adding four minutes for climb to cruising altitude, our estimated time in flight to Burbank is 1 hour and 58 minutes.

We receive taxi instructions at 1325 PST, and at the end of the runway we are cleared for takeoff.

1335:   airborne from SFO airport.

ENROUTE

As we begin our climb from takeoff to cruising altitude at 8,000 feet, we glance at our map and note that a course directly from the airport to the San Francisco VOR station (26 miles southeast of the airport) also leads to the Morgan Hill fan marker, at which point we shall enter Victor airway 100 to Fresno. We turn on the VOR receiver, and after allowing a couple of minutes for it to warm up we tune to the frequency of SFO (117.6 mc). Through our loudspeaker mounted in the roof of the cabin the identification signal comes through clearly, over and over: dit-dit-dit, dit-dit-dah-dit, dah-dah-dah.

The next step, getting the plane on course to the SFO omnirange, can be accomplished very simply in either one of two ways. The chart shows that the course lies in a general southeasterly direction. Consequently, we can turn to an approximate southeasterly heading and then rotate the course selector until the left-right needle is centered. At 106° the needle should be vertically centered in the dial. The to-from indicator should point to "to." To hold this 106° magnetic course to the SFO station we can turn to the same compass heading, 106°.

But a second and even simpler way to establish the initial courses along the route has occurred to us before takeoff. On our chart we drew in the course lines between stations and intermediate checkpoints. Now we can read the omnirange bearings directly from the compass roses printed around the stations. Thus, the bearing drawn from the SFO omnirange to the airport is read directly from the station, not from it. We simply subtract 180° to obtain the reciprocal, 106°. We rotate the course selector to this value, turn the aircraft to a magnetic heading of about 106°, and the left-right indicator is centered. We're on our first course.

Climbing at the rate of 500 feet per minute and indicating 122 knots, we notice at the end of 10 minutes after takeoff that the left-right indicator suddenly begins to oscillate. The red alarm flag appears on the dial and waves three times. Simultaneously, the to-from needle moves back and forth and presently comes to a firm stop in the "from" position.

These three indications show us to be directly over the SFO omnirange. If we were listening to the aural signal at the time of crossing the station, we would hear a surge in the aural signal volume followed by an indistinct or fuzzy signal.

1345: over SFO VOR.

After passing the station we glance at the map. Victor airway 100 follows a radial of 94° from SFO toward Fresno. It's not necessary for us to measure this course or apply the local variation, or even to determine the drift angle. The compass rose printed around the station shows the magnetic course or radial from SFO to be 94°. In Victor airway flying all we have to do is read the course. The

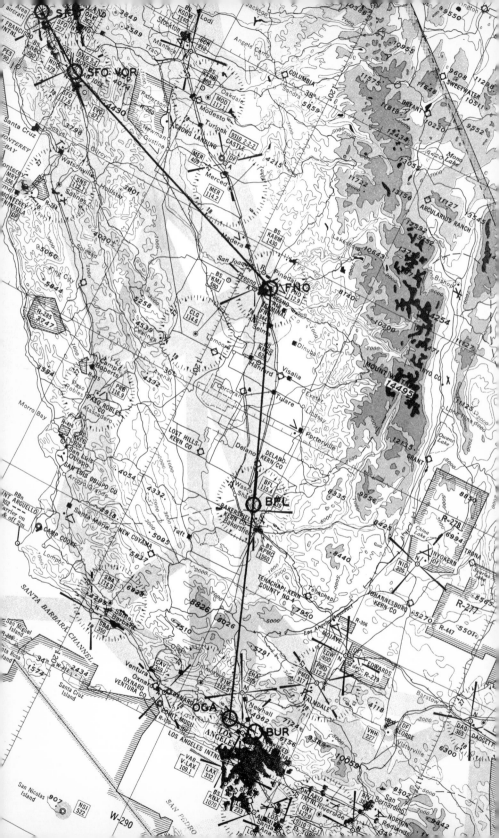

airway itself is a magnetic radial shown on the map as a straight blue line, the boundaries of the airway extending five miles on both sides of the radial.

We turn to a compass heading of approximately 94°. The to-from needle now points to "from," but the left-right indicator continues to show correctly whether the course is to the right or to the left, just as it did while flying toward the station.

1350: levelling off at 8,000 feet cruising altitude.

A few minutes later as we fly on out from the station we note that the left-right needle has edged off slightly to the right of center, even though the compass heading is still 94°. This means that we have drifted to the left of course while flying by compass heading rather than by the needle. Instead of making a sharp right turn to get back on course immediately, we increase the compass heading by only 5°– to 99°. This heading should bring us gradually back into the course and save some time. If we corrected sharply into the needle every time we got off course our track would consist of a series of zig-zags.

With the left-right needle eventually centered again, we are back on course.

1400: altitude: 8,000 feet.
    indicated airspeed: 140 knots.
    outside air temperature: + 15° C.
    true airspeed: 162 knots.
    forecast wind: 245/18 knots.
    dead reckoning groundspeed: 174 knots.

On the basis of this information we establish an estimate of 1405 for arrival time at the Los Banos fan marker, where Victor airway 100 bends slightly toward Fresno.

1407: over Los Banos fan marker.

The map shows Victor 100 extending along a radial of 270° from the Fresno VOR. Since we are flying toward the station rather than from it, we turn to a compass heading of approximately 90° (reciprocal of 270°), and tune in the Fresno omnirange (FNO−112.9 mc), 66 miles away. The aural identification signal comes in "loud and clear." We turn the course selector until the left-right needle is centered, and note that the to-from indicator points to "to."

All we're required to do now by way of navigation is to glance occasionally at the left-right needle and keep it centered. The omni will do the rest for us.

At this distance from the VOR transmitter the width of the omnirange course is about 15°. To check on the accuracy of the left-right indicator we can test it in flight by noting the number of degrees of change in the course selector required for full swing of the needle from the last dot on the left of the dial to the last dot on the right. This change should total approximately 20° at an altitude of 6,000 feet 75 miles from the VOR station.

1410: the sky is clear and visibility unlimited—above, that is. Below, haze reduces visibility to the point where it's almost impossible to identify objects. It's VFR flight weather according to the definitions, but pilotage under these circumstances is a genuine chore. This is a good time to have omni aboard.

According to the forecast the wind at 8,000 feet on this leg of the flight was supposed to have been 18 knots from 245°. This would cause us to drift 4° to the left. Without an omni receiver we should have to take this drift into consideration in establishing a heading, using either a driftmeter or enroute checkpoints to verify the accuracy of the forecast. If the winds should shift and we had no way of measuring the amount of change, we could be blown far off course and still not be aware of it. But omni, unlike the automatic direction-finder which merely points toward a transmitter, actually tells us what course to fly to get to the station.

1415: the left-right needle is pointing to the right of center; we're left of course. Conscientiously, we've been holding a compass heading of 90°—the magnetic course for Fresno that we started out on. Obviously we have drifted to the left. We rotate the course selector slowly until the left-right needle is again centered. The new course is 96°. This time we correct to a compass heading of 100° to keep the needle centered.

We decide that since we've drifted off course our estimated groundspeed also is probably in error, and a definite position fix is called for.

The map shows that a cross-bearing on the Coalinga VOR will give us a line of position that intersects our course line at a good angle. We tune in Coalinga (CLG–114.6), identify it, and then rotate the course selector until the needle is centered and the to-from indicator points to "from." The value on the course selector is 327°, our magnetic bearing from Coalinga. With a pencil and a straight-edge we draw a line on the map from the Coalinga VOR through 327° on the compass rose and extend it out to the area where it crosses Victor 100.

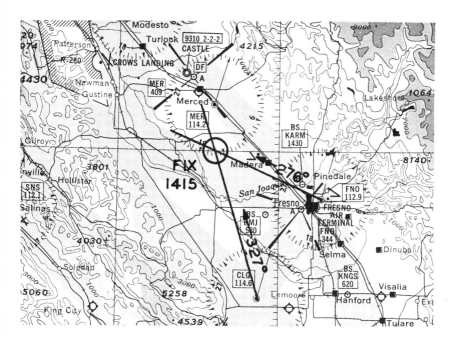

We already have our bearing on Fresno–96°, toward the station. We add 180° to that to obtain the reciprocal of 276°, and then plot that bearing on the map. The point where our CLG and FNO bearings intersect is our fix position for 1415.

We re-tune the FNO omnirange and continue on course toward the station.

Our groundspeed between SFO and the 1415 fix has been 164

knots, eight knots less than estimated on the basis of the forecast wind. Using the new groundspeed, we determine an ETA of 1427 for FNO.

The bearing on CLG, the process of re-tuning to FNO, and the plotting of the fix altogether have required no more than two or three minutes.

As we approach FNO the left-right needle increases in sensitivity and we make another minor admustment in our heading in order to keep it centered. At 1427 it oscillates from side to side, the red flag appears on the dial and waves three times and the to-from indicator swings over to the "from" position. Over Fresno omni.

Our course between Fresno and Bakersfield is along Victor airway 23. After passing FNO we turn to the Victor 23 outbound course of 142° magnetic, centering the left-right needle with the to-from indicator in the "from" position.

After establishing ourselves on the new course we pick up our microphone and call the Fresno omnirange station.

"Fresno radio, this is Executive two six zero seven. Over."

"Executive two six zero seven, this is Fresno radio. Go ahead."

"Executive two six zero seven over Fresno omni two seven at eight thousand, VFR flight plan, estimating Bakersfield five eight."

BFL is 82 nautical miles from FNO, so we plan to fly the first half of this leg outbound on the FNO omni and the second half inbound on BFL.

Meanwhile as we proceed along on course with the left-right needle centered and the San Joaquin valley unrolling below us, we take time to review the simple ease with which a lost aircraft can locate itself with the help of VOR. The first requirement—one which applies to almost any kind of position-finding procedure—is to settle down on a constant compass heading. Any reasonable heading will do as long as it's maintained for a while. Next, tune through the omnirange frequency band (112 to 118 mc) until a VOR station is picked up, identified, and located on the map. Then rotate the course selecror until the left-right indicator is centered and the to-from needle points to "to." All that remains is to take up a compass heading in general agreement with the course selected and fly to the station, keeping the left-right needle centered.

Or, if it is preferable to obtain a fix without flying directly to the station, the bearing from the station is plotted on the chart, followed by another bearing on a second station. A new course then can be flown from this fix to the original destination.

The omni method of locating oneself in an emergency is simpler, faster, and more reliable than the one that depends on the direction-finding loop. After a few hours of flight experience with omnirange any pilot can work this procedure in a matter of two or three minutes.

In any case, to our Burbank-bound flight this is an academic problem: we have one constant line of position from the visual course we are flying, and we can obtain a second one in a matter of seconds with a cross-bearing on either of several stations.

1440: altitude: 8,000 feet

      indicated airspeed: 145 knots.

      outside air temperature: $+20\,°C$.

      true airspeed: 170 knots.

      forecast wind: $200\,°/12$ knots.

      dead reckoning groundspeed: 161 knots.

1444: we obtain magnetic bearings of $91\,°$ from CLG and $139\,°$ from FNO. The resultant fix locates us two miles left of course,

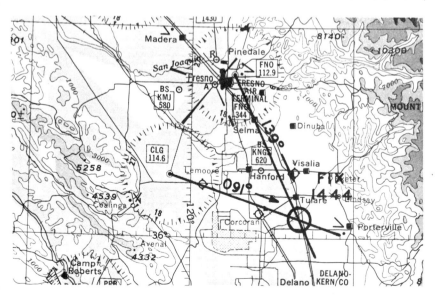

with a groundspeed of 163 knots. ETA BFL: 1447. Wind speed and direction between FNO and 1444 fix: 213°/11 knots.

We tune to the BFL omni (115.4 mc) and find that we bear 327° magnetic from the station. We rotate the course selector to the reciprocal of this bearing, 147°, center the needle, and head for Bakersfield.

1457: over BFL omnirange.

Our outbound course from BFL is 143°, but we find that it takes a compass heading of 146° to keep the left-right indicator centered. The drift correction angle is 3° to the right, a fact that is purely irrelevant since the omnirange determined it for us . . . and then promptly forgot about it.

Victor airway 23, the particular airway we are following on this leg of the flight, terminates at Wheeler Ridge, a reporting point 33 miles south of BFL. Victor 137, of which Victor 23 is a segment, veers off to the southeast and Palmdale. Consequently, in heading for Burbank to the south we have to proceed down low-frequency airway Amber 1, although this doesn't mean that we have to give up omnirange as a navigation aid. Like most medium-size aircraft, ours is also equipped with an LF receiver which we can use in conjunction with omni.

Our ETA over Wheeler Ridge is 1509. By holding the left-right needle centered on our 143° course from BFL, we have established a heading to make good this track. Now we re-tune our omni to Palmdale (PMD–112.2 mc) and set the course selector to a bearing of 276° from the station. At 1505 the needle is off center, but when it is eventually centered we shall know that we bear the same from Palmdale as Wheeler Ridge does. For the second bearing required for the fix at Wheeler Ridge we can tune our LF receiver to the Bakersfield range and fly a course out on the southeast leg, which has virtually the same bearing as the omni course we were flying from BFL.

If our aircraft were equipped with a dual omni installation we could leave one receiver on BFL VOR and the other on PMD.

1508: with the omni tuned to PMD, and the course selector set to 276°, the left-right needle is centered, and the to-from indicator

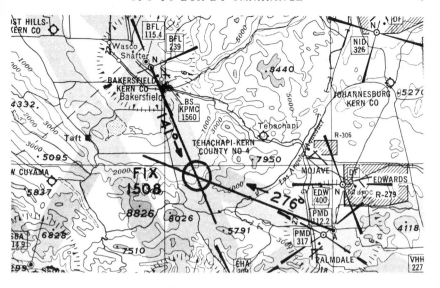

points to "from." On the LF receiver we hear the on-course signal
of the Bakersfield range . . . Wheeler Ridge at 1508.

We now tune the omni to Long Beach (LGB–115.7 mc) but the
signal is weak, according to the flag alarm: we are still more than
80 miles distant from the station, with intervening high terrain. We
tune the LF receiver to the Newhall range and approach the station
on the northwest leg.

1515: in spite of the still relatively weak visual indication of
the signal from the Long Beach omni, the scheduled weather broadcast comes in loud and clear on voice. Burbank's ceiling is unlimited, the wind is calm, the altimeter setting is 29.96, and surface
visibility is restricted to four miles by haze.

Our destination, Lockheed Air Terminal in Burbank, does not
have facilities for a standard VOR instrument approach or letdown,
so we decide to utilize the left-right needle feature of our omni
receiver to do a simulated instrument approach on the localizer
(but not the glide path) of the Burbank ILS.

By 1520 we note that the visual signal indication of the Long
Beach VOR is now strong enough to be used for reliable bearings,
and we turn the course selector to 299°. This is the bearing of the
Canoga Park radiobeacon (OGA) from the Long Beach omni, Canoga

Park being the point at which the procedure turn is made into the BUR localizer.

APPROACH, LETDOWN, AND LANDING

1522: over the Newhall range. We start our letdown to 6,000 feet, prescribed altitude at which we are to arrive over the Canoga Park beacon according to the standard ILS approach procedure. Our low-frequency receiver is tuned to the Canoga Park beacon, on which we are homing by means of the ADF. The omni is still tuned to LGB VOR and the left-right needle is off to the right of the dial but slowly approaching center.

1526: the ADF needle swings over suddenly, and the left-right needle is centered on the omni. Over Canoga Park.

We commence our letdown at the rate of 500 feet a minute, with an indicated airspeed of 105 knots, and at the same time begin our procedure turn. On the control unit of our omni receiver we switch from the "OMNI" position to "VAR-LOC," which cuts off omnirange reception and puts the receiver into the localizer frequency band. We tune to the Burbank localizer (109.5 mc) and continue with our procedure turn, letting down meanwhile to 4,100 feet.

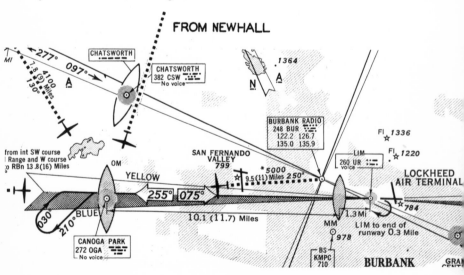

With the completion of the procedure turn, we are on a heading of 75°, located on the localizer beam with the left-right indicator centered. As an ILS deviation indicator it functions exactly as it did while we were flying the omnirange—if we get off to the right of course the needle points to the left, and vice versa. The localizer beam, however, has a yellow side, or sector, and a blue one, the former on the left side of the beam as we head toward the transmitter and the latter on the right. Our left-right dial has a corresponding yellow and blue sector painted on the bottom under the needle. When the needle points to the blue area of the dial it means that the aircraft is flying in the blue sector of the localizer and must be turned to the left in order to get back on the correct approach course. It adds up to the same thing as in omni flying: head toward the needle to get back on course.

We cross the middle marker at 1,300 feet, then the inner marker at 900, and at 1532 our wheels touch down on runway 7 at Lockheed Air Terminal, the left-right needle still centered.

Our flight from San Francisco has required just under two hours. The total time actually devoted to navigation, thanks to omnirange, probably has been less than 15 minutes. We can appreciate now as we taxi up in front of the hangar what omnirange has done to relieve the physical and emotional strain of cross-country flying.

4

Approach and letdown

Bad weather conditions at the terminal—low ceilings and re-stricted visibility—are still the greatest hazard to scheduled flight and to general safety in the air. In the last few years great progress has been made in eliminating this hazard, or, more accurately, in providing better facilities to enable the pilot to land his aircraft safely despite low ceilings and poor visibility.

For the most part, the established landing minimums at airports equipped with omnirange have not been lowered, but omnirange has simplified the problems of approach and letdown. Moreover, it has some features in common with the Instrument Landing System, which, together with radar, has done more than anything else to promote safety in landing and year-round scheduled-flight dependability.

As the heart of the airborne receiving equipment, both omnirange and ILS use the same cross-pointer indicator, with the exception of several VOR receivers designed for light planes. They operate in adjacent bands of the VHF radio spectrum—the former between 112 and 118 megacycles, the latter between 108 and 112 megacycles—and they naturally complement one another. One is designed to guide an aircraft accurately, simply and efficiently from point A on the map to point B; the other is designed to bring the aircraft down to a safe landing on the airport at point B, regardless of weather.

Strictly speaking, a detailed study of the Instrument Landing System does not fall within the bounds of this manual, but, in view of its present importance as an all-weather aid to VHF navigation and the features it shares in common with omnirange, a brief discussion is included in this chapter.

INSTRUMENT APPROACH BY OMNIRANGE

Omnirange approach procedures are approved by the **FAA** for 291 airports. Obviously, not all of the 455 omnirange stations in the U.S. have standard approach procedures inasmuch as many of them are located at intermediate points along the airways, not necessarily adjacent to major airports.

Directions for making omnirange approaches to terminals are contained on the 8"×10½" AL-VOR chart series published by the U.S. Coast & Geodetic Survey at 5¢ each.

To make an instrument approach by means of the old four-course range it was first of all necessary to identify the range quadrant or the leg on which the aircraft was approaching the station. This was not always as easy to do as it sounded. There were two "A" quadrants and two "N" quadrants and four equi-signal legs. Under conditions of extremely high winds, especially cross-winds, or in the instance of a lost aircraft trying to re-orient itself on a range, there were possibilities of confusing one quadrant with its opposite, or of mistaking one leg for another.

With omnirange, on the other hand, the approach may be made to the station from any direction, rather than a long one of only four established legs. There is no need to identify quadrants or legs since there can be but one magnetic course along the selected approach route. As long as the value of this course is set on the course selector and the left-right needle is centered, the aircraft is approaching the station directly, and its magnetic direction from the station is definitely known.

Let us assume, for the sake of example, that we are flying by omnirange from Ponca City, Oklahoma, to Tulsa. The Tulsa weather as reported on the teletype sequence: ceiling, 700 feet; visibility, two miles; light rain and haze. Instrument weather. The regular daylight instrument minimums are 500 feet and one mile. An IFR flight plan is filed.

The minimum enroute instrument altitude is 2,400 feet, but our enroute traffic clearance calls for a cruising altitude of 5,000 feet. The distance from the Ponca City VOR to the Tulsa VOR is 65 nautical miles. The estimated time in flight is 30 minutes, based on an average groundspeed of 148 knots, with three minutes included for climb to altitude.

Fifteen minutes after takeoff Air Traffic Control clears us to descend to 2,300 feet and cross the Skiatook marker at that altitude. With the left-right indicator centered and the course selector turned to 106° on the Tulsa omnirange (TUL-114.1 mc), we begin our descent from 5,000 feet. The Skiatook marker is 11.5 miles from the Tulsa omnirange station. Allowing about six minutes of our 30-minute estimated time enroute for this distance, it becomes apparent that we must descend at the rate of 300 feet per minute at 148 knots groundspeed in order to cross the marker at 2,300 feet.

After crossing the Skiatook marker (four consecutive dashes), we continue on the same course (106°) toward the Tulsa VOR. As we cross the station six minutes later we begin a turn to 332° magnetic, as prescribed by the standard VOR instrument approach procedure to Tulsa airport (see approach chart, page 56).

We turn the course selector to 332°, and the left-right needle is centered with the to-from indicator reading "from." While flying this close to the transmitter the left-right needle is highly responsive and should be kept just slightly to the left of center, so that the aircraft is on the right hand side of the radial without getting too far off course.

The wind is light—10 knots, from the west. The one or two degrees of crab angle necessary to keep the left-right needle centered during the approach are negligible, and would hardly be apparent in

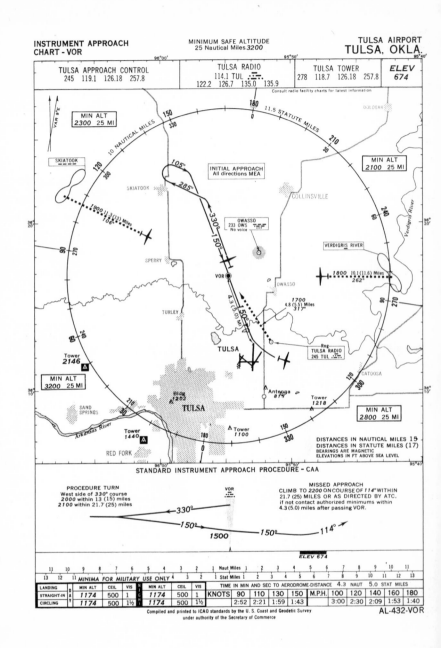

STANDARD INSTRUMENT APPROACH PROCEDURE – CAA

PROCEDURE TURN
West side of *330°* course
2000 within 13 (15) miles
2100 within 21.7 (25) miles

VOR

MISSED APPROACH
CLIMB TO *2200* ON COURSE OF *114°* WITHIN 21.7 (25) MILES OR AS DIRECTED BY ATC, if not contact authorized minimums within 4.3 (5.0) miles after passing VOR.

←—330°

—150°

1500

—150°

114° ➤

ELEV 674

11 10 9 8 7 6 5 4 3 2		Naut Miles	1 2 3 4 5 6 7 8 9 10 11							
13 12 11	MINIMA FOR MILITARY USE ONLY	4 3 2	1 Stat Miles 1	2 3 4 5 6 7 8 9 10 11 12 13						

LANDING		MIN ALT	CEIL	VIS		MIN ALT	CEIL	VIS		TIME IN MIN AND SEC TO AERODROME-DISTANCE 4.3 NAUT 5.0 STAT MILES						
STRAIGHT-IN	A	1174	500	1	C	1174	500	1	KNOTS	90	110	130	150	M.P.H.	100	120	140	160	180
CIRCLING		1174	500	1½	D	1174	500	1½		2:52	2:21	1:59	1:43		3:00	2:30	2:09	1:53	1:40

Compiled and printed to ICAO standards by the U. S. Coast and Geodetic Survey
under authority of the Secretary of Commerce

AL-432-VOR

the difference between the compass heading and the course selector setting.

Simultaneously with the turn to 330° after crossing the station we start letting down to 2,000 feet. We hold the heading of 330° for two minutes and then make a standard left-hand procedure turn to 285°, followed by a 180° turn to the right (to 105°). The course selector is now set to 150°, preparatory to intercepting the final approach radial back to the station. When the left-right needle is centered and the to-from indicator reads "to," we hold the course until we are over the station again, this time at 1,500 feet. The distance from the station to the end of runway 17-left, the active runway, is 4.3 miles. At the standard approach speed of 110 knots, the time between the station and the end of the runway is two minutes and 21 seconds. The minimum ceiling is 500 feet above aerodrome elevation, or 1,174 feet above sea level. In other words, between the station and the end of the runway we can descend 326 feet and still adhere to the regulations governing the minimum ceiling.

On our particular approach, however, because the ceiling is 700 feet above field elevation, we break out at 1,374 feet above sea level shortly after crossing the station. With two-mile visibility we proceed straight in toward runway 17-left and complete a normal landing.

The same procedure approach could be made to the station from any direction of the compass, except that the prescribed approach altitudes are different in each quadrant because of differences in the height of the surrounding terrain.

If we had not been able to establish visual contact at 500 feet altitude above field elevation and within 4.3 nautical miles after crossing the VOR station, we should have had to execute a "missed-approach" procedure. On the Tulsa VOR this consists of climbing to 2,200 feet on a magnetic course of 114°, or as directed by ATC.

A purely literary description of an omnirange approach and letdown may sound complicated, yet in actual practice it is surprisingly simple. Pilots are aware that it is much easier to fly by visual reference (watching a needle or indicator, for example) than by aural reference (listening to a signal). The eye is quicker than the ear, and what the eye sees makes a greater impression on the brain than what the ear hears. Omnirange flying is visual flying. It permits the pilot to devote more of his attention to the actual handling of the flight controls.

INSTRUMENT LANDING SYSTEM

The instrument Landing System (ILS) consists of three basic components: (1) the localizer radio beam, which provides lateral, or directional, guidance to the airport runway; (2) the glide path, which provides vertical guidance during the aircraft's descent to the airport runway; and (3) the markers (usually two) to provide radio position fixes along the approach course to the runway. Other facilities are used in conjunction with ILS, such as high-intensity approach lights, compass locator stations, and precision-approach radar, but these will be discussed only very briefly.

The localizer transmitter is located on the extended center line of the principal instrument runway of an airport, a short distance from the end opposite the approach end of the runway. It transmits one beam down the center line of the runway and out across the markers and another beam away from the runway in the opposite direction. The first is the front course and the second is called the back course. This back course of the localizer should be ignored if it is designated by the FAA as "not to be used." At some ILS locations it has been found necessary to screen off reflections from interfering objects near the transmitter, and in so doing a large amount of the energy radiating toward the back course is deflected, resulting in an erratic and unreliable beam.

The localizer transmitter provides an on-course signal at a minimum distance of about 25 miles from the runway at an altitude of 2,000 feet. The on-course signal, or beam, is approximately 70 feet wide at the landing point on the runway and widens out to nearly 5,100 feet at a distance of 10 miles from the transmitter. The right side of the beam, as seen from the point of view of the pilot approaching the runway on the front course, is modulated at 150 cycles per second, and is identified on maps, as well as on the pilot's cross-pointer indicator, as the blue sector. The left side, modulated at 90 cycles per second, is the yellow sector. The on-course signal, which is being received when the cross-pointer is centered, is the point where the signal strength between the two modulated sides is equal.

A three-letter station identification is transmitted intermittently in code, and voice transmissions of approach-control directions are made from the control tower on the same frequency.

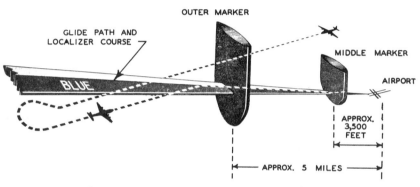

Schematic diagram of ILS approach and letdown.

If the localizer beam were turned on its side it would be the same as the glide path, with the upper side of the beam modulated at 90 cycles per second and the lower side at 150. The upper and lower sides of the glide path, however, are not designated as blue and yellow sectors. Instead, the horizontal needle of the cross-pointer indicator points up above center when the aircraft is below the glide path, and points down when the aircraft is above the glide path.

The glide path transmitter is so designed as to transmit a course at an angle upward of about 2.5 degrees above the horizon unless high terrain or other obstacles necessitate a steeper angle. Because of the inherent mechanical structure, all glide path transmitters pro- duce five other courses, all at much steeper angles. During a proper approach and letdown, however, these superfluous courses are not encountered and hence cause no trouble. At the point of ground con- tact on the runway the glide path is one degree wide; ten miles dis- tant from the transmitter it is about 1,380 feet thick.

The fan markers used in conjunction with the ILS localizer and glide path operate on a frequency of 75 megacycles. They radiate a vertical, fan-shaped field pattern. Except at certain military fields they consist of an outer marker, generally located about $4\frac{1}{2}$ to 5 miles from the runway on the front course of the ILS, and a middle marker, located about 3,500 feet from the approach end of the runway, also on the front course. The outer marker identifies itself by transmitting continuous dashes at the rate of two per second; the middle marker is identified by alternate dots and dashes.

The compass locators are low-powered non-directional radio beacons that operate in the low-frequency 200-400-kilocycle band and are identified by the intermittent transmission of two-letter codes. They are installed at the sites of the outer and/or middle markers for use with dual automatic direction-finding compasses in the aircraft. As used in conjunction with ILS, they serve the following purposes: (1) as an aid in the transition from low-frequency range to ILS—for example, in homing direct to the outer marker from the range station; (2) as a holding pattern—the pilot is aware at all times of his position relative to the outer marker, and (3) as a double check on passing over the outer and middle markers.

Another important adjunct to ILS is high-intensity lighting, the pilot's principal guide to the runway after establishing visual contact at or below the established instrument minimums. Theoretically, ILS makes blind landings possible. Actually, however, the high speed and heavy weight of modern transports make such landings difficult and unsafe. As a result, it is necessary to provide an approach and runway lighting system of extremely high intensity, one which penetrates fog, smoke, snow or rain but one also which can be controlled under conditions of varying visibility.

High-intensity lighting systems are now installed at most of the major airports in the U.S. The two basic systems are the "ladder," which uses horizontal bars at right angles to the line of approach and which is located in line with the left side of the runway extended, and the "slope-line," which consists of a row of bars on each side of the runway extended, with the bars so slanted that they indicate to the pilot his position relative to the correct approach path. The FAA maintains that the slopeline system permits routine landings with ceilings as low as 200 feet and visibility as restricted as a quarter of a mile.

The airborne ILS receiver equipment consists of the following units: the localizer and glide path antennas (usually mounted together on the fuselage atop the cockpit), a control panel near the pilot's seat, and the marker lights and cross-pointer indicator, which are located on the pilot's instrument panel. The control panel incorporates an on-off switch, a volume control, and a channel selector switch. Each localizer frequency has a corresponding glide path frequency. The channel selector switches are designed to switch the glide path receiver automatically to the localizer frequency.

Twenty separate VHF channels have been allocated for localizer frequencies, but at the present time only the following seven are in common use: 108.1 mc, 108.3 mc, 109.5 mc, 109.7 mc, 109.9 mc, 110.1 mc, and 110.3 mc.

The cross-pointer indicator is the same instrument as the one used in flying by omnirange. This is the instrument upon which the pilot focuses most of his attention (along with the airspeed indicator and altimeter, of course) while making an ILS approach. In omnirange flying, only the vertical pointer is used, to indicate whether the aircraft is flying to the left or right of a given magnetic course to a VOR station, or is directly on course. The vertical pointer serves the same function in an ILS approach except that it then indicates whether the aircraft is in the blue sector of the localizer beam (i.e., too far to the right), in the yellow sector (too far to the left), or is directly on course. During an ILS approach the horizontal pointer indicates when the aircraft is above, below or on the glide path. This pointer is inoperative in omnirange flying.

The localizer pointer is pivoted at the top of the dial and swings like a pendulum from side to side. The glide path pointer is pivoted at the left side of the dial and swings up and down like a semaphore. In the center of the dial is a fixed target circle with four perpendicular radial rows of dots, dividing the instrument into equal vertical and horizontal quadrants. On the left side at the bottom of the dial the scale is colored blue and on the right side yellow.

Regardless of the position or heading of the aircraft, the localizer pointer is always deflected into the color area in which the aircraft is flying. When an aircraft is flying in the blue sector of a localizer beam the vertical pointer is in the blue area of the dial. Since the blue sector of the localizer is on the right side of the beam as the aircraft approaches the runway, this means that the aircraft must be turned to the left in order to get back on the correct approach course. The opposite is true when the vertical pointer is deflected into the yellow area. When the pointer is centered vertically on the dial, the aircraft is located along the center of the approach beam.

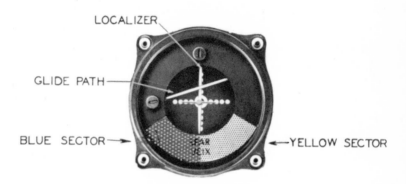

ILS indicator. The cross-pointers here show the aircraft to be near the center of the localizer beam and below the glide path. (from a Lear, Inc., photo)

"Follow the needle." This is the simplest way to make an ILS approach. Corrections to heading, however, should be relatively small since the pointer is highly sensitive: full-scale deflection is indicated when the aircraft is a mere $2\frac{1}{2}°$ to either side of the on-course. It must be sensitive to bring an aircraft down dead-center onto a runway usually no wider than 200 feet.

When the horizontal pointer is above it indicates that the aircraft is below the glide path. In effect it is warning the pilot: "The glide path is up there above you." When it points below the center line it indicates that the aircraft is too high—above the glide path.

The glide path indicator is even more sensitive than the localizer indicator. Less than 1½° separates an indication on the dial of "full up" and "full down." As a result, the aircraft must be aligned on the glide path well in advance of reaching the runway.

The procedure altitude at which the glide path is to be intercepted (generally at the outer marker) is listed on the ILS chart for the particular airport. Also on the chart is a tabulation of the rate of descent in feet per minute necessary to stay aligned on the glide path, at four standard-approach indicated airspeeds.

The fan markers used in conjunction with ILS all transmit on the same frequency of 75 megacycles. The airborne marker receiver is equipped with three small, round lights—purple for the outer marker, amber for the middle marker, and white for the airways marker—mounted on the pilot's instrument panel. These lights operate independently, each one indicating the crossing of the particular marker for which it is designed. The outer marker transmits a 400-cycle tone and the purple light flashes on and off in synchronization with this signal. The middle marker transmits a 1,300-cycle tone and lights the amber light.

These markers may be received aurally also. As a further aid to identification the tone signals are pitched, respectively, low, medium and high.

To indicate automatically that the ILS signals are being received correctly and in the proper strength, there are two safeguards inherent in the system. The first is the automatic alarm, consisting of two tiny red metal flags installed on the right side and at the bottom of the cross-pointer dial. The one on the right is the same flag that on many VOR receivers indicates when no signal, or a faulty signal, is being received from an omnirange station.

Both flags are actuated by tiny voltmeters. When no current is being received from the glide path receiver the red flag on the right side of the dial swings down across the face of the instrument. The red flag on the bottom swings up on the dial when no usable signal is being received from the localizer.

As a further precaution, nearly all airlines recommend that at least one of the pilots aboard an aircraft listen continuously to the

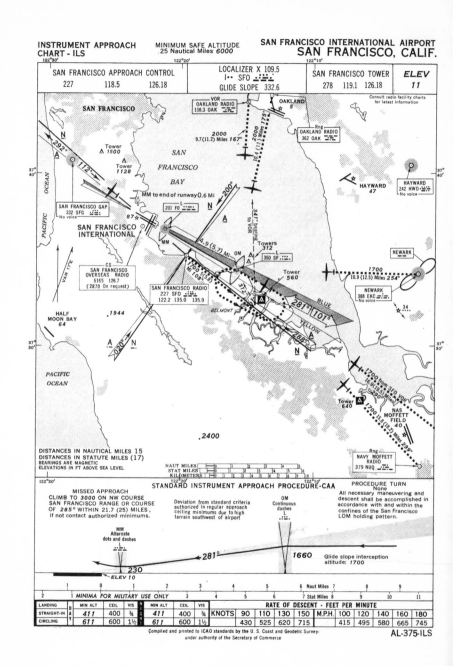

aural signal of the ILS transmitters whenever ILS approaches are being made.

Precision-approach radar is installed at most major airports to enable control operators to monitor the actual approaches of aircraft using the ILS. This furnishes a complete check on both the operation of the ILS components and the aircraft's progress toward a landing.

Let us visualize a standard ILS approach, by way of example, to San Francisco International Airport, under conditions of minimum ceiling and visibility (see accompanying chart for procedures discussed in this example). We shall assume that our aircraft is arriving over San Francisco from Seattle in the north, that there is no other traffic in the immediate vicinity of the airport, and that we have been cleared to begin an ILS approach to active runway 28-right. The reported ceiling is 400 feet, the visibility is one mile.

Letting down ten minutes before our estimated time of arrival over the San Francisco range station, we turn on the localizer and glide path receivers to allow them to warm up. After reporting over the Golden Gate intersection we complete the pre-landing checklist, slow the aircraft down to standard approach speed, and lower the flaps to the prescribed degree for landing. The flap setting should not be changed during final approach: an increase in the setting will cause the airplane to balloon above the glide path and a decrease will drop it below.

In accordance with the standard approach procedure, we cross the San Francisco range station at the prescribed altitude of 1,660 feet and continue out on a magnetic course of 108°. The ILS chart shows us that the distance from the range station to the Belmont intersection, at which point we are to begin our procedure turn onto the front course of the ILS localizer, is 5 miles, and the estimated time to reach the intersection at an approach speed of 110 knots indicated airspeed is 2 minutes and 45 seconds.

When we bear 161° magnetic from the Oakland VOR we are located at the Belmont intersection, and we commence a 180° left turn toward the localizer beam. During the course of this turn the localizer cross-pointer moves from the edge of the dial slowly toward the center as the aircraft nears the beam. Since the inbound magnetic course of the beam is 281°, when the aircraft is turned to a magnetic heading of 281° after reaching the center of the beam, the cross-pointer indicator should be centered, assuming of course either no-wind or a wind directly on the nose. For any cross-wind component, the final compass heading necessary to keep the pointer centered will vary from 281° by as many degrees as the drift-angle correction, plus or minus compass deviation.

After the airplane has reached the localizer on-course we hold the heading unless the pointer drifts off center to the edge of the target circle. In that case, the time required for the pointer to reach the edge of the circle is an indication of the amount of drift due to wind, and therefore of the amount of heading correction necessary to bring the aircraft back into the center of the beam.

It is advisable to turn onto the localizer beam far enough out from the outer marker so that the heading corrections necessary to keep the aircraft on course can be made before crossing the marker. This allows the pilot to concentrate more on tracking the glide path during the final approach.

Maintaining 1,660 feet, with the localizer pointer centered, we cross the outer marker and the purple light on the instrument panel flashes on and off. The glide path indicator, which has been dropping slowly down from the top of the dial while we were approaching the outer marker, is now centered. At this moment we are located directly on course and on the glide path.

With a steady, indicated airspeed of 110 knots, we begin descending immediately at the rate of 525 feet per minute, a rate calculated to establish visual contact just short of the airport. Here we reduce power (we have been in fairly level flight at 1,660 feet altitude since crossing the San Francisco range) in order to keep the glide path pointer centered. Although the glide path angle is constant and is fixed at between 2¼° to 3°, the approaching aircraft may, and probably will, either rise above the glide path or drop below it. The actual rate of descent is affected by the groundspeed, which is determined not only by the indicated airspeed during approach but also by the wind direction and velocity. Consequently it is necessary to adjust the power setting during final approach (correcting the trim appropriately at the same time) to hold to the glide path.

After passing over the outer marker we do not make any heading corrections greater than 5°. The beam is so relatively narrow at this distance from the runway that heading corrections greater than 5° may cause the aircraft to fly through the beam and require even greater corrections to get back on. When corrections are necessary they should be reduced proportionately as the end of the runway is approached. During the last two or three miles of the approach no heading corrections greater than 2° should be made.

Between the outer marker and the middle marker, then, during the most critical part of our ILS approach, we concentrate exclusively on:

(1) maintaining a constant indicated airspeed;
(2) adjusting the power setting for a uniform rate of descent in order to stay on the glide path;
(3) holding the airplane on the localizer beam by keeping the vertical needle of the cross-pointer indicator centered, and
(4) watching for the outer and middle marker signals, to determine our distance from the end of the runway.

At about 400 feet altitude, minimum daytime ceiling for landing on runway 28-right, we establish visual contact. In a matter of seconds after that, the amber light of the middle marker flashes on, and since the visibility is approximately one mile we spot the end of the runway directly ahead. Nothing remains now but to proceed with a normal landing.

The ILS is a remarkably simple and accurate method of making blind approaches to airports even under the most adverse weather conditions. With experience and practice any pilot can learn exactly how much correction to heading and readjustment of power are necessary to keep an aircraft centered on the ILS localizer beam and glide path. The rest—the coordination of controls, the mental arithmetic—will follow naturally.

Terminal omnirange transmitter located in center of airport. (Wilcox Electric Co.)

TERMINAL OMNIRANGE (TVOR)

Because of the relatively high installation and maintenance costs of ILS and approach radar, most medium-size and small airports can't afford them. To provide instrument letdown facilities many of these Class 2, 3, and 4 airports are equipped with "baby" omniranges, a low-powered version of the standard VOR station. These terminal omniranges, or TVOR's, have a power output of 50 watts, as compared to the 200 watts of the standard VOR, with maximum signal reception distance correspondingly shorter.

The TVOR transmitter is usually installed near the intersection of the most frequently used runways on the airport, but since it transmits the magnetic courses in all directions it permits the use of any runway. If, for example, the active runway is No. 18, the pilot simply flies an omni course of 180° magnetic until he is over the end of the runway, assuming of course that he is on a straight-in approach. For approaches from other directions, standard turns and letdown procedures are required. Inexpensive non-directional beacons or markers can be used in conjunction with TVOR.

The same airborne VHF receivers and indicators are used for both TVOR and conventional VOR, and the methods of using them for navigation are identical.

The LVOR (low-powered omnirange) is the same facility as the TVOR but it is installed along the airways as a gap-filler in the regular VOR system. Both TVOR and LVOR stations operate in the 108.0-112.0 mc band, on the even-tenth decimals (108.2, 108.4, etc.).

Omnirange receivers

It is not the aim of this chapter to recommend any particular omnirange receivers, but merely to take a brief look at the equipment currently available. All one can hope to accomplish in such a survey is to provide a general idea of the variety and cost of the receivers. In the end, the only reliable way to select equipment like this is to fly with it—to ask the local dealer for a demonstration and see the equipment at work under actual flight conditions.

The descriptive material that follows, and the prices where available, have been furnished by the manufacturers themselves, and all specifications are quoted from their current publications. Remember that designs are modified frequently and that prices fluctuate, both upward and downward.

AIRCRAFT RADIO CORPORATION (ARC)

The Type 15D VHF navigational receiving equipment manufactured by the Aircraft Radio Corporation of Boonton, N.J., combines in one system all the advantages of VHF navigation and communication. It can be used for receiving omniranges, ILS runway local-

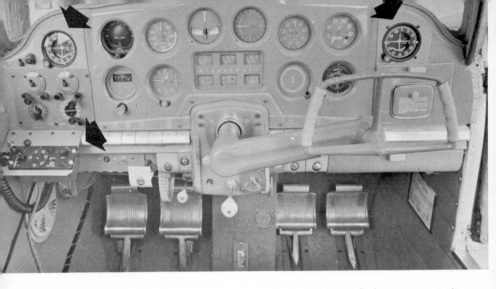

Dual ARC installation in Beechcraft Bonanza includes course indicators (upper left and right) and edge-lighted control unit (lower left). (Aircraft Radio Corp.)

izers, visual-aural ranges, and all VHF voice communications, including GCA radar approach instructions.

An important feature of the 15D is the three-in-one indicating instrument for the pilot's panel. This indicator, which fits a standard 3⅛" instrument hole, combines the presentation of the course selector, cross-pointer indicator, and to-from meter. The compactness of this instrument makes it ideal for dual VOR installation in smaller and medium-sized aircraft.

The VHF receiver is designed for reception of signals in the 108-135 mc band. It has automatic volume control of the delayed type, which allows the output to build up to about 170 milliwatts before taking hold. The normal output load is 300 ohms.

The function of the converter in receiving omnirange signals is to take the signal from the receiver and convert and interpret it in such a way that the bearing of the receiving antenna from the transmitter is determined. In other words, it measures the difference between the transmitted signal's reference phase (magnetic north) and the variable phase as received by the aircraft's antenna. This phase difference is then read on the course indicator as the bearing from the station.

The course selector operates in the conventional way. To fly a VOR course, tune in the station and rotate the cross-pointer azimuth knob until the index arrow indicates the value of the desired course. (A round index marker simultaneously indicates the reciprocal of this course.) If necessary, turn the aircraft to a heading that eventually centers the left-right needle, and then keep the needle centered. If the course is toward the station, the to-from indicator points to "to" until the station is crossed, after which it indicates "from."

To determine a bearing with the ARC course indicator, rotate the course selector knob until the left-right needle is centered. Read the value of the bearing under the index arrow, noting whether it is "to" the station or "from" it.

The control unit, usually located alongside the pilot's seat or below the instrument panel, remotely controls the ARC receiving equipment. It consists of an "on-off" power switch, volume control, tuning control, and two-position switch for selecting reception of either VOR signals or visual-aural range and localizer signals. An edge-lighted model is also available.

The "ram's horn" antenna incorporates two broad-banded antennas, one for use with VOR and runway localizer receivers, and one for use with ILS glide-path receivers. The antenna, which is priced at $98.00, can be used on all aircraft from helicopters to multi-engine transports.

The ARC 15D receiving equipment requires 2.8 amperes at 28 volts dc, or 5.6 amperes at 14 volts dc.

Total weight of the equipment, including antenna, with one rack: 25 lbs. Receiver size, including dynamotor and converter on rack and mounting: $7\frac{1}{8}" \times 11\frac{5}{8}" \times 13\frac{1}{8}"$.

Price: complete with all accessories: $2,118.84

NATIONAL AERONAUTICAL CORP. (NARCO)

From its plant in Fort Washington, Pa., this well-known company produces a wide variety of VHF navigation and communications equipment, including the popular Omnigator and Superhomer.

The Omnigator Mark II provides two-way VHF communications, VOR navigation, ILS localizer indication, and 75 mc marker beacon reception in a compact, single-unit package. The transmitter has 27-channel capacity, and the receiver has "whistle-stop" tuning from 108 to 127 mc. Course deviation and to-from indication of the omni receiver are combined in a single standard presentation. Continuous "to" or "from" sensing is indicated in a small window behind the left-right pointer. The course selector is horizontally mounted at the bottom of the control panel, similar to a magnetic

NARCO equipment in this Bonanza includes VOR Omnigator (at the left of instrument panel), Superhomer (right), and (below panel, at center), a Simplexer VHF communications transmitter-receiver. (National Aeronautica Corp.)

compass card, and is graduated in five-degree increments for accurate selection of course or bearing. Operation on VOR is the
same as with most of the other receivers described thus far.

Built into the Omnigator is a system that permits fast and accurate tuning of the VHF receiver to the same frequency as the
transmitter for simplex (same channel) communications with towers
and other ground stations. For example, to transmit and receive on
119.5 mc the transmitter is set to 119.5, the function switch is
turned to CAL, and the receiver is tuned until a high-pitched tone
is heard. The receiver is then set precisely to receive on 119.5.

Technically, the Omnigator is well made, and includes extensive

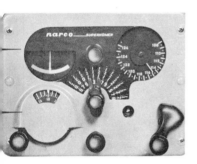 

*Control panels and indicators of the NARCO Superhomer (left) and Omni-
gator. (National Aeronautical Corp.)*

printed circuitry to save space and weight. Audio output has been
doubled over previous models to provide plenty of loudspeaker or
earphone volume under virtually any condition.

The Mark II comes complete with power supply, two antennas
and all necessary cables. It is available for either 12-volt or 24-
volt aircraft, with the latter being priced about $60.00 higher.
Weight, 17.9 pounds. Dimensions of panel space, 5½″ × 6⅞″; case
depth behind panel, 10¼″. Price, about $1,100.

The Superhomer is another single-package NARCO VHF navigation and communications unit, designed primarily for light aircraft and offered at about half the price of the Omnigator. It includes a 12-channel transmitter in the 121-123 mc band, and VHF
receiver for the 108-127 mc band, which includes the entire range

of ILS, VOR, tower, and traffic control communications.

Left-right indication of the course deviation needle is the same as on the Omnigator, but "to-from" indication is unique. To determine whether course or bearing is toward or away from the station, a knob to the right of the indicator is turned. This action displays the "to-from" flag, and the course deviation needle then points either to "to" or "from," as appropriate. The manufacturer says this system minimizes the weight, cost, and complexity of the equipment.

The Superhomer's course selector operates in two stages. The course dial is first tuned to the 30° point nearest the VOR bearing (or course). Precise bearing is then determined by turning a fine-tune knob which moves the course index left or right to center the course deviation needle.

The Superhomer has a self-contained power supply, weighs 11 pounds, fits standard aircraft glove compartment, and comes complete with two antennas and cables. Price, about $575.00.

THE NARCO OMNIPLEXER

The Omniplexer is a 2½-pound omnirange converter and display presentation that was designed for use with a NARCO VHF receiver-transmitter set called the Simplexer. The Simplexer receives between 108-128 mc, and the Omniplexer can be plugged into a receptacle provided for it in the receiver. The Omniplexer itself can be mounted pancake-style on top of the Simplexer, or separately if a more convenient cockpit location is available. Because of its small size, and relatively low price, it is well suited for dual installation in small and medium-sized aircraft.

The Omniplexer course selector is similar to the one on the Superhomer described above. The left-right and to-from indicators are combined in one display instrument. The left-right needle is the same as the Superhomer's. Turning the to-from switch electrically converts the left-right meter to a to-from indicator, and mechanically changes the meter scale to indicate whether the course selected is the one toward the station or the one away from it.

Power requirements: must be connected to allied NARCO power units and the Simplexer receiver; weight, of the Omniplexer only, 2.2 lbs.; panel space, 3⅛"×6½", case depth behind panel, 6⅝".

Price: less antenna, $195.00 (the Simplexer sells for about $500.00.

LEAR, INC.

Lear, Inc., LearCal Division, Santa Monica, Calif., offers 18 different combinations of units for omnirange navigation and VHF communications. The basic units of these combinations are:

1. Either "Omniscope" or "Omnimeter" VOR presentation.
2. VHF receiver.
3. VHF transmitter.
4. Low frequency receiver.
5. Marker beacon receiver.
6. Cross-pointer indicator.
7. VAR adapter.

The 18 combinations available provide a wide choice of equipment which may include as few as two of the above units or all of

Lear VHF radio installation in Cessna 195. Omnimeter (upper left on instrument panel) and VHF receiver (lower left). (LearCal Division, Lear, Inc.)

them. This permits the aircraft owner to start out with relatively inexpensive primary radio equipment and build his system progressively to the point where he has full use of all existing radio facilities.

The Lear Omnimeter consists of the familiar left-right needle presentation of omnirange flying. It is a three-in-one instrument, combining a rotatable 360° course selector, the left-right needle, and a to-from indicator. Although the design is slightly different from other omni indicators we have discussed, operation is identical. The course selector is rotated until the left-right needle is centered, and the aircraft is then flown into the needle, either toward or away from the station as indicated.

Lear Omnimeter presentation of VOR signals (left) and Omniscope presentation. (LearCal Division, Lear, Inc.)

The Lear Omniscope is an instrument that provides picture presentation of VOR signal reception. When signals are being received, a luminous circle is superimposed over the fixed 360° azimuth dial, a small pip on the circle indicates the magnetic bearing to the VOR station. If, for example, the pip indicates 320°, the aircraft is turned to a magnetic heading of 320° in order to fly to the station. When the transmitting station's signals are not strong enough to provide accurate bearings, the pip does not appear in the trace. When the signals are interrupted or distorted by intervening mountainous terrain, the scope pattern becomes a small flickering ring of light in the center of the dial.

Changes in heading made necessary because of drift are readily apparent in the Omniscope indication. When the aircraft passes over the station, the pip reverses itself 180°. To take a fix with the Omniscope, tune successively to two VOR stations and plot the fix using the reciprocals of the readings on the picture scope.

Lear ADF omnirange antenna mounted below the tail cone of a Bonanza. (LearCal Division, Lear, Inc.)

Of the 18 different combinations of Lear VHF radio and omni equipment, a typical one might include the following units:

1. Tunable VHF transmitter: two-watt, 12-channel, crystal-controlled, with two crystals supplied as standard; standard instrument panel or ashtray mounting also available.

2. Tunable VHF receiver: frequency range 108-127 mc, for all VHF communications and navigation; with new low-noise input circuit, high-stability tuner with increased signal-to-noise ratio.

3. Either Omniscope or Omnimeter dial presentation for omniranges.

4. Low frequency receiver and marker beacon receiver: standard broadcast (550-1,600 kc) and range (200-400 kc) bands, with separate circuit for automatic reception of 75 mc marker beacon signals; slide-rule type illuminated dial with provisions for external dimmer control.

The total weight of this combination (Lear-designated combination "D"), including antennas and accessories, is approximately 28 lbs.

Prices on request.

MITCHELL INDUSTRIES

Mitchell Industries, Inc., of Mineral Wells, Texas, manufactures two basic omnirange receiver-indicators, the "Avigator" and the "Avigator Jr."

THE AVIGATOR

The model AT99-45(A) is a VHF transmitter and receiver combined with an omnirange receiver-indicator and low-frequency receiver for aural direction-finding.

Instead of a course selector, left-right needle, and to-from indicator, the Avigator employs an omni magnetic bearing indicator. It is necessary only to tune in the VOR station and read the bearing as indicated on the 360° azimuth dial. This bearing is the direction of the aircraft from the station. For example, if the indicator reads 220°, this means the aircraft bears 220° from the station. To fly directly to this station, it is necessary only to turn the aircraft to a northeasterly heading which keeps the indicator reading 220°. The amount of crab necessary to hold this course is arrived at automatically, just as it is in flying with omnirange receivers that incorporate a left-right needle.

A neon tube inside the dial lights up when the station tuned in is exactly on frequency, indicating that the reading of the bearing is correct.

The Avigator has a six-channel transmitter, and a receiver for the frequency range of 108-130 mc.

A feature of the Avigator is low-frequency "whistle direction finding." To obtain a relative bearing on a broadcast or LF range station, tune in and identify the station, and then place the WDF switch in the ON position. All that can be heard with the switch in

Control panel and magnetic bearing indicator of the Mitchell Avigator. This model incorporates a low-frequency receiver for aural direction-finding. (Mitchell Industries, Inc.)

this position is a whistle. Rotate the manual loop control until the whistle fades. This is the null position of the loop. The signals transmitted from the station are masked by the whistle, but the loop sensitivity is increased to the point where the null is only a few degrees wide. Standard procedures for obtaining an aural null (relative bearing) can be used with the WDF switch in the OFF position.

The indicating panel of the Avigator has controllable edge-glow lighting.

The Avigator requires 21 volts, has a built-in vibrator for power supply, and weighs 21 lbs. The price, complete with antenna and all coaxial cables, is $781.00, federal excise tax included.

THE AVIGATOR JR.

Mitchell's Avigator Jr., Model AT91-47, is a somewhat similar but smaller version of the Avigator. It includes a six-channel VHF transmitter, and a receiver for the 108-130 mc band. The omnirange indicator (an optional feature) is a single-magnetic-bearing type, in which a pointer on the azimuth dial indicates the aircraft's bearing in relation to the station.

The Mitchell Avigator Jr. omni receiver and magnetic bearing indicator. (Mitchell Industries, Inc.)

A low-frequency receiver is also available on the Avigator Jr. model.

Voltage required: 6-12; power source: built-in vibrator; overall installed weight: 20 lbs.; price, with omni indicator, and antenna and cables, but without low frequency receiver, including federal excise tax, $475.00.

DAYTON AVIATION RADIO & EQUIPMENT CORP.

The complete VHF "Micro-Tuner" navigation and communication system manufactured by Dayton Aviation Radio & Equipment Corp. (DARE), Troy, Ohio, consists of five units: transmitter, receiver, omnirange indicator, omnirange converter, and modulator power supply.

The receiver is a tunable unit graduated in tenths of megacycles, with a micro-switch on the control panel for changing from VOR to localizer-VAR reception. It provides for coverage of all VHF navigation and communications facilities, and operates from either 12 or 24 volts dc. A remotely controlled model is also available.

The 22-channel transmitter, providing full coverage from 118 to 127 mc, can be installed separately or in a single instrument panel together with the receiver. The transmitter operates on either 12 or 24 volts dc, and is also available in a remotely controlled model.

The omni converter, in conjunction with the receiver and navigation indicator, provides accurate bearing information on all VOR

DARE VHF receiver-transmitter (left) and omnirange navigation indicator.
(Dayton Aviation Radio & Equipment Corp.)

stations. It is remotely installed in the aircraft. Size: $6\frac{1}{4}$"$\times6\frac{1}{4}$"$\times8\frac{1}{4}$". Weight: 4 lbs., 8 oz.

The navigation indicator, incorporating omnirange and localizer functions in a single instrument, is available for either single or dual installations. The course selector is a knob-actuated rotatable azimuth dial graduated in units of $5°$. The left-right needle is conventional, indicating whether the VOR course is to the left or to the right of the aircraft. The to-from indicator is set into the top of the navigation dial. It presents positive and clear indication on any usable VOR signal, and automatically becomes centered when the signal is unusable.

The entire navigation unit is incorporated in a standard $3\frac{1}{8}$" instrument housing.

The total weight of the DARE omni and VHF equipment, including transmitter and receiver, is about $18\frac{1}{2}$ lbs. The price of one available combination transmitter-receiver-omni set, including antennas and accessories, is $1,245.00.

COLLINS RADIO CO.

Collins makes a number of different instrumentation systems (primarily for airline, military, and larger executive aircraft), all of which include, in one form or another, omnirange navigation receivers.

The Collins 51R-3 is the basic VOR receiver. The 51R-3, together with its accessories, provide for reception and presentation of all radio services now available in the 108-136 mc VHF band. These include: (1) automatic indication of VOR signals, giving combined ADF and magnetic compass presentation on a radio magnetic indicator (RMI); (2) automatic VOR indication, with a cross-pointer meter, the course chosen by manual bearing selector, and including a to-from meter and flag alarm; (3) voice communication on localizer and omnirange as well as on all regular communications channels; and (4) tone-type ILS localizer, including flag alarm.

The receiver requires an external dynamotor power supply, and operates on either 14 or 28 volts dc with the appropriate dynamotor power unit. Five amperes are required at 28 volts dc or 11 amperes at 14 volts dc. For full instrumentation the requirement is 26 volts, 0.2 amperes, at 400 cps.

Any one of the 280 channels covered by the Model 51R receiver may be selected from the cockpit over a positive nine-wire control system. A tone-phase toggle switch is provided on the unit to permit the pilot to choose the appropriate glideslope or localizer service. Numerals and markings on the control unit are radium painted for good readability under all conditions. Control units are available for either vertical or horizontal mounting.

The Collins omni-bearing indicator (left) and omnirange course indicator. (Collins Radio Co.)

The omni-bearing selector permits the pilot to select any desired track to or from the VOR station and to fly along this track using the deviation indicator ID-48 in exactly the same manner as is done when flying inbound on an instrument approach localizer. As a further aid to track flying, the selector contains a to-from indicator which gives a positive indication, first, when the VOR signals are usable, and, second, when the omnirange station has been passed over. The pilot selects his bearing and sense on the selector as, for example, 90° "to" the station. As he flies along this track the to-from indicator indicates "to" the station.   When the station is passed over, the indicator changes to read "from" the station. When the indicator is in the middle or neutral position the pilot knows that he should not rely on the omni system since either the signals are too weak, the equipment is functioning improperly, or the aircraft is too far off the selected track.   The selector is designed for instrument panel mounting. Weight: 2 pounds.

The 337A-2 omnirange bearing indicator presents a continuous indication of the magnetic bearing of an aircraft to a VOR station. The indicator is designed for instrument panel mounting and may be used to provide the pilot bearing information in installations where lack of a gyro or fluxgate compass precludes installation of a radio magnetic indicator.   When this latter equipment is installed, the omni bearing indicator serves to combine omni and heading information to the radio magnetic indicator. A 400-cps. 26-volt, 0.2-ampere power supply is required to operate the indicator. Unit weight: 2.5 pounds.

The 332C-1 radio magnetic indicator gives the pilot continuous automatic presentation of heading and course with reference to the omnirange station.   This presentation is exactly the same as the ADF or radio compass, with the addition of a stabilized magnetic scale synchronized with the fluxgate or gyrocompass.   The two needles of the instrument may be driven (1) from a 51R receiver (omni bearing indicator) and (2) from regular low-frequency ADF equipment; for a dual 51R installation, each needle may be connected to indicate bearing to a separate omnirange station.   The synchronized magnetic scale is driven by a servo motor, coupled electrically, through a type 333B servo amplifier to the fluxgate or gyro compass. The needle driven from the omnirange equipment always points toward the station while the magnetic scale presents aircraft heading. Weight of the 332C-1 is two pounds.

A servo amplifier is required to drive each radio magnetic indicator from the fluxgate or gyro compass. Two types are available for this purpose. Type 333B-1 amplifier is designed for accessory frame mounting and Type 333B-3 is provided with a base for separate mounting.

The Collins approach horizon (left) and radio magnetic indicator. (Collins Radio Co.)

The radio magnetic indicator or omni bearing indicator in practice is used to determine a course to the omni station. However, precise flying of a selected track with either of these instruments is difficult because a small error in the aircraft's position with respect to the track shows up as a correspondingly small deviation in the instrument pointer. On the other hand, a very precise job of track flying can be done using a standard deviation indicator (cross-pointer) with the omni bearing selector. With this latter system the desired track is selected on the omni bearing selector and left-right signals are fed from the receiver to the vertical pointer of the deviation indicator. Full-scale deflection of the pointer corresponds to a 10° offset from the selected track. Thus the deviation indicator provides a vernier method of flying a selected track, while the radio magnetic indicator provides continuous orientation and a simple means of displaying heading and course information to the pilot but with reduced precision of track flying. The receiver also furnishes signals for actuating the vertical flag alarm of the indicator. So long as the flag is down the pilot has a positive indication that the omnirange system is functioning correctly. The deviation indicator is designed for instrument panel mounting. Weight: one pound, 14 ounces.

To fly any desired omnirange course with the Collins equipment, the pilot merely tunes in and identifies the station, and then sets the value of the magnetic course on the omni-bearing selector. Deviation from this course is shown by the vertical needle of the deviation indicator in the identical manner of other sets described earlier. Information in the manner of the ADF is also available from the needle of the Collins radio magnetic indicator. This needle points directly toward the station, like the needle of an ADF on the low-frequency radio ranges. However, the azimuth scale of the radio magnetic indicator is automatically synchronized with the magnetic compass through a servo amplifier link, thus enabling the pilot to home the aircraft directly to the station or to use the radio magnetic bearing to the station as read on the scale underneath the arrow of the needle.

The to-from indicator, like those of other omnirange receivers, swings from "to" to "from" when the aircraft crosses over a VOR station. The Collins equipment, however, presents an added feature. If after crossing a station and proceeding on the same course for a distance the pilot wishes to make a procedure turn and return to the station on the same track, he switches a knob on the track selector. This knob moves a shutter in front of the counter numerals obscuring the value of the track the aircraft has been flying and setting up in its place the reciprocal of that track. At the same time an internal switch, operated by the same knob, reverses the to-from indicator which now switches over from "from" and points to "to." The cross-pointer indicator continues to point in the proper direction of the course.

The radio magnetic indicator may be used with either VOR receiving equipment or an an indicator for one or two low-frequency ADF's. As an ADF indicator it operates as do the standard compass repeaters on the instrument panel, but with the addition of a stabilized magnetic scale. This scale, in effect, performs the work of an extra crew member who occupies himself in continuously resetting the scale of the indicator to agree with the magnetic compass. The system layout of the VOR receiving equipment provides for coupling either one of the radio magnetic indicator needles to the omnirange receiver so that direct ADF-like bearings can be taken on VOR stations. The second needle can be used for low-frequency ADF bearings. This arrangement provides for continuous position fixes when the bearings are plotted on a chart.

COLLINS INTEGRATED FLIGHT SYSTEM

Collins has developed a completely integrated system of flight instrumentation which, although designed primarily for ILS approaches, is also quite useful for enroute navigation by omnirange. The three most important features of this new system are (1) pictorial presentation of the aircraft's position relative to the selected course, (2) reduction of the number of instruments required, and (3) simplification of those that are required.

The two basic instruments of this new system are the course indicator and approach horizon. The first displays pictorially the aircraft's position relative to the course, and the second, an instrument similar in appearance to the familiar artificial horizon, displays the attitude of the aircraft and presents steering information. This latter instrument also provides all the information necessary for making good an ILS course on final approach. The other two instruments required in the Collins integrated flight system are the conventional airspeed indicator and altimeter.

The approach horizon is a roll and pitch reference on which is superimposed position information with respect to the glideslope and steering information for precise ILS flying. The horizon bar and bank indicator are similar in appearance and action to a conventional horizon. Pitch information is displayed by vertical movement of the small airplane in the center of the instrument which serves as a pitch indicator moving up and down as the attitude of the aircraft is changed.

On this same instrument is superimposed displacement information with respect to the glideslope. The pointer at the left hand side of the instrument moves vertically, picturing the aircraft's position with respect to the glideslope.

The course indicator is a directional reference or compass card which provides a properly oriented pictorial presentation of the aircraft's heading and displacement in respect to the ILS or VOR course. This heading reference is driven by the aircraft's directional gyro and displays continuously the aircraft heading as read against

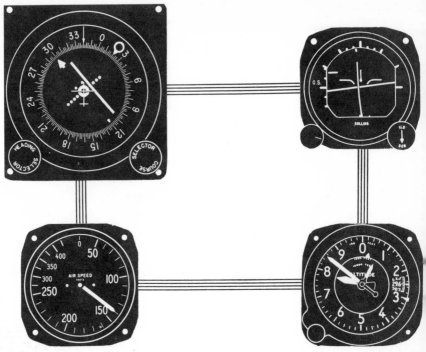

*Basic instruments of the Collins Integrated Flight System: course indi-
cator and approach horizon (top), airspeed indicator and altimeter (below).*

the lubber line of the instrument. For ease in flying selected headings, the card is provided with a marker which may be set by means
of the heading selector knob.   In the accompanying illustration a
heading of 20° has been selected. The marker riding with the card
shows the amount and direction of deviation from the selected heading.

The inner position of the course indicator provides a graphic
picture of the aircraft's heading and displacement with respect to a
selected localizer or VOR course. To select a localizer or omnirange
course the position indicator is rotated by the course selector knob
to the desired course as indicated by the arrow pointer read against
the compass card. The position indicator then rotates with the card
as the aircraft heading is changed. Left-right deflection voltages
from the aircraft's localizer or VOR receiver cause the course line

bar to move across the face of the instrument, thus showing the air-craft's displacement from the selected course. Since the bar also rotates as the aircraft's heading is changed, this bi-directional motion causes it to simulate exactly the selected course with respect to the aircraft heading. In the illustration on page 90, the pilot holding a heading of 340° sees that he is taking a cut of 40° toward his selected omnirange course of 300°. If he continues on this head-ing, the course line bar will move downward to the left, picturing graphically his approach to the course.

"To" and "from" indication for flying omnirange courses is provided by an indicator which appears on the appropriate side of the instrument's center. If the course chosen is "to" an omnirange station, the indicator will appear on the broad arrow side of the center.

The pictorial presentation of course line deviation information eliminates the sensing and ambiguity problems associated with the usual type of crosspointer indicator. When the miniature air-plane is pointed toward the course line bar, the aircraft is approach-ing the selected course. This is true even in localizer service, regardless of whether the flight is inbound or outbound on either the front or back course of the localizer.

The system is very well adapted to flying omnirange courses. Information relative to bearing and displacement in respect to any selected VOR course appears pictorially on the course indicator. Since the sensing of the indicator is always correct there is no possibility for misinterpretation. To intersect a course it is only necessary to fly the small airplane in the center of the instrument toward the course line bar.

While the steering computer feature of the system is not employed for flying omnirange, it can be used to advantage in flying compass headings. With the right hand knob on the approach horizon in the HDG position, steering information with respect to a heading (as selected on the course indicator) is presented on the steering pointer. To maintain this heading it is only necessary for the pilot to maneu-ver the aircraft to keep the pointer centered.

In addition to altitude, glideslope, and steering information, the

approach horizon provides flag warning services in respect to the
ILS and VOR receivers.   The flag marked GS is operated from the
output of the glideslope receiver while the one marked LOC/VOR
receives signals from the localizer and omnirange receiver.

BENDIX RADIO

The Bendix NA-3 omnirange navigational system is designed to
permit maximum utilization of omnirange, ILS localizers (both 90-150
cps and phase comparison), visual-aural ranges, tower communication, company communication, and a portion of the military communication band (132-135.9 mc).   It is the commercial counterpart of a
system designed by Bendix for the Air Force.

The Bendix TA-18A VHF transmitter transmits on each of the
channels spaced 100 kc from 118.1 mc to 135.9 mc. Built-in crystals
are used in a "crystal saver" circuit to provide operation on the 17
channels with an overall frequency tolerance of .007%.   The limit of
line-of-sight distance to the radio transmissions practically eliminates interference between stations on the same frequency if the
stations are located so that the aircraft cannot "see" both stations
at once.

The MN-85B receiver of the NA-3 system is a crystal-controlled
superheterodyne.   It will tune to each of the channels spaced at 100
kc intervals from 108 mc to 135.9 mc.   By means of the Bendix
"crystal saver" circuit, or monitor, crystal-controlled operation on
these 280 channels is possible with 21 crystals which are installed
in the receiver at the time of manufacture.   The receiver has the
standard aircraft half ATR form factor with rear mounted cable connector.   The antenna cable connector is on the front of the receiver.

Frequency selection in the receiver is accomplished from a remote
position.   Two concentric knobs are graduated in frequency.   The
larger, nearest the panel, is graduated in megacycle steps.   The
smaller is graduated in steps of 1/10 of a mc.   The scale is back-
lighted for maximum visibility.   A minimum of interconnecting wires

The Bendix Omni-Mag, three-in-one instrument presentation, and (right) the Bendix radio magnetic indicator. (Bendix Radio Division)

is used between the remote position and the receiver. This is in accord with the standard wiring established by the airlines and the radio manufacturers for this kind of equipment.

THE OMNI-MAG

The indicating unit of the Bendix NA-3 system is the "Omni-Mag," mounted on the pilot's instrument panel. It works in conjunction with the VOR and localizer receiver, a glide path receiver, and a gyro-stabilized magnetic compass system to present flight information previously shown on several indicators.

The Omni-Mag minimizes the usual computations necessary for a VOR or ILS orientation problem, and in station or runway approaches it shows the pilot a continuous "motion picture" of the selected course, the aircraft heading, and its position relative to the course. In this presentation, the Omni-Mag eliminates the need for separate course selectors and cross-pointer indicators.

The Omni-Mag provides selection of any omnirange or localizer course. A sliding bar continuously shows position of the aircraft on or off the selected course. A pivoted pointer continuously shows the aircraft's magnetic heading with relation to the selected course. A second sliding bar shows the vertical position of the aircraft with relation to the glide path.

In the Omni-Mag picture the pilot sees the vertical slide bar as the omnirange course. He sees the free end of the pivoted magnetic heading pointer as the nose of the aircraft. When the value of the course is set into the dial's course window and the aircraft is turned so that the "nose" pointer is straight up, the aircraft heading is equivalent to the heading set into the window. Turning the aircraft to the right or left of the heading in the window causes the nose pointer to swing to the right or left of the chosen course.

Bendix calls Omni-Mag navigation "flying by picture" because of the similarity between what the pilot actually sees through the windscreen when flying VFR and what he sees on the Omni-Mag.

When cross-winds exist, it is necessary to hold the aircraft nose at some drift angle to the VOR course, maintaining the same picture on the Omni-Mag that would be seen through the windscreen when flying VFR. Any change in the cross-wind component during the flight becomes apparent by movement of the course-line bar away from the center of the dial. The pilot corrects for this simply by turning the nose pointer toward the bar long enough and steeply enough to regain a position on the course. The aircraft is then turned to a new crab angle. In this way the current drift angle is automatically presented throughout the flight.

THE RADIO MAGNETIC INDICATOR

As an auxiliary presentation of VOR data for the pilot, the Bendix radio magnetic indicator (RMI) is also available as a part of the NA-3 navigational system. It combines VOR indication with the indication of a Pioneer fluxgate or other remote indicating magnetic compass. This gives a heading-sensitive indication of direction toward the station. It is directly comparable to the indication of a standard ADF azimuth indicator. The RMI always points toward the VOR station regardless of aircraft heading. The reading of the pointer against the lubber line indicates the change in heading required to fly directly toward or away from either station. The scale is rotated by the fluxgate compass. The reading of a pointer against this scale is always the magnetic bearing to the omnirange station. An MN-69 A radial converter indicator must be installed when the RMI is used to give VOR indication. It is important to remember that the VOR data is not aircraft-heading sensitive. The instrument indicates magnetic radial directly to or from the range station regardless of aircraft heading.

SPERRY GYROSCOPE CO.

The Sperry Integrated Instrument System is a combination of three panel instruments aimed at simplicity of operation in flying VOR courses and making instrument approaches and letdowns. It provides a realistic pictorial presentation of both aircraft heading and position with respect to VHF courses. The system is based on standard accepted instrument presentation.

The three instruments in the system—gyrosyn compass, horizon flight director, and pictorial deviation indicator—replace the standard RMI repeater, the gyro-horizon, and the ILS deviation indicator, and in addition provide two new kinds of instruments—the flight director and a pictorial presentation of radio beam position.

THE C-6 GYROSYN COMPASS

The compass has a master indicator with RMI presentation: a rotating dial compass card and two radio pointers driven from either VOR or ADF receivers. The compass card, operating as a master indicator of the gyrosyn compass system, is a primary direction instrument of the RMI repeater type. The master indicator is driven from a remote directional gyro.

A rotatable course marker is provided on the compass card of the C-6. Setting this marker to a given magnetic heading simultaneously sets the heading for the flight director. This operation not only locates the setting on the primary direction instrument but also

The Sperry radio magnetic indicator (upper left), horizon flight director (upper right), and pictorial deviation indicator (lower left). (Sperry Gyroscope Co.)

eliminates the necessity of having a separate heading selector. Up to eight repeaters can be installed.

THE HZ-1 HORIZON FLIGHT DIRECTOR

This is a horizon-indicating instrument which has no connection with omnirange flying except insofar as it is used in helping to keep the aircraft in proper flight attitude. It gives a sensitive indication of pitch and roll by means of a bar-less horizon.

THE R-1 PICTORIAL DEVIATION INDICATOR

This instrument provides indication of displacement from a selected omnirange course (or ILS localizer) in the conventional manner. It also incorporates a course selector, the function of which is identical to the others already described. The pictorial presentation of course position is obtained by mounting the course deviation indicator in the case and driving it by a servo as a remote compass repeater. The meter is in the center position when the aircraft heading is the same as the course selector setting. As the aircraft heading changes from this setting, the meter rotates accordingly to show pictorially the angular difference between the beam and the aircraft heading. No compass graduations are provided in this instrument since they are provided on the primary heading instrument.

Except when the radio is tuned to an ILS frequency, the horizontal glide path pointer is automatically held out of view.

One of the important features of the pictorial deviation indicator is the method of indicating "to" and "from" during VOR operation. The course deviation pointer is made in the form of a narrow converging "V." When the aircraft is flying toward the station, the "V" converges at the top of the instrument. As the station is crossed and the aircraft flies into the "from" zone, the receiver causes the "V" to rotate 180°. The result is relatively fast rotation of the meter, which conspicuously indicates to the pilot that he has passed the station. This "to-from" presentation resembles somewhat the action of an ordinary ADF which also swings around 180° when the aircraft crosses the station to which the ADF is tuned.

6

Accuracy and maintenance

It probably goes without saying that omnirange navigation is only as accurate as the airborne omnirange receiver and the ground transmitter. Pilots can't do anything about transmitter operation (which is in the capable hands of FAA technicians) but there are a number of ways in which they can guarantee the accuracy of their receivers— or at least determine the amount of error.

CHECKING THE RECEIVER

In itself the omnirange receiver is a wonderfully precise instrument, but like all fine electronic equipment it is subject to a certain amount of wear and tear that can eventually result in false indications. This is not only hazardous, it is also disconcerting.

How are VOR receivers checked for accuracy?

There are four principal methods, described below in order of decreasing reliability.

1. FAA TEST SIGNAL

This is the simplest and most accurate way of checking an omni receiver. Unfortunately, the facilities for the test signal are available at only a few of the larger airports, such as LaGuardia in New York City, Midway in Chicago, Kansas City Municipal, Miami International, and the like.

If there is a VOR test signal on the airport, all that's necessary is to turn on the receiver and let it warm up for five minutes. The aircraft can be located anywhere on the field. Tune to the omni channel used for the test signal. With the left-right needle centered, the bearing indication on the course selector should be 0° "from" or 180° "to." The difference between the actual indication on the course selector and 0° "from" or 180° "to" is the error of the receiver.

A reasonable amount of receiver error is plus or minus 4°. When the error is greater than 4°, a maintenance check is in order.

In the radiated signal test, as in the others described here, it is important to check on receiver sensitivity. In other words, there should be no activity of the red alarm-flag on sets with this particular kind of equipment, and on the other models the needle should be fully deflected to "to" or "from" indication.

2. AIRPORT CHECK POINTS

At nearly 200 medium-size airports in the United States the FAA has designated a specific check point for VOR receivers. This is usually a point near a ramp, taxiway, or other convenient spot, to which the aircraft should be moved and parked for the test. A sign located at the checkpoint indicates the correct "to" and "from" courses that should be received at that point. For example, "DCA 176-356," which means Washington, D.C., omnirange, with a correct magnetic course of 176° toward the station and 356° from it. Either course may be used for the test. The heading of the aircraft has no effect on the bearing indication. If the error is less than plus or minus 4°, the receiver is in good shape.

All FAA-designated airport and airborne check points, as well as radiated-test-signal sites, are listed in the Airman's Guide. If you don't have a copy of the Guide, ask any airport tower controller where the nearest check point is located.

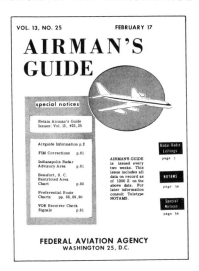

VOL. 13, NO. 25   FEBRUARY 17

AIRMAN'S
GUIDE

special notices

Retain Airman's Guide
Issues: Vol. 13, #23, 25

Airguide Information p.2

FIM Corrections   p.61

Indianapolis Radar
Advisory Area   p.81

Beaufort, S. C.
Restricted Area
Chart   p.80

Preferential Route
Charts   pp. 88, 89, 90

VOR Receiver Check
Signals   p.91

AIRMAN'S GUIDE
is issued every
two weeks. This
issue includes all
data on record as
of 1200 Z on the
above date. For
later information
consult Teletype
NOTAMS.

Radar-Radio
Listings
page 3

NOTAMS
page 54

Special
Notices
page 54

FEDERAL AVIATION AGENCY
WASHINGTON 25, D.C.

3. DUAL RECEIVER CHECK

A pilot fortunate enough to fly an aircraft equipped with dual omni receivers can make a quick, accurate check of one receiver against the other without recourse to designated check points or radiated test signals. The readings on both indicators should agree within plus or minus $4°$, which, incidentally, is the generally accepted maximum tolerance for instrument flight. If they deviate by more than $4°$, they should be tested against a radiated test signal or airport check point.

4. AIRBORNE CHECKS

Airborne VOR receiver checks at certain designated points near terminals and along the Victor airways are also available, although they are of necessity not as accurate as the ground checks. For these tests it is necessary to fly toward a selected landmark on a course to or from the particular omnirange station. When the pilot is over the landmark he centers the left-right needle and determines how much the course selector reading varies from the published bearing at the check point. The allowable tolerance on this check is plus or minus $6°$.

The same sort of procedure can be improvised by a pilot in areas where there are no **FAA** designated check points. Find a prominent landmark on the chart and measure its magnetic bearing from a VOR station at least 20 miles distant. Fly over the landmark at a reasonably low altitude. The difference between the chart-measured bearing and the course selector bearing is the receiver error, which should be less than plus or minus 6°.

VOR RECEIVER MAINTENANCE

Most errors in omnirange receivers can be corrected with minor adjustments, but the actual maintenance work should be entrusted only to well-equipped repair stations with a good deal of experience in the field.

Although you shouldn't attempt your own omnirange maintenance work, there are a number of things you can do to keep the receiver in top working condition.

Never start the engine when the receiver is turned on. Use the aircraft's electrical accessories in such a way that the generator and battery aren't overloaded. Most small VOR receivers draw eight to nine amperes at a nominal 12 volts. Actual voltage should be between 13.8 and 14.2. Using the receiver at voltages above 14.5 can cause damage and shorten the life of tubes and other components. Low voltage can reduce receiver sensitivity and cause false readings in some types of receivers.

A good voltmeter is inexpensive insurance against unwittingly using so much electrical equipment simultaneously that voltage drops to dangerous levels.

To avoid the electrical "noise" that often produces false VOR readings, a clean electrical system, carefully bonded (not just grounded), is necessary.

Antenna location may affect accuracy of bearings in some instances. Follow the advice of an experienced installation man in locating the antenna.

Tubes should be replaced when they fall below certain power limits, of course, but new tubes indiscriminately added may cause more trouble than they prevent, since most sudden tube failures occur in the first 20 or so hours of service. New tubes also may change the calibration of the receiver and require re-tuning of associated circuits.

Inaccuracies in VOR receivers usually develop gradually. Sudden error can appear, but it is extremely rare. Slow deterioration of parts is the usual cause of erratic readings.

STATION ERRORS

The FAA maintains as nearly constant a watch as practical on the accuracy of the signals being transmitted from all omnirange stations. The transmitters are monitored from the ground at frequent intervals, but it is only from the air that the true accuracy of the radials can be determined. To that end, all stations with suspected errors are flight-checked by one of several methods, and the results

★ROCKY MOUNT-RADIO: April 28, VOR cmsnd. Freq: 116.5 mc. Ident: RMT. Lctd at lat 35-58-42, long. 77-42-09; 4.2 n mi E Rocky Mount Arpt. Monitoring category (1).

WILMINGTON-RADIO: VOR quad 65-235° flgt-checked to shoreline only. (3-9)

on test basis only. (11-10) FLD: Helicopters lndg and take-off use caution to avoid 55' unlgtd overhead high voltage p-line running W from ctl twr to arpt bndry. Due to non-visibility twr unable to ctl tfc on taxi strip between Rnwys 16 and 23 and final apch leg and first 1300' Rnwy 23. (11-10)

NORTH DAKOTA: BISMARCK ARPT: Obstn lgts apch end Rnwy 26, 35 inop. (11-30)
FARGO-RADIO: April 18, LF rng and Z mrkr, Barnesville and Glyndon, Minn. and West Fargo, N. D. Fan Markers shut down until approx June 18. (5-3)
GOLVA-RADIO: VOR has severe course disturbance area 2 n mi in diameter at 4-5n mi out on radial 240° at 4300'. (7-31) DME coverage 20°-35°, 90°-95° and 175°-225°, 35 n mi at min en route alt. (1-1)
LANGDON ARPT: NW/SE Rnwy clsd, const. E/W Rnwy lgtd. Lgts avail. on req. (11-1)
**RHAME ARPT: Abandoned. (3-29)
**SANISH ARPT: Abandoned. (3-29)
OHIO: AKRON ARPT: Due to non-visibility twr unable to ctl tfc SSW of airdock on apch to Rnwy 36L. First 800' E end Rnwy 9-27 and NE end 6-24 landfilled oiled and rolled - use daylgt hrs only at pilots' discretion. (12-10)
AKRON-CANTON ARPT-TOWER: ILS back course has flyable bend 4 to 2 n mi from stn, displaced 3.5° E Rnwy 18 centerline throughout area of bend. ILS glide slope usable 200' weather minimum. (2-14)
CINCINNATI-RADIO: VOR has light to moderate visual and aural interference 360°-60° from stn to 52 n mi at min en route instr alt. (2-23) DME coverage 60°-150°, 35 n mi at min en route alt. (1-14)
CINCINNATI-ORE: single-eng tfc on NW/SE Taxiway from Rnwy 18 to 200' SE of Rnwy 18 unless such tfc remains on fld side of this taxiway. After lndg on rnwy in use acft taxi straight ahead to nearest intsxn. No 180° turns on rnwy prior to rcvg approval from twr. Prior to departure acft with no

Check the Airport and Radio Notices section of the Airman's Guide for information on flight-checked VOR radials and unusable courses.

are published in the Notices to Airmen (Notam) section of the Airman's Guide. These notices usually take the form of a warning that
such-and-such VOR has a maximum usable distance of so many
miles in a certain direction at minimum instrument altitude, or that
moderate scalloping exists in the radials in the northwest sector of
such-and-such VOR, or that radials 0, 90, 100, 130, and so on have
been flight-checked and found to be unreliable.

Actually, the accuracy of omnirange course alignment through the
360° of azimuth is excellent, especially when compared to that of
the old LF ranges.   Each VOR radial is normally within 2° of its
published value.   On certain stations some sectors may contain
slightly larger errors, but no course published as usable in the Airman's Guide is displaced more than 3½° from its theoretical location.
Nevertheless, certain minor irregularities may be observed in using
VOR facilities, such as apparent course roughness, infrequent brief
flag alarm activity, course deflections and/or limited distance range.
Pilots should be on the alert for these eccentricities especially
when flying unfamiliar routes.

It is suggested that the Notam section of the Airman's Guide be
consulted before departure on an instrument flight.

STATION CALIBRATION

VOR stations can be calibrated mechanically from an aircraft in
flight by recording the voltage applied to the left-right needle
(course deviation indicator) as the aircraft circles the station at a
radius of from six to 15 miles. The course selector is advanced in
10° steps to keep the left-right needle on center and to provide   a
recording whereby the indicated magnetic bearing from the omnirange
station may be obtained.   The indicated bearing is compared with
the magnetic bearing, as measured by a theodolite operated on the
ground at the VOR station.

7

Distance measuring equipment

Distance Measuring Equipment (commonly referred to as DME) is an essential part of the VORTAC system of airways which is planned for full operation within a few years. Along with the omnirange, DME has also been adopted by the International Civil Aviation Organization as the standard world-wide navigation aid.

There are actually two kinds of DME currently in operation, each of which requires different airborne receiving equipment. Civil DME is installed at a number of VOR and ILS sites, but the primary distance-measuring facility is DMET, which was adopted from the military TACAN system (see Chapter 9). As far as pilot operation of the DME receiving equipment is concerned, however, they are virtually the same, and the references to DME in this book include both systems.

At this writing the available airborne DME equipment is still too expensive for the average private aircraft owner, but to the airlines, military services, and FAA it is a jet-age necessity in precise fixing and traffic control. Unquestionably the equipment will come within the financial reach of more and more pilots as production increases and prices are lowered.

Operating in conjunction with VOR, DME provides the pilot with a continuous position fix by telling him how far his aircraft is from the ground station. With the distance information from DME and azimuth information from the VOR, the pilot can pinpoint his position at any moment almost automatically. The actual electronic equipment involved in DME is highly complicated, but the manner in

105

which the distance information is presented to the pilot couldn't be simpler.

HOW DME OPERATES

In some respects, DME operates a little like radar. The radar transmitter sends out a signal which is received back at the source after the signal bounces off a target. In DME, however, the signal is transmitted from an aircraft and received at a ground station which then transmits the pulses back to the aircraft on a different frequency. The airborne DME receiver measures the amount of time required for the round-trip of the signal, and then translates the time

Bendix DME indicator, with range set for 0-200 miles. For close-in work the range can be set for 0-40 miles. (Bendix Radio Division)

measurement into distance from the aircraft to the ground station. An indicator in the aircraft records this distance automatically and continuously.

These two-way transmissions occur automatically many times a second. If the signal being received by the airborne equipment is lost for a period of less than eight seconds, the interrogator goes into a "velocity memory" state and continues to indicate mileage changes at the rate shown when the "memory" period started. An amber light tells the pilot when the equipment is in "memory." The object of this feature is to prevent interruption of the mileage display caused by momentary signal loss. When signal loss continues for more than eight seconds, the interrogator goes into "search." With the equipment in this position, the indicator pointer revolves rapidly until the signal is again received from the ground transponder.

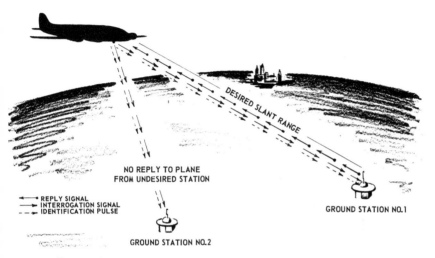

NO REPLY TO PLANE
FROM UNDESIRED STATION

DESIRED SLANT RANGE

GROUND STATION NO.1

REPLY SIGNAL
INTERROGATION SIGNAL
IDENTIFICATION PULSE

GROUND STATION NO.2

Principle of transmission and reception of DME signals.

DME measures slant distance, rather than distance over the ground. In other words, it measures the distance between the ground station and the aircraft's position above the ground. However, the navigational error introduced by slant measurement, except when the aircraft is located near the station, is negligible. In passing over the station, the DME indicator shows the approximate height of the aircraft, rather than zero miles. The ground antenna is designed to radiate a circular pattern with energy transmitted in a horizontal rather than vertical direction, and for this reason DME reception is sometimes interrupted briefly when the aircraft is over the station. During these periods the DME goes into "search" for a short while.

The DME ground station receiver-transmitter unit is called the transponder. In addition to proceeding through its cycle of receiving signals from the airborne interrogator and sending out replies, the transponder also transmits identification signals at regularly spaced intervals synchronized with the identification code of the VOR or ILS station with which it is paired. DME and VOR transmission is arranged so that a pilot tuning to the frequency of any VOR station also automatically tunes in that station's DME equipment.

The accuracy of the airborne DME interrogator is designed to be comparable to that of radar. At a distance of 25 miles from the transponder, for instance, the error should be no greater than plus or minus ½ mile.

The DME frequencies are in the 960-1,215 mc band in the UHF portion of the radio spectrun.

A FIX WITH DME AND VOR

A pilot turns his channel selector switch to the frequency of a VOR-DME station. After the station is identified he turns the course selector until the left-right needle is centered. He reads his magnetic bearing to or from the station. The DME indicator tells him his distance to or from the same station. . . . He has a precise fix. That's all there is to it.

The pilot can use this information in either one of several ways, depending upon what he wants to do with it:

(1) If he wants to establish a new course or heading he can plot the fix on a chart simply by laying his plotter along the correct VOR radial (as read from his course selector) and then making a pencil mark at the distance indicated by his DME from the station. The new course is plotted from this fix-point.

(2) If he wants the fix as the basis for a voice position report all he is required to do is pick up his mike and transmit the distance

and azimuth information as read directly from the VOR-DME indicators; for instance, "Oakland radio, this is seven-zero-one-one hotel, one-two-zero degrees magnetic and three-two miles from the Oakland omni at eight-thousand on the hour."

(3) If he is flying a prescribed Victor airway radial, he can check it constantly with VOR bearings, and make proper corrections to heading when necessary, on the basis of distance remaining to fly to the next station.

AN INSTRUMENT APPROACH WITH VOR-DME

Reliable VOR-DME instrument approaches can be made to almost any airport located within a reasonable distance of the transmitters. This permits access to many fields that would otherwise be shut down during IFR weather conditions—fields that ordinarily serve corporation, private, and charter aircraft rather than the airlines.

Here is an example, selected because the airport (Leighton, Pennsylvania) has no radio navigation facilities of its own and because it lies in a valley between high ridges. Without DME, an instrument approach from the Allentown VOR to Leighton would be possible only with very high ceiling and visibility minimums. (See illustration on page 110.)

Leighton airport, with an altitude of 562 feet, is 14 nautical miles from the Allentown VOR-DME. The procedure calls for an approach from Allentown on a radial of 304° at 2,100 feet until the DME indicates 12 miles, which is a distance safely past the ridges. The ceiling is 1,000 feet above the airport elevation, or 1,562 feet above sea level.

Twelve miles out from Allentown (as indicated by DME), the pilot starts a fairly rapid descent—approximately 500 feet per minute. He breaks out over the center of the airport, makes a tight circle of the field and lands. If the ceiling had been lower than measured, the pilot would have commenced a missed approach procedure at 14 miles from Allentown, making a left turn to 238° and climbing out of the valley to 3,000 feet.

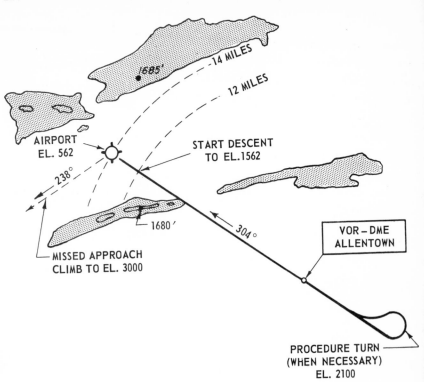

A pilot flying this approach is dependent on the accuracy of the DME to prevent passing over the airport toward the high ground beyond it. A number of actual flights on this approach and letdown at Leighton have shown various DME readings of 13.5, 14, 13.6 and 13.8 miles when the aircraft were over the airport—a high degree of accuracy considering the hilly terrain surrounding the field.

DETERMINING GROUNDSPEED

DME makes it easy to determine groundspeed at any point along a course within signal-receiving distance of a station. Some pilots use a stopwatch or clock with sweep-second hand to determine the number of seconds required to fly one, two, or three miles. A computer is used to establish the actual number of miles per hour or knots. The easiest method is to note the number of miles change in the DME readings over a one-minute period, and then multiply the total by 60. For example, if the DME reading decreases in one minute from 26 to 22 nautical miles, the groundspeed is 240 knots. No written or computer calculations are needed.

The accuracy of groundspeeds determined by DME naturally increases as longer periods of time are allowed for the changes in distance. Even with short-range DME groundspeeds, however, ETA's for destination and intermediate checkpoints can be established much more accurately than with the aid of previous facilities. Moreover, DME makes it possible for the pilot to re-check his ETA whenever he suspects a wind shift. He is wholly independent of the scattered fan markers and other checkpoints along the airways, since the distance remaining shows continuously on the instrument panel.

HOLDING PROCEDURES

DME makes it possible to establish many new kinds of traffic holding patterns and to increase the accuracy of the ones established originally for the older facilities. The patterns are flown on a basis

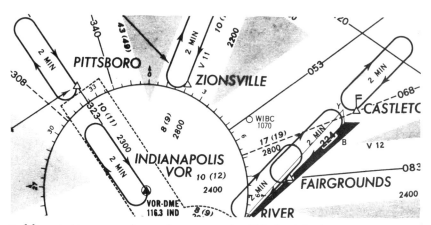

Holding patterns such as these are simplified with distance measuring equipment.

of actual distances covered, rather than on the basis of the one- and two-minute time-patterns.

Some DME holding patterns are the familiar race-track shape, established 7-15 miles from the VOR-DME station; others are 12-20 miles distant. One precise holding procedure uses two different VOR radials for the long sides of the race-track pattern. This produces a slightly egg-shaped pattern, since the radials are not parallel, but doesn't introduce any difficulties at reasonable distances from the station where the radials differ by only $3°-5°$.

Radar observers monitoring some of these DME holding procedures have reported "tight and exact" patterns, even though some of the flights were conducted under conditions of 50-knot winds.

DME also makes it possible to fly an arc around a station at a selected distance from the station. The pilot selects a DME reading, representing the radius of his circular course, and then holds the reading constant. He can determine his progress around the orbit by measuring the VOR radial at intervals, or he can pre-set the VOR to show when a given radial is intercepted.

LONGITUDINAL SEPARATION

Aircraft not equipped with DME and flying in the same direction at the same altitude along a Victor airway are separated longitudinally by units of time: five minutes if the first aircraft has filed an airspeed at least 25 miles greater than that of a succeeding aircraft, 10 minutes where radio facilities permit a frequent determination of position and speed, and 15 minutes where such facilities are scattered. With high-speed aircraft the separation may amount to as much as 65 miles.

DME does away with much of this extravagant use of the airspace. When two aircraft heading in the same direction at the same altitude are equipped with DME they have a constant check on the distance that separates them. Ground traffic controllers can direct them to different headings or altitudes if one aircraft begins to close on the other, or under conditions that might approach the hazardous the pilots can change their own headings and altitudes if they are in communication.

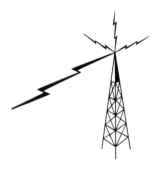

8

The course-line computer

The simplest way to fly by VOR-DME is directly from station to station, with the receiving equipment providing an automatic and continuous fix in terms of bearing and distance to or from a given station. In this case the omni also indicates any deviation of the aircraft from the selected course to or from the station. However, when an aircraft is flown off airways, to one side or the other of an omni station but still within signal reception range, the omni can not show deviation from a selected course.

To provide such information, an ingenious electronic calculator called the course-line computer was developed a few years ago. For one reason and another, however, it seems not to have been widely accepted, and at the present time it is in limited use only. Nevertheless, it was an interesting experiment in pointing up the navigational possibilities of distance-bearing information, and a few paragraphs on the equipment may be of interest.

The navigational principle behind the operation of the course-line computer is called "R-Theta," usually designated R-θ, the latter being the eighth letter of the Greek alphabet. In this system R represents the distance from a fixed point, such as a VOR-DME station, since it would be the radius of a circle drawn at that distance around

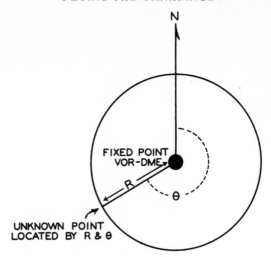

the fixed point. The theta symbol (θ) represents the bearing from the same fixed point, that is, the angle between the station and the aircraft measured from magnetic north.

The diagram shows how a course could be flown between two points (A and B) with the distance from a VOR-DME station computed for pre-selected bearings. In flight it would be possible to

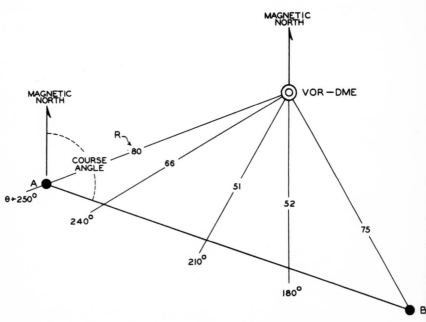

check the DME indicator as each of these pre-selected bearing lines was crossed (you would know when you reached that point by the angle indication on your omnirange receiver) and thus determine your position with relation to your course.

For example, the calculations for a flight from A to B show that the 180° bearing line crosses the course 52 miles out from the station. If the DME indicator reads 54 miles when the 180° line is crossed in actual flight it means that you are two miles to the right of course and the heading must be corrected to the left to get back on the course A-B.

As we said earlier, it would be possible theoretically to fly a VOR-DME course like that. Actually, however, not only would it involve too much work but the track of the aircraft would probably be represented by a zig-zag line instead of a straight one.

The course-line computer does the work for you. Moreover, its calculations are instantaneous, continual, visual, and precise. It tells you when your aircraft deviates from course, regardless of where or in which direction you are flying.

The computer absorbs radial information from the omnirange, and distance information from the DME. The lateral deviation from course is indicated by the left-right needle. The along-track distance to your destination is presented by means of a "projected distance" indicator.

THE AIRBORNE EQUIPMENT

In order to see what the course-line computer actually can do let's take a look at the equipment made by the Collins Radio Co. It's called the NC-101 navigation computer, and consists of five separate components:

1. The navigation computer itself.
2. The course indicator.
3. The card reader.
4. The waypoint selector.
5. The distance indicator.

The system is designed to enable a pilot to fly a selected course to any chosen waypoint or destination, neither of which need have any radio navigation facilities. It is necessary only that the aircraft be within the service area of a VOR-DME station or any two radio transmitting stations.

The system indicates deviation from the selected course line in a pictorial presentation of the aircraft's position on the course indicator, and shows the distance to or from a waypoint or destination by means of the distance indicator. By means of the card reader it automatically tunes the VOR-DME receivers and supplies pre-coded input reference data necessary for the computation. This feature reduces the pilot's work load and lessens the possibility of human error. Station frequencies and navigation reference information are entered into the computer through the medium of the punched card.

Course indicator (left), distance indicator, and waypoint selector of the Collins NC-101 course-line computer. (Collins Radio Co.)

The waypoint selector is a standard 3" instrument panel indicator with two controls for selecting a given ground location as waypoint. The magnetic bearing of the waypoint from a selected "master" station and the distance from the station to the waypoint are set on two digital counters reading azimuth in degrees (0 to 360) and distance in miles (0 to 99).

The card reader takes a manually inserted punched card and reads the holes punched in the card to automatically tune the two navigation receivers and to obtain input data required by the computer. Data for five different station pairs are accommodated on a single punched card. The navigation receivers may be tuned manually when the computer is not in use.

The distance indicator shows continuously the distance in miles from the aircraft to the selected waypoint or destination. Distance is presented as a pointer indication against a circular scale calibrated from 0 to 150 miles. Flag alarms are provided to indicate proper functioning of the computer and associated VOR receiver. When the computer is switched to give distance to touchdown in an ILS approach the distance indicator reads 0 to 15 miles full scale.

The course indicator provides for the selection of any course, and pictorially displays the aircraft's position with reference to the selected course line. When the navigation computer is not in operation the course indicator provides for omnirange course selection in addition to to-from and course deviation information. It also provides indication of aircraft heading and a means for heading selection. The instrument, in other words, presents the pilot with a map-like picture of his heading and position relative to his desired course.

The navigational computer (left) and card reader unit of the Collins course-line computer. (Collins Radio Co.)

Here are the progressive steps in the use of the Collins computer for enroute navigation by means of a VOR-DME station:

(1) Select a VOR-DME station that will be at all times within range of the aircraft until it reaches the waypoint. The VOR-DME station can be tuned either manually or by means of the punched card system.

(2) On the waypoint selector set the azimuth and distance of the waypoint from the VOR-DME station. The azimuth and distance can be measured directly from an aeronautical chart.

(3) Set the aircraft's course to the waypoint on the course indicator. This course is also measured from the chart.

(4) Fly the picture presented on the course indicator by watching for indications that the aircraft is left or right of course. Heading, course, and to-from indications also must be noted.

(5) Watch the distance indication to or from the waypoint as shown on the distance indicator. When 0 miles are indicated (with the course deviation bar centered under the course pointer), the aircraft is over the waypoint.

(6) After crossing the waypoint, continue on course until the next VOR-DME station is within range, then repeat steps (1) through (5) above, selecting new frequency, waypoint, and course.

As we said earlier, the course-line computer is in limited use only, but if it or some similar equipment were adopted generally it would make possible the creation of an entirely new air traffic control system based on multiple airways. This would be akin to making a six-lane superhighway out of a narrow two-lane road.

The present system of handling instrument traffic on two-lane airways wastes an enormous amount of airspace, especially considering that provision must be made for both 500-knot jets and 100-knot private aircraft. Separation between aircraft on the same airway at the same altitude can slow operations down to the hazardous point.

The multiple-lane airways made possible by the course-line computer would seem to be the solution to this problem. With a single row of VOR-DME stations to define the center line of the airway, it will become practical to utilize the course-line computer to fly an number of properly spaced parallel lanes at each altitude level. Such a system would eliminate traffic bottlenecks and help to achieve the goal of all-weather, on-time flight reliability.

9

VORTAC

For a number of years now the U. S. Air Force and Navy have utilized a short-range navigation system of their own which provides distance and bearing information in much the same manner as VOR and DME. This system is called TACAN (for "tactical air navigation"). Admittedly, TACAN has several advantages over VOR-DME as an accurate navigation aid, but the advantages are of more interest to the military services than to civilian users of the airways.

The VOR-DME system was planned and developed in the beginning by both the FAA and the military as the standard system calculated to meet U. S. navigational and traffic control needs at least until 1975. Later, however, experimental TACAN was introduced, and the Air Force and Navy came out strongly in favor of it. The FAA meanwhile had gone ahead and completed its nation-wide VOR installation as planned, and was well along in the DME program when a choice between the rival non-compatible systems became a public issue.

On one side were the FAA, nearly all civilian pilots, and the owners of private and business aircraft. On the other side were the Air Force and Navy. Somewhere in between were the airlines. The advocates of VOR-DME did not deny that TACAN was somewhat more accurate and more adaptable to the military's special needs, but argued that it would be absurd to scrap the whole multi-million dollar VOR-DME program merely because the military had committed itself to a different system. The idea was to have a common system of navigation which would be used to advantage by sports plane and jet fighter alike. Not even the United States could afford the dubious luxury of two new systems, to say nothing of a third one, the old low-frequency airways which are still operating.

There was not only the public investment in facilities to consider but also the fact that thousands of private and business aircraft owners had already spent millions of dollars to install omnirange receivers which would be useless if TACAN were to become the common navigation system. On the other hand, the

Lightweight, transistorized omnirange receivers like the Lear "VORTRAN" can be used with all current VOR facilities and those planned for the next 15 years. Both bearing indicator and converter are completely housed in a 3½-inch case, and weight less than 2½ pounds. (Lear, Inc.)

military could not effectively use VOR-DME as a tactical means of navigation: they wanted a system which could function equally well from aircraft carriers, submarines, and combat zones — all operations for which VOR-DME was never intended.

The controversy was not settled until 1956 when a government-appointed committee representing all of the interested parties compromised on VORTAC — half VOR-DME and half TACAN. This is the system which is now in the process of construction, the system which is planned to be operational not only in the U. S. but internationally as well.

The VORTAC compromise means that the VOR part of the system will remain essentially as it is, and the distance-measuring feature of TACAN will be integrated gradually into the VOR system until approximately 300 ground transmitters are functioning by the target date of 1960. The goal of 1,087 combined VORTAC stations is expected to be reached by 1965. Meanwhile, the Air Force and Navy will continue to develop and test the complete TACAN system for their own purposes.

As we pointed out earlier, the omnirange is not a perfect navigation aid. It is subject to errors in both transmission and reception, as well as errors of interpretation. Good airborne receiving equipment is still not as cheap as comparable low-frequency equipment. Then, too, there is the British short-range Decca system, a competitor as a navigation aid, both in accuracy and simplicity, which has some advantages over VORTAC.

For better or for worse, however, the decision was made in favor of VORTAC as both the national and international system at least until 1975, by which time presumably there will be something better to replace it. The point is that VORTAC is a good system, it is operating, and the performance is more than just acceptable.

Where does the average private or commercial pilot fit into the VORTAC picture?

TACAN means nothing to him since it is basically a military system. The distance-measuring feature of TACAN is still somewhat beyond his realization at this point, especially since the receiving equipment costs around $5,000. Moreover, the pilot of a Cessna 175, a Piper Comanche, or even an Aero Commander, cruising at speeds between 125 and 225 mph, doesn't really require distance-measuring equipment. Omnirange alone will provide him with all the fixes he ordinarily needs in flying the Victor airways. DME is at its most useful in instrument weather and high-density traffic, especially airline and military operations.

A word or two about TACAN operation may be in order.

The TACAN bearing-information ground transmitter is somewhat similar to the VOR transmitter, but it operates in the ultra high frequency band (UHF) rather than VHF. High-elevation sites for the transmitter are theoretically unnecessary, since surrounding

Receiving components of integrated VORTAC equipment. Top, course indicator and radio magnetic indicator. Bottom, DME interrogator, range indicator, antenna (flush antenna optional), and control box.
(Federal Telephone and Radio Co.)

terrain does not interfere with the signals to the same degree that it does in VOR operation. The transmitter is portable, which means that it can be disassembled for military operations and moved quickly to new areas as required. It can also be used effectively aboard aircraft carriers.

TACAN receiving equipment operates very much like VOR-DME. The pilot tunes to a station frequency common to both the bearing and distance transmitters, rotates a course selector to the desired magnetic course, and then keeps a left-right needle centered to fly the course to the station. To determine a bearing he turns the course selector until the needle is centered, or if the aircraft is equipped with a radio magnetic indicator he simply reads the bearing under the azimuth pointer. The distance signals indicate automatically and continuously the aircraft's distance in miles (and tenths) from the station.

One of the typical integrated airborne VORTAC receivers (made by Federal Telecommunications Laboratories) weighs less than 50 pounds, and the components are somewhat simpler and more compact than those which make up a comparable VOR-DME system. The VORTAC package includes an omnirange course indicator, a bearing adaptor, an interrogator for the distance measuring equipment, a distance indicator, a control box, and an antenna which can be flush-mounted.

VORTAC or TACAN, the point to be emphasized again is that omnirange will continue to be the basic radio navigation aid in the U.S. for the next 15 years at least. The new distance measuring facilities—just like the present DME—will be a supplementary aid, a vital one in jet aircraft operations but still a luxury to the average pilot who flies for business or pleasure.

Appendix

Study questions

All of the following study questions are based on the material contained in the text. The correct answers are listed on pages 135-140.

GENERAL

1. What are three major disadvantages of the low-frequency radio range?

2. In what frequency range does VHF (including omnirange) operate?

3. Name at least two of the proposed traffic control and navigation facilities which will be installed with the completion of the long-range program.

4. Approximately how many omnirange transmitting stations are in operation in the U.S.?

5. What is surveillance radar?

6. Name at least three advantages offered pilots by the omnirange facilities.

7. What is precision beam radar?

8. What combination of the VHF facilities simplifies off-airway navigation and traffic control?

129

OMNIRANGES

9. Assuming no mountainous terrain intervenes, VOR signals ordinarily can be received by an aircraft at 1,000 feet altitude when within a radius of 50 miles of the station. True or false?

10. Using the analogy of the rotating light beacon, how would you explain the principle of omnirange transmission?

11. What kind of antenna is used with the airborne VOR receiver?

12. How many courses at any given altitude level does a VOR station offer a pilot?

13. What is line-of-sight transmission?

14. An aircraft flying at 4,000 feet altitude is tuned to a VOR station located at an elevation of 3,000 feet, but a mountain range 8,000 feet high intervenes between the transmitter and the aircraft. Normally, how would the pilot's VOR reception be affected?

15. How is 180° ambiguity on VOR bearings resolved by the VOR receiver?

16. What are the steps necessary to determine the bearing of an aircraft to or from an omnirange station?

17. In flying a desired course toward an omnirange station, what instrument indication would show you that your aircraft had drifted to the right of that course?

18. In flying away from the station, what instrument indication would show you that you had drifted to the right of course?

19. How can an exact position fix be obtained with the use of VOR facilities only?

20. What is the normal reception range of VOR signals at medium-high altitudes?

21. How far apart, on the average, are VOR transmitters placed?

22. If, while visually flying a VOR course, you wished to listen to a voice weather broadcast from the same station, what would you have to do?

23. At what speed does the variable-phase signal of an omnirange rotate?

24. At what instant are the reference and variable signals of a VOR exactly in phase?

25. What determines the azimuth angle of any point around the compass, as transmitted by a VOR station?

26. What part of the VOR transmitter antenna radiates the reference-phase signal?

27. What units of the antenna radiate the variable-phase signal?

28. The phase angle of VOR depends upon the direction of the receiving antenna from the omnirange station. True or false?

29. What is an omnirange "radial?"

30. In flying toward a VOR station you set the course selector to the magnetic value of the course you want to make good to the station. You then turn the aircraft to a heading calculated to hold the selected course. Unless the aircraft is more than 90° from the selected course, the "to-from" indicator should point to what?

31. What does the phrase "steering into the needle" mean?

32. You are flying an omnirange course of 96° directly toward a station. The left-right needle is centered and steady, and your deviation-free compass reads 103°. What would this tell you about the amount of crab into the wind?

33. What are the three main instrument indications when an aircraft crosses directly over a VOR station?

34. Is it possible to fly a course to an omnirange station by means of the left-right needle and without reference to a compass?

35. How would you know if a VOR station to which you are properly tuned is temporarily inoperative or the signals are not being received?

36. How, in effect, does omnirange compensate for cross-wind or drift?

37. What is the single greatest difference between omnirange indication and an LF radio direction-finder?

38. The left-right needle always points directly toward an omnirange course, regardless of whether the aircraft is heading toward the station or away from it, under what circumstances?

39. How does a VOR station identify itself?

40. While approaching a VOR station to which your aircraft receiver is tuned, you call the station on voice to report your position and ETA. When the voice communications begin, the red flag comes up on your cross-pointer dial and the VOR visual course-indication is temporarily interrupted. True or false?

41. If you became lost while flying an aircraft equipped with omnirange, what would be simplest way to establish a definite fix?

42. Do VOR stations broadcast weather reports?

43. What do the letters "Ph-Loc" on the omnirange control unit mean?

44. What is the most significant factor limiting the range at which VOR signals may be heard?

DME AND THE COURSE-LINE COMPUTER

45. Define DME.

46. The mechanism that is the "heart" of the DME system is called what?

47. What is the basic difference between radar and DME?

48. What is the maximum number of aircraft that DME ground stations are designed to respond to?

49. What is the most important limiting factor in the useful range of DME?

50. What is the maximum reliable range of current airborne DME equipment?

51. What is the DME "interrogator?"

52. In what frequency band do DME stations operate?

53. Why are the signals of an airborne DME transmitter unevenly spaced?

54. What feature of the combination VOR-DME facilities simplifies tuning in on the proper frequency?

55. DME facilities are also available for use in conjunction with ILS. True or false?

56. What function does the course-line computer serve?

57. In order to take advantage of the course-line computer, an aircraft must be headed either directly toward or away from a VOR-DME station. True or false?

58. What is the meaning of the symbols "R" and "θ" as applied to navigation with the course-line computer?

59. From what facilities does the course-line computer receive the information which it converts into a position-fix?

60. How would it be possible to maintain an accurate course which describes a circle around a VOR-DME station, assuming the aircraft is equipped with DME?

61. Explain how the course-line computer makes possible multi-lane airways?

62. How will the course-line computer affect air traffic control?

63. In order to fly and maintain a given course with the course-line computer, three values must be set up on the computer's dials. What are these values?

64. How does the course-line computer indicate deviation from course?

65. What is the function of the projected-distance meter?

66. How would a pilot flying by course-line computer know when he is over his destination?

Answers to study questions

GENERAL

1. (1) Static interference with the reception of signals, (2) complicated and time-consuming orientation procedures, and (3) eccentricities such as bent beams and multiple courses.

2. 108-144 megacycles.

3. (1) The block system of air traffic control, and (2) airborne equipment for the pictorial presentation of all surrounding air traffic.

4. 455.

5. Radar used to guide aircraft and direct traffic on the approaches to an airport.

6. (1) The pilot flies by eye instead of ear, (2) there is no static to interfere with the reception of signals, and (3) confusion as to which of two possible quadrants the aircraft is located in is eliminated.

7. A precision instrument-approach and letdown system in which an operator watching a radar screen on the ground "talks" the pilot down onto the runway by means of voice-radio directions.

8. Omnirange, distance-measuring equipment, and the course-line computer.

OMNIRANGES

9. True

10. If the identification flasher of an airport light beacon is adjusted so that it flashes each time the beacon itself sweeps past magnetic north, and if the beacon rotates clockwise at a constant rate, one's direction from the beacon can be determined. This is accomplished by starting a stopwatch at the instant of the beginning of the green flash, and stopping it when the rotating beam sweeps past the observer. If the number of degrees the beacon revolves each second is multiplied by the number of seconds on the stop-watch, the observer obtains his magnetic bearing from the beacon.

11. A special V-type dipole antenna.

12. A theoretically infinite number. Actually, however, the number is limited to 360 because of the impossibility of flying or holding a heading within less than one degree.

13. A characteristic property of VHF signals, in which the signals ordinarily continue straight out into space rather than bounce back and forth between the earth and the ionosphere, as do low-frequency radio waves. VHF signals can be received only slightly below a line-of-sight course from the transmitter.

14. The aural signal will fade and/or disappear, and a red flag will appear in the cross-pointer indicator.

15. By the to-from indicator which points to "to" when the aircraft is headed toward the station and "from" when it is headed away from the station.

16. (1) Tune in and identify the station, (2) turn the course selector until the left-right pointer is centered, (3) check the to-from meter to determine whether the bearing is to or from the station, and (4) read the magnetic bearing on the course selector.

17. The cross-pointer indicator would point to the left of center.

18. The cross-pointer indicator would still point to the left of center.

19. By crossing bearings from two VOR stations.

20. 150 miles.

21. Approximately 100 miles.

22. Nothing but put your headphones on (assuming the aircraft is not equipped with a cockpit loudspeaker). Voice transmission is simultaneous with directional signals.

23. At 1,800 rpm.

24. At the instant when the rotating signal reaches magnetic north.

25. In all directions other than magnetic north the positive maximum of the variable signal occurs at some time later than the maximum of the reference signal. The fraction of the cycle which elapses between the occurrence of the two maximums, at any point in azimuth, identifies the azimuth angle of that point.

26. The antenna that is located in the center of the five transmitter antennas.

27. The antennas arranged in a square pattern around the center antenna.

28. True.

29. A radial is the magnetic bearing of an aircraft from or to a VOR station, as established by the VOR transmitter's phase difference.

30. "To."

31. It means that if the cross-pointer needle points to the left the aircraft must be steered to the left to return to course, and vice versa.

32. It would indicate that your aircraft is crabbed seven degrees to the right.

33. The cross-pointer needle swings back and forth, a red flag appears in the same dial, and the needle of the to-from indicator moves from "to" to "from."

34. Yes, but in practice it is much simpler to fly by a gyro-compass or magnetic compass heading which tends to keep the left-right needle centered.

35. The to-from needle would move into the neutral area and the red flag would appear in the cross-pointer dial.

36. In keeping the left-right needle centered, the pilot automatically takes up a compass heading which compensates for wind-drift.

37. The omnirange not only tells the pilot what magnetic course to fly toward or away from a station but it also compensates for drift. The radio direction-finder merely points toward a station.

38. When the course selector and the magnetic compass are in general agreement, i.e., when one is not the reciprocal of the other.

39. By intermittently transmitting in code its own three-letter station designation.

40. False. VOR voice transmission is simultaneous with visual course signals.

41. (1) Maintain a constant heading while you tune through the VOR frequency band (112-118 mc) until you pick up a station; (2) identify the station and locate it on the map; (3) turn the course selector until the left-right needle is centered and the to-from needle points to "to;" (4) turn to a compass heading in general agreement with the course selector and fly to the station, or (5) plot the reciprocal of the bearing on your chart, take a bearing on another VOR station, and then set a new course to your destination from the resultant fix.

42. Yes, most stations are equipped for weather broadcasts simultaneous with visual course signals.

43. Phase-localizer, a development of the Instrument Landing System, which uses the same cross-pointer indicator as VOR.

44. Line-of-sight transmission.

DME AND THE COURSE-LINE COMPUTER

45. DME is the abbreviation of distance measuring equipment. It tells the pilot, visually, his distance from any given VOR-DME ground station and, used in conjunction with omnirange, gives him an instantaneous, continual position check, using the facilities of only one station. It will enable traffic controllers eventually to keep a more precise check on traffic and thus to speed up the arrival and departure of aircraft from busy terminals.

46. The transponder.

47. In radar the transmitter sends out a signal that is received back at the source after the signal bounces off a target. In DME the signal is transmitted from an aircraft and received at a ground station which transmits the pulses back to the aircraft on a different frequency.

48. 50.

49. Line-of-sight transmission.

50. 115 miles at line-of-sight transmission.

51. The airborne DME equipment which transmits pulses to a ground-station transponder and converts the response into distance out from the station.

52. Within the 960-1,215 mc band.

53. The signals are unevenly spaced in order to prevent the pulses from one aircraft from becoming evenly spaced ahead of a stream of reply pulses intended for another aircraft.

54. DME station channels are paired with corresponding VOR frequencies, which means that the pilot who turns his channel selector switch to the frequency of a VOR station automatically also tunes to the corresponding DME station channel.

55. True.

56. The course-line computer takes radial information from VOR and distance from DME and converts it instantaneously into the exact position of the aircraft in terms of lateral deviation from a course.

57. False. The course-line computer is designed primarily for off-airway flying, regardless of the position or heading of the aircraft.

58. R represents the distance from a fixed point (such as a VOR-DME facility) and 0 represents the bearing from the same point.

59. It receives radial or bearing information from VOR and distance information from DME.

60. By turning on gyro-compass headings which maintain constant distance-from-the-station indications on the DME.

61. With a single row of VOR-DME stations to define the center of the airway it will be possible for aircraft equipped with the course-line computer to fly any number of properly spaced parallel lanes at each altitude level.

62. It will permit faster, more efficient dispatching of aircraft, eliminate traffic bottlenecks and airport stacking, increase the regularity of schedules, and result in more efficient airspace and airport utilization.

63. The proposed course angle, bearing of the destination from the VOR-DME station, and distance of the destination from the station.

64. The left-right indicator points to the left of center if the course is to the left, and vice versa.

65. The projected-distance meter records the distance remaining to be flown to the destination.

66.. With the left-right needle centered, the projected distance meter would indicate zero miles.

Glossary of terms

used in VHF radio navigation

AMBIGUITY: The condition which obtains when a navigation facility defines an LOP without indicating the direction of an object with respect to an observer. In omnirange flying, 180° ambiguity is resolved by the to-from indicator which points to "to" when an aircraft is headed toward a station and to "from" when it is headed away from a station.

APPROACH PATH: The part of the flight path in the immediate vicinity of a landing area where such flight path is intended to terminate in a landing on a runway.

AZIMUTH: Angular bearing measured from 0° in a clockwise direction to 360°. In omnirange flying, all azimuths, or bearings, are measured from magnetic north.

BEARING: Angular measurement, clockwise in degrees. Bearings are either (1) true, as measured from true north, (2) magnetic, as measured from magnetic north, or (3) relative, as measured relatively from the heading of an aircraft.

COURSE: A direction of intended travel expressed as an angle from a reference direction, usually measured clockwise from true or magnetic north. As applied specifically to omnirange flying, a course is one of a theoretically infinite number of radials transmitted from the VOR station. Airborne receiving equipment translates the radial information

141

into designated magnetic courses (or bearings) of the aircraft to or from the station.

COURSE-LINE COMPUTER: An airborne mechanical "brain" which absorbs radial information from omnirange stations, and distance-measuring information from DME, instantly and continually computing an aircraft's position on the basis of this data. Position is provided in terms of lateral direction from a proposed course and of distance to destination.

COURSE-LINE DEVIATION: The difference between an aircraft's track (actual course made good) and it course (projected or planned path). The deviation is expressed in terms of either angular or linear measurement.

COURSE SELECTOR: A manually operated control on airborne VOR receiving equipment which indicates magnetic course or bearing values from or toward an omnirange station. For example, with the left-right needle (deviation indicator) centered, and the to-from needle pointing to "to", a value of 270° set on the course selector indicates that the aircraft is flying a magnetic course of 270° directly to the VOR station.

DEAD RECKONING: Determination of position by advancing a known position on the basis of such known or assumed factors as time, wind speed and direction, heading, true airspeed, groundspeed, etc.

DF (also D/F): Direction-finder or direction-finding. Generally refers to aircraft radio receiving equipment that determines the direction from which signals transmitted from the ground are received. ADF = automatic direction-finder. MDF = manual direction-finder.

DIPOLE ANTENNA: A special radio antenna, commonly a V-type, one-half wavelength long, for the airborne reception of VHF omnirange signals.

DISTANCE MEASURING EQUIPMENT (DME): An electronic navigation aid that measures the distance in miles from an aircraft to a ground station. Pulses sent out from an aircraft are received at a ground station which then transmits the pulses back to the aircraft. The time required for the round trip of the signal is measured by the airborne DME unit and translated into distance. An indicator on the aircraft instrument panel records this distance automatically and continuously. DME, used in conjunction with omnirange, presents the pilot of an aircraft with a constant position-fix.

FAN MARKER: A VHF radio facility with a fan-shaped or bone-shaped radiation pattern. Fan markers are located near airports and at airway intersections to provide navigational position fixes.

FIX: Definite determination of geographical position by either visual, radio, or celestial means, without reference to any former position.

FLIGHT PATH: The projected path of an aircraft between departure and destination, or between any two intermediate checkpoints. Flight path is generally interpreted to mean both lateral and vertical direction, i.e., course and altitude.

FLIGHT PATH DEVIATION: The difference between the flight track of an aircraft and the flight course expressed in terms of either angular or linear measurement.

FREQUENCY: The number of cycles completed per second by an electric current, a sound wave, or a vibrating object.

GLIDE PATH: Also called "glide slope." An inclined course or path extending upward at an angle from the point of desired ground contact.

GONIOMETER: In omnirange transmission, a motor-driven instrument used in conjunction with four stationary antennas to produce a rotating signal field.

HF: High frequency radio (3,000 to 30,000 kilocycles).

HOMING: The method of bringing an aircraft directly into or over a destination or intermediate checkpoint by means of constant reference to a target, object, or navigation facility located at that destination or checkpoint. Commonly, to home-in on a radio facility in air navigation means to follow an aural or visual bearing toward that station.

INSTRUMENT LANDING SYSTEM (ILS): A VHF radio navigation system designed to guide aircraft through approaches, letdowns, and landings during conditions of extremely adverse weather. Primarily, ILS consists of (1) a localizer beam to furnish directional guidance to the airport runway, (2) a glide path beam to furnish vertical guidance down the correct angle of descent to the runway, and (3) fan markers to provide accurate radio fixes along the approach course.

ILS MARKER: A VHF radio facility, the signals of which define specific areas along an ILS localizer course line. An ILS marker is either a boundary, middle or outer marker, depending upon its location.

INTERROGATOR: The airborne distance measuring equipment (DME) unit. It is designed to provide reliable measurement of distance from the ground unit up to a range of 115 miles at line-of-sight altitude.

IONOSPHERE: (Also called Heaviside layers.) Layers of ionized gas in the region 50 to 400 miles above the surface of the earth. Radio waves below a frequency of approximately 40 megacycles are reflected off the ionosphere back to earth under certain conditions.

LEFT-RIGHT NEEDLE: Cross-pointer indicator of the airborne VOR receiving equipment. It is the same instrument as used to indicate course deviation in ILS approaches and letdowns. When the needle is centered, the aircraft is on course. The needle points to the left of center when the aircraft is right of its course, and vice versa.

LF: Low-frequency radio (30-400 kilocycles). This band includes the obsolete four-course radio ranges.

LINE OF POSITION (LOP): A locus of the possible positions of an aircraft, as determined usually from a bearing on a radio transmitter or from observations of a celestial body.

LINE-OF-SIGHT TRANSMISSION: The straight line of a radio signal as sent out by a VHF transmitter. VHF radio waves do not follow the curvature of the earth.

LOCALIZER: A radio navigation facility which offers lateral guidance to aircraft in relation to a runway center line.

MARKER: A radio navigation transmitting facility which provides a distinct signal to designate a limited area in the airspace above its transmitter. (See also "Fan Marker.")

MEGACYCLE (mc): One million cycles per second.

MF: Medium frequency radio (300-3,000 kc).

MICROSECOND: One millionth of a second.

MULTI-LANE AIRWAY: Proposed multiple-lane flight paths or routes between larger cities. Such airways will be made possible through the development of the course-line computer, which enables pilots to keep a continuous check of actual position even when not flying directly toward or away from VOR-DME stations.

OMNI-BEARING: Magnetic bearing to or from an omnirange station.

OMNI-BEARING CONVERTER: An instrument which combines omnirange information with aircraft heading information to operate the pointer of a Radio Magnetic Indicator (q.v.). An omni-bearing converter becomes an omni-bearing indicator when a pointer and dial are added.

OMNI-BEARING INDICATOR: An instrument which provides automatic, instantaneous and continuous indication of the bearing to or from an omnirange station.

OMNI-BEARING SELECTOR: An instrument the dial of which can be set manually to any desired omnirange bearing. The instrument controls the left-right needle or course-line deviation indicator. See also "Course Selector."

OMNIMATIC: Trade name of the automatic airborne omnirange receiver and transmitter manufactured by Lear, Inc.

OMNIRANGE: (Latin "omnis," meaning "all," plus "range.") A radio station which produces a theoretically infinite number of courses, or radials, which radiate from the station like spokes from the hub of a wheel. Directional information is generated at the station and transmitted to an aircraft. Airborne receiving equipment intercepts the signal and converts it into a visual directional indication in terms of magnetic courses to or from the station.

PHASE: In omnirange transmitter operation, the stage to which a rotating signal and a non-directional signal have advanced, considered in their relation at the assumed instant of starting.

PHASE DIFFERENCE: In omnirange transmitter operation, the difference at any given instant between the two radiated audio frequency signals. The difference in phase between these two signals varies with change in azimuth.

PHASE-LOCALIZER (Ph-Loc): A localizer radio station which transmits two signal components for phase comparison.

POSITION: The location of an aircraft generally in terms of geographical coordinates and altitude. Geographically, the position of an aircraft flying within the continental U.S. is usually stated in reference to identifiable cities, topographical features, or fixed radio navigation facilities.

PRESET COURSE OR BEARING: In omnirange flying a desired course or bearing the value of which can be set in advance on the airborne course-selector. When the aircraft reaches this course or bearing, the left-right needle becomes centered.

RADAR: Radio detecting and ranging equipment. Radar is based on the principle that ultra-high-frequency radio waves travel at a known, constant speed, and are reflected back from objects within line-of-sight transmission. The waves are beamed outward by directional antennas, and the reflected waves are picked up by an ultra-high-frequency receiver. The elapsed time for the round-trip of the waves is measured electronically and translated into terms of distance and angle of the reflecting object.

RADIAL: One of a theoretically infinite number of courses which radiate from a VOR station, like spokes from the hub of a wheel.

RADIO BEACON: A radio navigation transmitter the signals of which are designed to provide directional information for aircraft or ships in relation to the radio beacon station.

RADIO FREQUENCY (r-f): Any frequency in the spectrum of electromagnetic waves having a value below that of heat but above the highest audio frequency.

RADIO MAGNETIC INDICATOR (RMI): An instrument which presents a combined display of an aircraft's heading and the bearing to or from an omnirange station.

RADIO RANGE: Four-course, low-frequency radio station providing radial equisignal zones.

RADIO WAVE: A combination of transverse electric and magnetic fields, each building up and collapsing at a radio frequency and capable of travelling through space at the speed of light.

RECEIVER: Equipment for converting radio-frequency energy into visual or aural frequencies.

REFERENCE PHASE: Of the two signals transmitted by a VOR station, one is non-directional and has a constant phase throughout its 360° of azimuth. This signal is called the "reference phase." It is radiated from the center antenna of a five-element group.

RELATIVE BEARING: A bearing or angle, usually measured clockwise, in relation to the fore and aft axis, or heading, of an aircraft.

REPLY: A radio-frequency pulse, or combination of pulses, transmitted by a transponder as a result of an interrogation from another source. DME (distance measuring equipment) is based on such an interrogation and the resultant reply by a transponder.

RESPONDER: Receiving unit in a transponder. Its function is to receive the signals transmitted from a beacon.

R-THETA: The principle upon which VOR-DME navigation is based. R represents the distance from a fixed point, since it would be the radius of a circle drawn at that distance around the fixed point. The Greek letter 0 (theta) represents the direction or magnetic bearing from the fixed point.

SELECTIVITY: The degree to which a radio receiver is capable of receiving signals of one frequency or band of frequencies while at the same time discriminating against signals of all other frequencies.

STEERING INTO THE NEEDLE: In flying the omnirange, when the left-right needle (or cross-pointer indicator) moves off center, it indicates that the aircraft is deviating from the selected course or flight path. To return to the course the aircraft must be steered toward, or into, the needle. Thus, when the needle points to the left it indicates that the aircraft has deviated to the right of course and must be turned back to the left in order to return to course.

TO-FROM INDICATOR: An instrument of the airborne omnirange receiving equipment which indicates whether the reading of the course selector (the bearing or course of a VOR station) is toward the station or away from it.

TRACK: In navigation, the actual course or path of an aircraft over the surface of the earth. In U.S. usage, course means the projected or desired path between any two points, while track, as defined above, is the path actually made good. Theoretically, at least, track and course can be the same, but in practice seldom are.

TRANSPONDER: As applied specifically to distance measuring equipment, the ground receiver-transmitter unit. It receives radio-pulse interrogation signals and transmits reply pulses in return.

TRUE BEARING: The bearing of a place or object as measured clockwise from true north.

TRUE COURSE: The direction of intended travel, projected in the horizontal plane and measured as an angle clockwise from true north.

TRUE HEADING: The direction of a line along which an aircraft is pointed, measured angularly in the horizontal plane clockwise from true north.

UHF: Ultra-high (radio) frequencies. The band ranges between 300 and 3,000 megacycles. Air-to-ground and ground-to-air communications will be conducted by UHF in the near future.

VARIABLE PHASE: Of the two signals transmitted by a VOR station, the one which rotates at a speed of 1,800 rpm, varying in phase with azimuth, is called the "variable phase." It is produced by a group of four stationary antennas connected in pairs to a motor-driven goniometer.

VCIX: Visual course cross-pointer indicator.

VELOCITY OF LIGHT: 186,280 statute miles per second; 328 yards per microsecond.

VHF: Very high (radio) frequencies (30-300 megacycles). This frequency band includes, among others, omnirange, ILS, and control-tower frequencies.

VOR: Abbreviation of VHF radio omnirange.

WAVE LENGTH: The distance travelled in one cycle by a periodic disturbance.

Z MARKER: A VHF radio navigation facility located at an airway radio range to provide for positive position-fixing above the transmitter.

Index

PACIFIC STANDARD TIME
plus 8 hrs. = G.M.T.

MOUNTAIN STANDARD TIME
plus 7 hrs. = G.M.T.

CANADA
UNITED STATES

WASHINGTON

OREGON

IDAHO

MONTANA

NORTH

NEVADA

CALIFORNIA

UTAH

WYOMING

SOUTH

NEBRASKA

COLORADO

ARIZONA

NEW MEXICO

LOS ANGELES

PHOENIX

ALBUQUERQUE

UNITED STATES
MEXICO

EL PASO

GOLFO DE CALIFORNIA

NCISCO - LOS ANGELES

NEV

CALIFORNIA

OCEAN

LEGEND		CONVERSION TABLE
	Controlled airway - Alternate airways not shown	NAUTICAL MILES TO STATUTE MILES

		NAUTICAL MILES	STATUTE MILES	NAUTICAL MILES	STATUTE MILES
V 1508	Transcontinental Airway - V 1500 Series	10	11.5	30	34.5
▲	Compulsory reporting point	11	12.7	40	46.0
△	Non-compulsory reporting point	12	13.8	50	57.5
	Limit of CAA Regions	13	15.0	60	69.0
KANSAS CITY	CAA Regional Office	14	16.1	70	80.6
SALT LAKE CITY	Air Route Traffic Control Center	15	17.3	80	92.1
	Flight Advisory Area boundary	16	18.4	90	103.6
120	Nautical miles between reporting points	17	19.6	100	115.1
(LAX)	Location identifiers	18	20.7	200	230.1
		19	21.9	300	345.2
○	Radio facility	20	23.0	400	460.3

•••••• Routes within which there is positive air traffic control
of all aircraft at all times at altitudes of 17,000 feet MSL